On Infantry

Recent Titles in
The Military Profession
Bruce Gudmundsson, Series Editor

On Air Defense
James D. Crabtree

Steel Wind: Colonel Georg Bruchmuller and the Birth of Modern Artillery
David T. Zabecki

John A. English and
Bruce I. Gudmundsson

The Military Profession

Westport, Connecticut
London

Library of Congress Cataloging-in-Publication Data

English, John A. (John Alan)
On infantry / John A. English and Bruce I. Gudmundsson.—Rev. ed.
p. cm.—(The Military Profession, ISSN 1074-2964)
Rev. ed. of: A perspective on infantry. 1981.
Includes bibliographical references and index.
ISBN 0-275-94588-X (alk. paper).—ISBN 0-275-94972-9 (pbk. : alk. paper)
1. Infantry. 2. Infantry drill and tactics. I. Gudmundsson, Bruce I. II. English, John A. (John Alan) Perspective on infantry. III. Title.
UD145.E53 1994
356'.1—dc20 94-12071

British Library Cataloguing in Publication Data is available.

Library of Congress Catalog Card Number: 94-12071
ISBN: 0-275-94588-X
0-275-94972-9 (pbk)
ISSN: 1074-2964

First published in 1994

Praeger Publishers, 88 Post Road West, Westport, CT 06881
An imprint of Greenwood Publishing Group, Inc.

Printed in the United States of America

The paper used in this book complies with the Permanent Paper Standard issued by the National Information Standards Organization (Z39.48-1984).

10 9 8 7 6 5 4 3 2 1

Contents

Introduction to the Revised Edition

When the first edition of this work, then called *A Perspective on Infantry*, appeared in 1981, it seemed as if infantry would soon go the way of horse cavalry. With all eyes focused on the defense of Western Europe against an attack by Soviet conventional forces, with the literature of World War II still dominated by the memoirs of the German *Panzer* commanders, and with debates over the purchase of hardware taking the place of serious military thought, the armies of the developed world paid little attention to the humble foot soldier. A dozen years later, the end of the Cold War and the consequent movement of regional and intramural conflicts from backdrop to center stage has cured many armies of this myopia. Military power is no longer calculated solely in terms of throw-weight or numbers of first-line fighter aircraft, tanks, or armored personnel carriers. When questions of whether to intervene in Somalia or Bosnia come up, the unit of account that matters is, as it was at the beginning of this century, the infantry battalion.

The current revival of interest in infantry is not limited to soldiers and statesmen. The past decade or so has seen a significant improvement in both the quantity and quality of published military history. This body of work has changed the way that we look at the wars and armies of the past century and, in particular, has uncovered a number of facts of interest to the student of infantry. The volumes that make up this corpus are too numerous to list in so short an introduction. Their study, however, played an important part in the preparation of the revised version of this book.

Readers who are interested in identifying them need only look at the notes appended to each chapter.

In addition to exploiting a great deal of recent scholarship, the revised edition of *On Infantry* differs from the first in a number of important respects. Restructured to serve (with the already published *On Artillery*, as well as the soon to be published *On Armor* and *On Air Defense*) as part of a series, this version of *On Infantry* is somewhat narrower in scope than its predecessor. This has resulted in the loss of some material, but a considerable gain in the form of a fuller treatment of the main themes of the book—the role played by combat psychology, the relation of infantry to the other arms, and the importance of the squad. Much of the material lost, such as the important questions of antitank defense and the cooperation between infantry and tanks, will be resurrected in subsequent works in this series.

It would be impossible, in a work of this size, to deal with all of the recent battles and campaigns in which infantry has played a central role. For that reason, many important conflicts are not mentioned. Thus, the Russian Civil War, the Russo-Polish War, the Gran Chaco War, the Spanish Civil War, the Chinese Civil War, many campaigns of both World Wars, and the Falklands/Malvinas War, to name but a few of the many conflicts of our bloody century, are neglected. For the most part, the decision not to examine these conflicts was a lack of readily accessible source material. I have nonetheless attempted to cast my net widely enough to give readers a reasonably complete view of the role played by infantry in twentieth century armies.

The revision of *On Infantry* would not have been possible without the help of many people. Dan Eades was both the instigator of the project and its patient godfather. John English was kind enough to suggest that I do the revision and generous enough to give me *carte blanche* in carrying it out. John Sayen, President of the Institute for Tactical Education, lent me office space, computer equipment, and books, as well as permission to use material that originally appeared in *Tactical Notebook*. Colonel and Mrs. Dominique Beau were charming hosts and good friends during my research trip to France in the summer of 1991. My family—my parents Barbara and Ivar, my brothers Brian and Peter, my wife Lee-Ann, and my children Brian and Kathleen—provided considerable material as well as unflagging moral support.

Bruce I. Gudmundsson
Quantico, VA, June 1994

On Infantry

1.

The Open Order Revolution

The years between the beginning of the Crimean War (1854) and the outbreak of the Great War of 1914–1918 saw the first major transformation of infantry tactics since the introduction, at the beginning of the 18th century, of the bayonet. As with earlier transformations, the agent of this change was technology. In particular, the device that caused the revolution in infantry tactics of the second half of the nineteenth century was the rapid-fire rifle.

The chief symptom of this change was the replacement of "close order" formations with "open order" deployments. That is to say, while there were many variations on the basic theme, soldiers on the battlefield were farther apart from one another than had been the custom for most of recorded history. This soon led to a recognitioin that the organizational and, above all, psychological framework appropriate to close order fighting would not do on the "emptier" battlefield of the time.

"The difficulties of command when men are in extended order," wrote a German company commander at the end of the nineteenth century, "are heightened by the din and other distracting influences of battle, especially in close and broken country. The best test of the training and discipline of troops is their behavior in extended order, for the less the leader is able to exercise personal control over his command, the more must the intelligence of each individual soldier be developed, and the more should he be encouraged to think and act for himself."[1]

Rifles had been used in European warfare for more than a century prior to the Crimean War. Hard to master and slow to load, they had, however, been weapons for specialists who had little in common with ordinary infantrymen. Similarly, rapid-fire firearms in the form of muzzle-loading, smoothbore muskets had long been available and, indeed, had formed the primary weapon of the eighteenth and early nineteenth century infantry. Just as the price of the accuracy of early rifles was slow loading, the cost of the relatively high rate of fire of smoothbore muskets was abysmal accuracy.[2]

The new weapons that started to appear in the third and fourth decades of the nineteenth century eliminated this dichotomy. The most popular were the rifles developed by the French Captain Minié and his imitators. These were rifled muzzle-loaders that used an expansible conical bullet. During loading the relatively small bullet slid easily down the barrel. Upon the firing of the rifle, however, the bullet expanded to the point where there was sufficient contact between the bullet and the rifling of the weapon to impart the desired spin. The net result was a weapon that optimistic (but nonetheless still reasonable) men could provide with 1,000-yard sights.

The other approach, attempted in many places but only made practical in Prussia, was to replace muzzle-loading with breech-loading. The early weapons of this sort were not nearly as accurate or reliable as the Minié type weapons. For short periods, however, they were capable of somewhat higher rates of fire. What was more important, the Prussian "needle-gun" and the less successful breechloaders of that generation were both more accurate and much more easily loaded than the smoothbore muskets they replaced.[3]

As is often the case with revolutions, the first battles in which these new weapons were used saw a strange mixture of the old and the new. Though fought by armies dressed in Napoleonic uniforms and, quite often, commanded by veterans of the Napoleonic wars, the Crimean War (1854–55) provided, at the very least, an opportunity for the "thin red line" to be thinner than it ever had been. The Franco-Austrian War in Italy (1859) was the occasion, thanks to the failure of the Austrians to use the sights on their new rifles, for a brief "Indian Summer" for close order tactics.

The battles of the three wars of German unification—the Danish War of 1864, the Austro-Prussian War of 1866, and the Franco-Prussian War of 1870–71—were fought by units which might stand in line and trade volleys like the grenadiers of Frederick the Great, disintegrate into swarms of individual riflemen, or adopt one of the "compromise" formations like the "company column." The same can be said for the American Civil War. By far the most extensive "civilized" war of this period, its many battles and engagements were fought in an almost infinite variety of ways that ranged from the primitive to the nearly modern.

Part of this confusion was a result of the newness of the new weapons. It is, after all, far easier to adopt a new weapon than to adapt to its potential. The lack of a consensus on the best way to make use of the new rifles, however, reflected a deeper problem. For while almost all observers recognized that the greater range of the rapid-fire rifle increased the distance at which soldiers could kill each other and that, as a result, the parade-ground tactics of the past were no longer valid, there was no unanimity when it came to evaluating the response of the individual soldier to his new environment.

Those who believed that most soldiers had sufficient motivation to fight as individuals saw no problem in releasing swarms of skirmishers on the battlefield. Such skirmishers, after all, had long played an important role in paving the way for decisive action of formations in close order. The only change mandated by the new weapons was to reverse this relationship. The skirmisher would now become the decisive element in the infantry battle. Troops in close order would be relegated to a supporting role—as reserves standing ready to "feed" the skirmish line, as a means of providing psychological support to the skirmisher, or as an insurance policy against a cavalry charge.

The skirmishers of the eighteenth and early nineteenth century, however, had been specialists. They were often distinguished by special skills and special equipment—either rifles or muskets that were more accurate than those which equipped the aptly named troops of the "line." The most salient characteristic of skirmishers of the period before 1850 was their loyalty. Whether they were Croats from the Austrian borderlands, Prussian *Jäger*, American riflemen, Scots Highlanders, or Nepalese Gurkhas, the troops trusted to skirmish were motivated by what can only be called a warrior's code. In an age when the only virtue required of most infantryman was the passive obedience of a cog in a machine, skirmishing tended to be a job for men whose world view, to say the least, was "pre-industrial."

This link between new tactics and old values had an ironic twist. The same forces that had made the new rifles possible—the growth in scientific knowledge, the continuing industrial revolution, better communications, and increasing urbanization—also tended to erode the very values necessary to successful skirmishing. This applied both to the communities that had traditionally provided recruits to skirmishing units as well as those units themselves. Thus, for example, the young German *Jäger* of the middle nineteenth century was not only less likely to have been raised in the woods, but would also practice customs—such as the carrying of colors and marching in step—that his predecessors would have regarded as alien.

What was true of units that had specialized in skirmishing was even more true of units which, from their very beginnings, had known nothing but close order fighting. Men raised in the increasingly predictable and orderly environments of nineteenth century towns and villages could not be expected to be at home on the empty battlefield. Men who were products of at least a few years of formal schooling, the beginnings of mass culture, and military training programs consisting mostly of drill, could not easily resist the temptation to hide themselves in the mass. In short, at a time when weapons technology favored soldiers who were both self-reliant and selfless and possessed of both loyalty and initiative, the social and military institutions of Europe and North America were producing men who were both self-absorbed and docile.

The result, as seen on the battlefields of the American Civil War, the Franco-Austrian War, and the Franco-Prussian War, was infantry that was often incapable of fighting in open order. The officers that recorded this incapacity described scenes that struck at the very heart of military discipline. Men who were otherwise fine soldiers would, when deployed as skirmishers, fail to move forward against enemy fire. Instead they would find ways of avoiding direct participation in the battle. The most shameless of these skulkers would simply hide in a hollow or clump of bushes. The more inventive would, rather than exposing themselves in order to find good targets, fire blindly from positions of complete safety.

The solution offered by most of the military writers who documented this phenomenon—the Germans Fritz Hönig and Jakob Meckel, the American Emory Upton, and the Frenchman Ardant du Picq—was a return to close order tactics. These revived close order tactics were, to be sure, a great deal more flexible than those of the eighteenth century. The goal, after all, was less to regulate the actions of the infantrymen than to provide those actions with motive power. The science which governed these new formations was not geometry but psychology.[4] The image conjured up in the mind's eye was no longer a picture of a mechanical time piece ticking away the hours but a vision of an irresistible river channeled by a cunning engineer, or a mob both inspired and directed by a charismatic leader.

It is important to note that the new close order tactics differed from the old in form as well as spirit. In the age of the smoothbore musket, the battalion had been the basic unit for both fire and movement. That is to say, in most battlefield situations, battalions were the smallest organizations which were given separate tasks on the battlefield and could do things like take advantage of terrain. In the new close order tactics the basic tactical unit was much smaller. Depending on the army or the period, it was either a small company or a large platoon. Thus, instead of a group of

400–600 musketeers, the basic "playing piece" was shrunk to an organization of fifty to a hundred riflemen.

Because of this, the close order tactics of the late nineteenth and early twentieth centuries were far more flexible than those of the period before the introduction of rapid-fire rifles. The three rank lines of men marching in step of the eighteenth century had given way to two or even one rank lines of men walking or even running. The great columns of the Napoleonic Wars—columns in which thousands of men had been packed together in a compact mass—had likewise given way to battalion formations in which there was considerable distance between the little two-deep lines formed by the companies or platoons.[5]

In places where there was a good supply of "natural skirmishers"—on the Northwest Frontier of India, in neighboring Afghanistan, in the Boer Republics of South Africa, and in mountainous nations such as Switzerland and Montenegro—the revived close order tactics were not well received. Modern rifles fit in nicely with the way that both these societies and the armies that defended them were organized. In the conventional armies of Europe and North America, however, the new doctrine spread rapidly, achieving the acme of its popularity in the last decade of the nineteenth century.

This revival of close order tactics coincided, quite understandably, with the attainment of positions of influence by men who had been young infantry officers in the 1860s and 1870s; the wide circulation of the works of Upton, du Picq, Meckel, Hönig, and their lesser known imitators; and the publication of civilian works on mass psychology such as Gustave Le Bon's *Spirit of the Crowds*. It also coincided with the next great improvement in infantry firearms—the introduction of the magazine rifle firing bullets propelled by smokeless powder.

The magazine in the new rifles—the most famous of which are the German Mauser and the British Lee-Enfield—gave them a rate of fire that was far greater than that of the single shot weapons they replaced. This rate of fire was further enhanced by the fact that smokeless powder left much less of a residue than black powder and thus reduced the chances that a barrel would become fouled in the course of a battle. Smokeless powder also reduced the smoke that was produced with each shot fired. This facilitated aiming, eased target acquisition, and greatly reduced the tell-tale cloud of smoke that tended to form in the vicinity of men firing black-powder weapons.

The last battles of the nineteenth century—those of the Second Anglo-Boer War (1899–1902) and the Spanish-American War (1898)—dealt a strong blow to the advocates of close order tactics. Reports coming from those battlefields were full of descriptions of units in close order paralyzed, destroyed, or, at the very least, decimated, by unseen assassins armed with the new weapons. Many veterans of these battles came home convinced that the well-ordered mob was no match for marksmen capable of moving and firing as individuals.

Building upon a half century of work by such organizations as the American and British National Rifle Associations and uniformed supporters of skirmisher tactics, the partisans of what were often called "Boer tactics" enjoyed three or four years of ascendancy. While American and British infantry units came to resemble full-time rifle clubs, French and German conscripts practiced the art of crawling forward over the recently harvested grain fields that provided their countries' closest approximation to the South African Veldt.

A more general and more lasting result of the wars of the turn of the century was a change in military fashion. In the dozen years that followed that conflict, nearly every army in the world began to replace their brightly colored uniforms with less ornate clothing dyed in subtle shades of brown, green, or gray. Such clothing had long been used in colonial warfare. Its general introduction, however, required that generals and war ministers be convinced that the tangible benefits of reduced visibility outweighed the psychological benefits provided by pomp and ceremony.

The failure of the French infantry to adopt such a uniform is the exception that proves the rule. In 1903, the French military authorities began looking for a replacement for the red and blue uniform that French infantrymen had worn since the 1830s. Clearly influenced by the recent fighting in South Africa, one of the first proposed replacements consisted of a bluish-gray tunic and trousers topped off with a wide-brimmed "Boer" hat. Other proposals were variations on the same theme, with cork helmets, képis, and grayish-green taking the place of bluish-gray. Such drabness, however, did not sit well with either the French populace or their representatives in the Chamber of Deputies. As a result, the French infantrymen who went to war in 1914 did so in the uniforms of 1870.[6]

The high water mark of the influence of the skirmisher school seems to have been reached about 1904 or 1905. At that point, the enthusiasts of "Boer tactics" (as they were often called at the time) began to give ground to a second revival of the close order school. The immediate cause of this renaissance was a series of reports coming from the battlefields of Manchuria, where, in 1904 and 1905, the Russians and Japanese engaged in what has often been called the "dress rehearsal" for the Great War. These reports, particularly those dealing with the earlier battles, generally described the Japanese victors as faithful practitioners of close order fighting.

While not an entirely reliable means of evaluating a war in which the infantry tactics of both sides seem to have gotten progressively more open as time went on, the reports of the successful employment of close order tactics had great effect. One reason was the widespread view that the Russo-Japanese War, though a conflict between two Asian powers over control of Chinese territory, was a closer analogue to a future European War than the Second Anglo-Boer War. Another cause was the clear line of paternity connecting European theory and Japanese practice. For not only had senior Japanese officers been personally trained by Jakob Meckel, one of the most eloquent German advocates of close order tactics, but the Japanese infantry had been trained according to a verbatim translation of the 1888 edition of the German drill regulations—a book that leaned heavily in the direction of the close order school.[7]

Reports from the battlefields of the next major European conflicts—the two Balkan Wars of 1912 and 1913—would have tended to discredit the close order school.[8] Before the pendulum of professional opinion could swing back in the direction of the skirmisher school, however, the Great War broke out. As a result, there were infantrymen in 1914 whose tactics were no better suited to the rapid fire weapons—magazine rifles, quick-firing artillery, and the occasional machine gun—of the day than the bright-colored uniforms of the French. At the same time, there were other soldiers who had both retained their faith in skirmisher tactics and recognized its implications—in particular the need to stress both individual initiative and marksmanship.

The grenadier and foot regiments of the Prussian Guard practiced tactics that put them firmly in the close order school of tactics. The same can be said for many French units as well as some Russian outfits that had not benefited from the reforms that had followed the Russo-Japanese War. *Jäger* battalions and many (but not all) of the other units that had historically specialized in skirmishing retained their traditional approach to tactics.[9] British professionals and soldiers from mountain states such as Switzerland, Serbia, and Montenegro could easily be described as practicing skirmisher tactics.

The bulk of the infantry of the world's European style armies, however, practiced a mixture of the two styles. The intervals between men varied according to the regulations set down by war ministries, the standards set down by an inspector or corps commander, or even the local practices of a particular regiment. The standard of marksmanship, the degree to which the private soldier was expected to display initiative, and training in such things as individual cover and concealment also varied widely. Within certain armies—particularly those of Germany, Austria-Hungary, and

Italy—the tendency towards variety was encouraged by decentralized administration. Thus, for example, the tactics of the infantry of one German corps might differ greatly from those of its neighbor.

While the differences in tactics among various infantry organizations were marked, there was also a strong consensus on a number of points. The greatest was the importance of rifle fire. Advocates of close order tactics wanted to pack a large number of riflemen into a small space in order to concentrate fire power as well as to prevent fear of enemy fire from turning into panic or inaction. Advocates of skirmish tactics feared the effects of enemy fire on troops that were too close together. Both opinions were based on a healthy respect for the ability of the well-handled magazine rifle to put out a heavy volume of accurate fire.

It was perhaps for this reason that the infantrymen of the decade preceding 1904 displayed little interest in the machine gun. The obvious advantage of this latter weapon was its firepower. Firepower, however, was something that, thanks to the magazine rifle—the infantry already had in abundance. The obvious disadvantages were weight and complexity. At a time when military journals were still filled with worries about *riflemen* running out of ammunition, a 50-kilogram device that promised to consume even more ammunition was unlikely to prove popular.

The exception that proves this general rule is the fondness for machine guns displayed by elite light infantry units. The men of these organizations—German *Jäger*, French *Chasseurs*, Greek *Evezones*, Rumanian *Venetori*—expected to be put into situations where their rifles—though generally handled better than those of the ordinary infantry—would not suffice. These included the holding of mountain passes and other defiles, covering the mobilization of the bulk of the army (and therefore defending against much larger forces), and cooperating with the action of large cavalry units. (Even when dismounted, cavalry suffered from a severe shortage of firepower. When the men needed to hold the horses are taken into account, a dismounted cavalry brigade could put fewer rifles into the firing line than a battalion of infantry.)[10]

A second area for broad consensus was organization. With the exception of the *levée en masse* of Montenegro, the infantry of Europe was formed into battalions of about a thousand riflemen each. If these battalions were of ordinary ("line") infantry, they were almost always broken up into four identical companies, each of which consisted of 250 or so riflemen. If, on the other hand, the battalions were of elite light infantry, additional elements were often added. In Germany, for example, a *Jäger* battalion of 1914 consisted of four rifle companies, a machine gun company (of six

Maxim machine guns), and a small company of *Jäger* mounted on bicycles.[11] The aforementioned *Chasseur*, *Venetori*, and *Evezone* battalions were each provided with, in addition to their four rifle companies, a section of two machine guns.[12]

Companies were divided into three or four elements whose names betrayed their relative novelty. The Germans and Austrians called them *Züge*, which might be translated as columns. The French rather prosaically called them *sections*. The British, the last major army to adopt the four company battalion and also the last to have subdivisions of this sort, revived the eighteenth century word "platoon." Beginning with the Germans, who tended to have more faith in their lieutenants than most people, these subdivisions were increasingly placed under the permanent command of a subaltern officer. When officers were in short supply, senior NCOs took their place. In 1913, the French even created the rank of *adjudant-chef* to provide this latter category of platoon leader with additional prestige.[13]

Introduced for tactical purposes—particularly moving men into the firing line—platoons didn't always have a place in the administrative chain of command. The same could be said for half-platoons (*demi-sections* in France, *Halbzüge* in Germany) and squads (*groupes*, *Gruppen*). These latter units also served as a way of feeding the firing line with men and, once they were there, controlling their fire. In the case of Germany, tactical subdivisions of the company, being formed at the morning formation from the men available for duty, had no permanent character. Thus, the German lieutenant or senior NCO who led a platoon in combat and the young NCO who led a squad was responsible for such things as making the best use of cover, the maintenance of direction, and, most of all, fire discipline. If one of the men of these tactical units showed up on parade with unshined buttons or uncombed hair, on the other hand, it was a matter for the company commander, the first sergeant, and the sergeant in charge of the chief administrative subdivision of the company, the "corporalship" (*Korporalschaft*).[14]

Most European infantry battalions were formed, sometimes by twos, sometimes by fours, but mostly by threes, into regiments. By 1914, most of these regiments had received a small number (usually between two and eight) of machine guns. These were either (as in Germany) formed into a regimental machine gun company or (as in Great Britain and France) distributed among the battalions. The tactics for integrating the rather concentrated firepower of these latter weapons with the better understood effect of musketry, however, had yet to be worked out. As a result, the ability of the infantry battalion, regimental, or brigade commander to influence a fight was largely a result of the skill with which he handled his riflemen.

Three or four regiments made up the infantry strength of a division (see Figure 1). In most cases where there were four infantry regiments forming a "square" division (e.g., France, Germany) the regiments were paired to form brigades. Three regiment "triangular" divisions (such as those of Greece and the Ottoman Empire), on the other hand, tended to lack this intermediate headquarters. The major exceptions to this rule were Belgian *divisions d'armée* (with three mixed brigades of two infantry regiments and an artillery battalion each), British infantry divisions (with three brigades of four battalions each), and German second line formations (mixed brigades of four infantry battalions, one artillery battalion, and one or two cavalry squadrons each).[15]

The third area of broad agreement concerned the relative importance of infantry. Though the thirty years prior to 1914 had seen considerable growth in both field and heavy artillery, nearly every person who took the trouble to form an opinion on the subject was convinced that infantry was the arm that decided the battle. This axiom had two important corollaries. The first was that all other arms existed to facilitate the action of infantry. They were, to use a phrase that had yet to come into vogue, "supporting arms." The second was that infantry had to act decisively.

It was this need to achieve decision that led every European-style army, even those which leaned heavily towards skirmisher tactics, to stress the use of the bayonet. Long range rifle fire was an excellent means of driving an enemy to ground, inflicting casualties, and even gaining a certain moral ascendancy over an enemy. Driving an enemy from his position, or putting him in a position where he must choose between surrender and death, required a more immediate threat than that provided by long range sniping.

The first battles of the Great War provided few doctrinal lessions to the officers who had spent their adult lives preparing for such a conflict. Casualties, particularly among the infantry, were heavy. That, however, had been expected. Infantry trying to cross open fields in order to drive an enemy from a prepared position often failed and almost always suffered significant losses. That, too, should have been no surprise to those with even a nodding familiarity with the military literature of the day.

Practitioners of close order tactics, when fighting enemies using similar methods, found their approach worked as advertised. Prussian Guardsmen, for example, discovered that the tactics that had served so well at Solferino were workable as long as the conditions that made them possible—a line of enemy soldiers who were not masters of the sights on

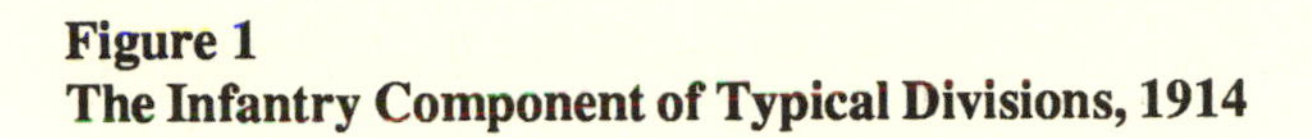

Figure 1
The Infantry Component of Typical Divisions, 1914

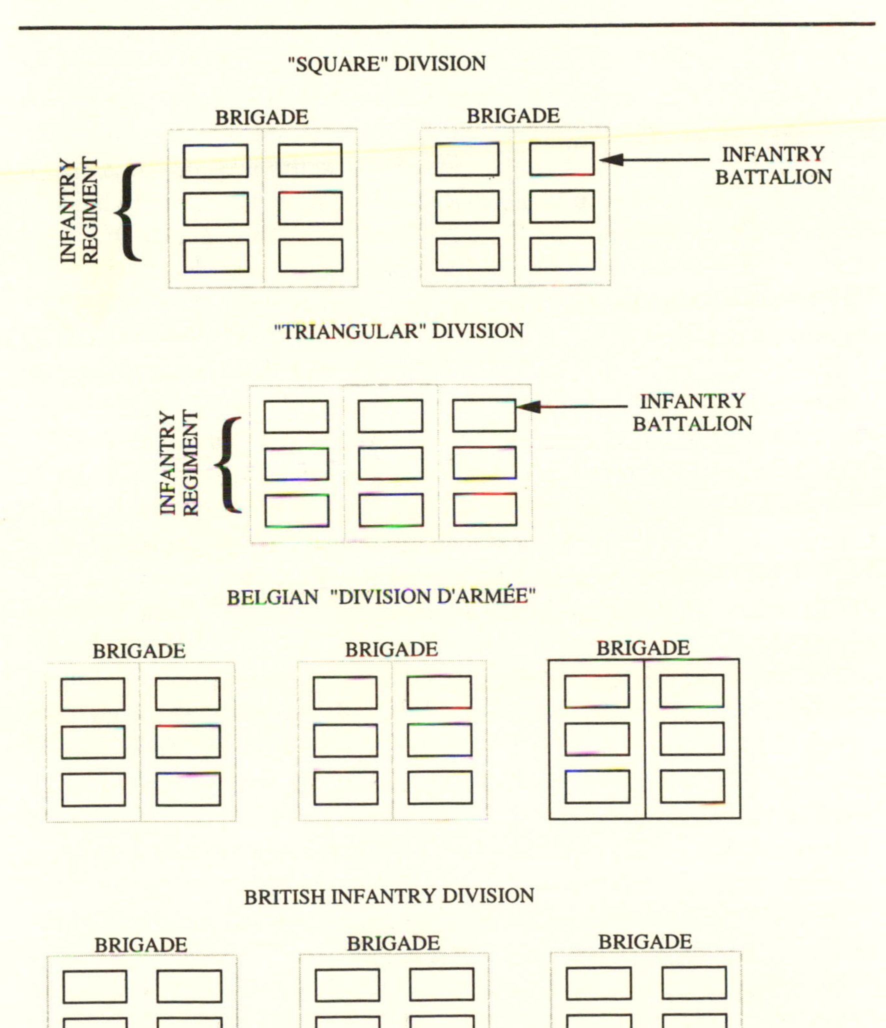

their rifles—held true. When faced with those adept at skirmish tactics, the shoulder-to-shoulder firing lines proved far too lucrative a target. Thus, the same regiments of the Prussian Guard that had performed so well against the French in August and September of 1914, failed, despite considerable sacrifice, to make any headway against the British in October and November.[16]

Against an enemy who had been able to make modest preparations—the choice of a position with a clear field of fire, a shallow ditch to protect the firing line, and the installation of a handful of machine guns—the defects of close order tactics soon became clear. This was dramatically illustrated by a side–by–side attack of the two Hessian infantry brigades on September 9, 1914 near a town in East Prussia called Gerdauen. The ground was flat and often devoid of cover. With their artillery fully occupied in a futile attempt to knock out the defiladed Russian batteries, the German infantry had to attack without any fire support beyond that provided by the regimental machine guns.

One brigade, the 43rd, dissolved into sections of about twenty-five men who moved forward by short rushes. The brigade commander left the peculiarities of this movement to his subordinates. All he asked was that there be five to ten paces between each man, that there be 300 meters between the sections, and that the riflemen hold their fire until they had reached a position about 300 meters from the enemy. At that point, they would be closer to the Russian infantrymen than the Russian artillery dared to fire and could therefore begin the firefight without the distraction of being shelled.

The movement of the 43rd Brigade over the open field took about seventy-five minutes and cost about a hundred casualties. Three-quarters of these casualties were suffered in a single company. This outfit, commanded by a reserve officer who was either unable or unwilling to let his command dissolve into a cloud of skirmishers, had attempted to attack in close order. The other companies lost, on average, only one man to death or serious wounds. In percentage terms, the company that attacked in close order lost 50 percent of its men. The companies that attacked in open order lost an average of 1.67 percent of their men.[17]

The other German brigade attacking at Gerdauen, the 44th, failed to follow the example of its sister unit. Instead, it attempted to advance in close order. Benefiting from a small woods, this unit was able to get within 800 meters of the Russian line. Once out of the woods, the fifty-man platoons, with less than a meter separating each man from his comrades to the left and right, proved a lucrative target for the Russian rifles, field guns, and machine guns. Losses were so heavy that the attack fell apart.

The very panic whose avoidance had provided the close order tactics with their *raison d'être* caused the survivors to run back to the shelter of the woods.[18]

Whether an attack like that of the German 43rd Brigade would have resulted in so few casualties if the enemy had consisted of the British infantry or had been supported by the French artillery of 1914 is doubtful. By the end of the 1914 campaign, however, the advantages of open order tactics were clear to almost all participants. By the middle of 1915, even the infantry of Prussian Guard—units of which had suffered heavily while trying to charge Siberian Riflemen at Gorlice-Tarnow in May of that year—had given up close order tactics.

The triumph of the open order, however, was not to last long. Even before the peacetime debate had been settled by the cruel arbiter of the battlefield, the seeds of a third approach to infantry tactics were being sown. Appearing at first to be a means of dealing with a special case—the peculiar conditions of trench warfare on the Western Front—this third approach was eventually to become the dominant form of infantry combat in the twentieth century.

NOTES

1. William Balck, *Modern European Tactics*, trans. Louis R. M. Maxwell (London: Sands and Co., 1899), I, p. 105.

2. The best way to get a sense of the relative virtues (and corresponding vices) of the two sorts of weapons is still the report of a test made by Gerhard von Scharnhorst during the early 1800s. An English translation printed as an appendix to Peter Paret, *Yorck and the Era of the Prussian Reform, 1807–1815* (Princeton, NJ: Princeton University Press, 1966).

3. For a detailed history of this replacement, see Dennis Showalter, *Railroads and Rifles, Soldiers Technology and the Unification of Germany* (Hamden, CT: Archon Press, 1975).

4. "Psychological elements are all-important in war, and tactical formations should assist to develop them. It is on psychological considerations that the principles of attack and defense and of the training and leading troops should be based." Fritz Hönig, *Der Taktik der Zukunft*, quoted in Balck, *Modern European Tactics*, I, p. 23.

5. For a detailed description of how the revived close order tactics were supposed to have worked, see Jakob Meckel, "A Summer Night's Dream," serialized in the May, July, and August 1993 issues of *Tactical Notebook.*

6. Anonymous, "Bekleidung, Ausrüstung, und Feldfahrzeuge der Französischen Infanterie," *Vierteljahresheft für Truppenführung und Heerskunde*, 1/1913, pp. 158–165.

7. Leibmann, "Die deutschen Gefechtsvorschriften von 1914 in der Feuerprobe des Krieges," *Militärwissenschaftliche Rundschau*, 4, 1937, p. 460.

8. For more on the Balkan Wars of 1912–1913, see the series on that conflict beginning in the January 1993 issue of *Tactical Notebook.*

9. See, for an anecdotal description, Anton Constantin von Zobeltitz, *Das Alte Heer, Erinnerungen an die Dienstzeit be allen Waffen* (Berlin: Heinrich Beenken, 1931), pp. 42–43.

10. A typical cavalry brigade of 1914 consisted of two regiments of four squadrons of 150 men. This yielded a total of 1,200 men, 300 of whom would be needed to hold the horses of those who had dismounted. The 900 men left to carry carbines thus compare unfavorably with the thousand or so riflemen of a typical infantry battalion.

11. In 1914, the authorized strength of the bicycle company was three officers and 124 men. Germany, Heer, Generalstab. *Taschenbuch des Generalstabsoffiziers* (Berlin: E. S. Mittler, 1914), pp. 18–32, quoted in "Etatstärke der deutschen Truppenteile und Einheiten 1914," *Der Feldgrau*, August 1964, p. 97.

12. Unless otherwise indicated in the notes, all organizational information in this chapter is taken from the 1913 edition of a widely circulated yearbook on the world's armies, *Von Löbells Jahresberichte über das Heer- und Kriegswesen* (Berlin: E. S. Mittler, 1913).

13. It is interesting to note that the NCOs who served as platoon commanders were not necessarily the most senior NCOs in the company. In the case of both the British and the Germans, the command of officerless platoons was given to NCOs who ranked one grade below the company first sergeant (color sergeant, company sergeant major, *Feldwebel*). R. J. Kentish, "The Case for the Eight Company Battalion," *Journal of the Royal United Service Institution*, July 1912, pp. 891–927. (Reprinted in *Tactical Notebook*, December 1993).

14. Zobeltitz, *Das Alte Heer*, pp. 100–103.

15. For details on Belgian organization, see "Plans for Oversized Divisions," *Tactical Notebook*, January 1993; For details on German second line formations, see the July 1993 issue of *Tactical Notebook*.

16. For some excellent descriptions of the tactics used by the infantry regiments of the Prussian Guard throughout the Great War, see Ernst von Eisenart Rothe and Martin Lezius, *Das Ehrenbuch der Garde, die preußische Garde im Weltkriege 1914–1919* (Berlin: Wilhelm Kolk and Verlag Oskar Hinderer, n.d.).

17. These figures assume that out of the twenty-four rifle companies in the brigade, the eight that had been in brigade reserve did not take part in the attack. If they did, in fact, take part in the attack, the average loss for the companies that had moved forward in open order would have been slightly over 1 percent. These figures also assume that the brigade's two machine gun companies, which supported the attack by long range fire, took no casualties.

18. Wilhelm Balck, "Über den Infanterieangriff," *Militär-Wochenblatt*, Number 29, Volume 104, 4 September 1919, pp. 562–66. The 43rd and 44th Brigade formed the 22nd Infantry Division of the XI Corps. After a month of campaigning, the platoons were down to an average of fifty men and the sections (*Halbzüge* or "half-platoons") were thus reduced to about twenty-five combatants.

2.

The Grip of Hiram Maxim

The machine gun has often been blamed for the four years of stalemate that still dominates our image of the Great War of 1914–1918. The armies of Europe, we have been told by no less an authority than Basil Henry Liddell Hart, were locked in the "grip of Hiram Maxim." Insofar as getting trench warfare started, the accusation is unfair. Once started, however, trench warfare provided the machine gun with an ideal medium for steady growth. by the end of the Great War, an impartial observer might even go so far as to say that the infantry consisted of two types of troops—those who served machine guns and those who specialized in destroying them.

First-line infantry units in 1914—made up of young, well-trained men led by professional officers and NCOs—were provided with an uncannily regular proportion of two machine guns for every thousand rifles. Second-line units, though often employed as if they were composed of younger, better trained men, had far fewer, if any, machine guns. Stocks of machine guns held in reserve, moreover, were nearly nonexistent. Once a frontline machine gun was broken, destroyed, or captured, the chances of it being replaced were very small. It is therefore not surprising that the many anecdotal accounts of small unit combat in 1914 show few instances where machine guns were the decisive factor in stopping an attack.

The tactical effect of these relatively rare machine guns was further diminished by the less than optimal tactics used by most machine gunners. The authors of pre-1914 machine gun manuals had tended to view machine gun fire primarily as a supplement to the fire of magazine rifles. Words such as "reserve of fire" reinforced the notion that the machine gun was little more than a mechanical substitute for a section or platoon of riflemen. Combined with a general fondness for opening fire at the greatest possible range, this view resulted in machine gun fire that had roughly the same effect on the enemy as long range rifle fire.

The inability of such a small addition in firepower to prevent the continuation of mobile warfare in 1914 is well illustrated by what happened in the Balkans Wars of 1912 and 1913. The machine guns used in the Balkans were of the same types as those used in 1914. In proportion to the number of riflemen involved, these machine guns were present in only slightly smaller numbers than those of 1914.[1] Nonetheless, trench warfare in the Balkans was, as it had been in the Russo-Japanese War, intermittent. The surrender of a fortress, the clearing of a pass, or even the taking of a series of field fortifications was often sufficient to permit the resumption of open warfare.

The cause of the position warfare that reigned unbroken over the Western Front from the end of 1914 to the end of 1918 must therefore be sought elsewhere. A small part of the blame for the start of trench warfare can be laid at the feet of the field artillery of the German, French, Belgian, and British armies. Not only were the guns and howitzers of 1914 more numerous than those of the Balkan Wars, they were also better handled. Given that the most widely used projectile of 1914 (time-fused shrapnel) was deadly to men in open fields but a mere irritant to those in trenches, the net result of the extra field artillery was to strengthen whichever force was on the defensive.

The real culprit, however, seems to have been the railroad. Railroads permitted the rapid mobilization of armies of unprecedented size. These armies were so large that, even after suffering losses in the hundreds of thousands, they still had enough men to occupy, however precariously, every important terrain feature along a front that stretched from Switzerland to the North Sea. The same railroad also made it possible for them to be kept in place with a steady stream of supplies and replacements. If, moreover, one of these pieces of ground were threatened by attack, the railroad could carry, in a matter of days or even hours, the reserves needed to bolster the defense.

It did not take long for the armies involved in position warfare to realize that the name of the game was economy of force. The key precondition for success—whether in holding ground or attempting to solve the "riddle of the trenches"—was the accumulation of reserves. The key precondition to the accumulation of reserves was learning how to hold ground with the smallest possible number of men.

That the machine gun had an important role to play in economizing on manpower was obvious to most concerned. Even before true machine guns (as opposed to multi-barrel weapons like the Gatling or Nordenfelt guns) had been perfected, their potential for defending permanent fortifications had been widely appreciated. Now that most of Europe's infantry was intimately concerned with defending field fortifications, few disputed the need for additional machine guns. And few complained as machine gunners gradually took responsibility for producing the bulk of small arms fire needed to defend most positions.

More controversial by far were the implications of extensive use of the machine gun. If machine gun fire had replaced rifle fire as the backbone of the defense, why risk so many lives by packing riflemen in the firing trenches? If machine gun fire was so important to the defense, was not the destruction of machine guns the chief task of the attacking forces?

At first, trenches were packed because there were many men and few trenches. Once time and the advice of the all-too-rare officer of engineers made the construction of more extensive works possible, however, infantry commanders on both sides continued to insist on putting the bulk of their riflemen in the forward trenches. Because this practice was rarely questioned in the Allied armies, there is very little evidence of formal justification. On the German side, where this practice was opposed from the beginning by a number of thoughtful officers, the rationale was clear. General Erich von Falkenhayn, who was simultaneously Chief of the General Staff and War Minister during the first two winters of trench warfare, justified his insistence on the packed forward trench on psychological grounds. Like Jakob Meckel, Fritz Hönig, and Ardant du Picq, Falkenhayn believed that once control of troops had been lost, it was very difficult to regain.

To be fair, General Falkenhayn did not insist that the forward trench be held by riflemen standing shoulder-to-shoulder on the parapets. What he did require was that forward trenches be held at all costs. If the slightest portion was taken by the enemy, it was to be retaken immediately. Commanders who failed in this latter task were sacked.[2] Given these parameters, it is not surprising that most commanders put the majority of their riflemen in the forward trenches.

The irony of this arrangement was that it was not only contrary to established German teaching for position warfare but was also a repudiation of classic notions about the defense of fortresses. Prior to 1914, German engineers designed fortifications—both field and permanent—under the assumption that, given enough time and sufficient shells, a determined enemy could pulverize any trench, outwork, or fort. Defenses were therefore to be arrayed in depth, with plenty of fallback positions which prevented any single breach from becoming a critical rupture.[3]

Unfortunately for the tens of thousands of Germans needlessly slain by his policy, Falkenhayn was less interested in the classical tradition of siegecraft than in the more recent discipline of combat psychology. Against the French attacks of the winter of 1914–1915—attacks that were sometimes made without even the pretense of artillery support—this approach proved workable.[4] Once the Allied armies obtained sufficient artillery, they began to use it to systematically bombard the German infantrymen crowded into their forward trenches.[5]

The result of these bombardments, some of which lasted for more than a week, was, as one might expect, horrendous casualties on the part of the German battalions unlucky enough to be on front-line duty when the offensive began. This, in turn, often resulted in the capture of the German forward trenches. The capture of the German forward trenches, however, rarely translated into a deeper penetration, for the forces that triumphed over whole battalions of riflemen were often stopped by a few dozen well-sited machine guns and artillery pieces located behind the forward trenches.[6]

As might be expected, it did not take long for frontline German commanders to realize that machine guns had replaced rows of riflemen as the "backbone of the defense." The corollary to this realization, that the riflemen packed in the forward trenches would be both more useful and less vulnerable if kept in reserve behind the line, did not take long to develop. Nonetheless, despite much protesting both within and outside his headquarters, Falkenhayn held fast to his dictum of *Halten was zu halten ist*—"Hold what is to be held"—until his dismissal in the late summer of 1916.

Falkenhayn's failure to acknowledge the central role played by machine guns in the defense of German-held territory did not prevent him from recognizing that machine guns were fast becoming an important element in Allied defenses. Thus, while Falkenhayn's belief in mass psychology prevented the Germans from altering their defensive tactics, his desire to deal with enemy machine guns made him a supporter of offensive tactics based on very different principles. In particular, Falkenhayn made possible the formation of the first assault battalion (*Sturmbataillon*). Though it soon developed techniques for dealing with a variety of problems in trench warfare, the first assault battalion was initially formed to experiment with ways of dealing with machine guns.[7]

The central idea behind the tactics of the first assault battalion was the use of squads (*Stosstrupps*) of specialists (*Stosstruppen*) who dealt with each machine gun as an independent tactical problem. The weapons carried by these specialists varied greatly: pistols, pickaxes, different kinds of hand grenades and grenade launchers, carbines, daggers, captured Lewis guns, and flamethrowers were among the weapons tried in the first year of the assault battalion's existence. The specific techniques for using these weapons also varied. The common denominator for all of this variety was as simple as it was radical—the squad had become a combined arms unit in its own right, capable of combining the actions of different weapons to produce a decisive effect upon an enemy.[8]

The squad was not an invention of the Great War. Beginning in 1854 with the Prussian Army, the late nineteenth century saw most armies adopt the practice of dividing their infantry platoons into units of ten or so men led by a junior non-commissioned officer. These squads (called *groupes* by the French, *Gruppen* by the Germans), existed chiefly as a means of supervising rifle fire. Squad leaders designated targets, estimated distances, provided settings for sights, commanded the opening and ceasing of fire, organized volleys, controlled the rate of fire, watched the ammunition supply, and passed on the commands of platoon and company commanders. A secondary function was the control of movement. Where the terrain failed to provide covered avenues by which a platoon might move forward, the squads might be released to move independently, and thus take advantage of more modest cover.[9]

The few cases where pre-1914 squads were expected to act are in keeping with this theme of fire control and supervised movement. A squad might be sent out on a patrol and, indeed, as the nineteenth century progressed, training in patrolling seems to have received increased emphasis in many armies. The mission of a squad on patrol, however, rarely involved decisive combat. A weak enemy (e.g., an enemy patrol caught unawares or a lone courier) would be overwhelmed. A strong enemy would be avoided. Even if the encounter eventually resulted in sustained fighting, the role of the squad would be limited to buying time while the rest of the company or battalion arrived to form a proper firing line.

It was immediately obvious that these new kinds of infantrymen could not be motivated by the same sort of mass psychology associated with long lines of interchangeable riflemen. To perform his tasks on the battlefield, each member of a *Stosstrupp* would have to first provide his own forward impetus. Once forward, he would have to fight without supervision, actively cooperating with his teammates. If the tactical situation changed, as it often did, this cooperation would have to take the form of improvisation.

A partial solution to the problem of motivation was found in the selection of the *Stosstruppen*. At first, they were drawn from the ranks of the pioneers—men who were already used to working in small groups under fire. The next wave of recruits consisted of *Jäger*, men who were used to patrolling as squads and operating their weapons as individuals. Finally, as units of *Stosstruppen* were formed throughout the German army, the extensive use of volunteers from conventional units provided a mechanism by which soldiers could select themselves for this highly individualistic sort of fighting.[10]

Though often psychologically alone in what the Germans of the time called "the emptiness of the battlefield" (*Das Leere des Schlachtfeldes*), *Stosstrupps* did not act in a vacuum. An integral part of their tactics was the extensive use of heavy weapons—machine guns, infantry guns, and trench mortars—to provide a framework within which the *Stosstrupps* maneuvered. In the case of the larger assault units, these weapons were an organic part of companies and battalions. In the case of smaller assault units, these weapons were often borrowed for an operation. In either case, the success or failure of a storm troop operation depended heavily upon the closeness with which the *Stosstrupps* cooperated with the heavy weapons teams.

The framework provided by heavy weapons units performed three essential services for the *Stosstrupps*. The first was the suppression or destruction of enemy heavy weapons. The second was the isolation of the area in which the *Stosstrupps* were operating. The third, which was particular to trench warfare, was the sweeping of the surface of the ground through which *Stosstrupps* would move. This served to trap enemy troops in their trenches and thus make them vulnerable to one of the definitive techniques of Great War *Stosstruppen*—the "rolling up" (*Aufrollen*) of a trench. Though there were many variants of the basic technique, the essential ingredient was a small team moving rapidly from one bend of a trench to another, throwing grenades around each corner and larger charges into dugouts.

Artillery, which played a big role in creating the environment in which the *Stosstruppen* thrived, played a relatively minor role in *Stosstrupp* tactics. The main contribution of the German artillery seems to have been in assisting the infantry heavy weapons with the work of isolating the battlefield. The chief means of doing this were barrages (barriers of exploding shells) and counter-battery fire (the bombardment of enemy batteries). The effects of both types of artillery action were temporary. Barrages inhibited both the movement of reinforcements and orderly retirement. Counter-battery fire was rarely successful in knocking out guns, sometimes successful in silencing enemy batteries, but almost always successful in diverting the attention of at least some of the enemy artillery away from the infantry battle.

Another contribution of the artillery was the preparatory bombardment, a short but intense storm of shells that often preceded an attack. This type of artillery fire was a two-edged sword whose disadvantages sometimes outweighed its advantages. The chief disadvantage lay in the warning that a preparatory bombardment gave the enemy. This, of course, could be minimized by keeping the bombardment as short as possible. Conversely, false preparatory bombardments were useful deception measures.

The chief advantage of preparatory bombardment lay in the destruction of the intregrity of the defense. That is to say, a well-constructed defense consisted of mutually supporting elements—machine guns sited to protect each other, mortars which covered areas that machine gun fire could not reach, and the like. A preparatory bombardment that knocked out one of these elements—even if it was only a single machine gun—would create a small gap in the defense. If they acted quickly enough, the *Stosstruppen* could find and exploit this gap before the defenders could plug it. This was true even though the *Stosstruppen* had no way of knowing before the bombardment which *particular* machine gun would be knocked out.

Like the skirmish tactics of eighteenth century light infantry, which developed fastest in regions (such as North America) and periods (such as 1763–1796) characterized by the absence of large battles, *Stosstrupp* tactics developed on the Western Front at a time when the German Army there was on the strategic defensive. This is not to say that the Germans weren't involved in offensive action; the period from November 1914 through March 1918 was full of German attacks. With the exception of the idiosyncratic German offensive at Verdun, however, these attacks rarely involved the simultaneous employment of more than two divisions. Even much of the Verdun operation might well be described as a series of these small scale attacks rather than a single continuous battle.

German small scale attacks of the Great War took two forms. For the purpose of taking terrain, the Germans employed the "attack with limited objectives" (*Angriff mit begrenztem Ziele*). For purposes where the Germans did not wish to occupy the ground over which they fought, the Germans employed the trench raid.[11] In terms of the tactics employed, these two forms were very similar. Indeed, the chief difference between an attack with limited objectives and a raid was what happened after the initial attack. After a raid, the raiders withdrew to their own lines. After an attack with limited objectives, the attackers sought to retain their hold on the ground just taken.

In both cases, the relatively small scale of the German attacks proved favorable to the development of *Stosstrupp* tactics. Trained *Stosstruppen* were always a minority of the German infantry. The fact that attacks were small and intermittent allowed units of *Stosstruppen* to act as "flying circuses" that moved from one part of a front to another. Within each corps or division, the fact that only a portion of the infantry was attacking permitted a greater concentration of heavy infantry weapons and artillery than would otherwise be the case. The availability of additional artillery was particularly important, for the greater the number of tubes firing, the shorter and more intense the bombardment.

The intermittent nature of German attacks on the Western Front also permitted *Stosstrupp* tactics to mature at a rapid rate. After most attacks, the *Stosstruppen* were relieved by ordinary infantry and withdrawn to safe and comfortable billets far behind the lines. While this caused a good deal of bad blood between the *Stosstruppen* and their more pedestrian comrades, it made possible the instant exploitation of lessons learned and the refinement of techniques.

Some of the ingredients that went into *Stosstrupp* tactics were present in the other armies which fought on the Western Front. The British and the French soon became as keen on trench mortars and machine guns as the Germans. The Canadian and Australian troops that fought alongside the British developed considerable expertise in trench raiding. Neither the French nor the forces of the British Empire, however, made the full transition from the linear tactics of the nineteenth century to the *Stosstrupp* tactics of the twentieth.

The exception that proves the rule is the system advocated by a young French officer, André Laffargue, in a pamphlet called *The Attack in Trench Warfare* (*Étude sur l'Attaque dans la Période actuelle de la Guerre*).[12] From the point of view of artillery and heavy weapons, Laffargue's tactics bore a vague resemblance to those of the *Stosstruppen.* When it came to the employment of small units, however, Laffargue remained wedded to the doctrine of mass psychology.

An attack conducted according to *The Attack in Trench Warfare* was to begin with the destruction of the first German trench by the fire of heavy trench mortars. Additional preparation fire would be provided by the ubiquitous 75–millimeter field guns. The first wave of the attacking infantry would then form a skirmish line and move forward. Strict attention was to be paid to the maintenance of alignment "as on parade," in order to carry along those who would fall back and restrain the "enthusiasts."

Those wire obstacles that had not been destroyed by the fire of the artillery would force the skirmish line to lie down. Individual soldiers would then cross the obstacle and commence firing once they reached the other side. When all had crossed, the line would reform and continue its march towards the enemy trench, which would be taken in a single rush. Instead of employing the varied arsenal of the *Stosstruppen*, Laffargue's infantrymen would rely heavily on the favorite weapon of the mass psychology school of tactics, the bayonet.[13]

Printed with the express blessing of General Joffre and distributed throughout the French Army, Laffargue's pamphlet seems to have been well received. Explicitly designed for ordinary troops (*une troupe normale*), it reaffirmed the central tenet of the French military orthodoxy of the time—the mass army of citizen soldiers.[14] Calling for companies to dissolve in order to move but reassemble to fight, it provided the suppleness needed to reduce exposure to artillery fire without challenging cherished notions about close combat. Finally, by advocating that companies push forward without regard to the progress of neighboring companies, Laffargue may have helped suppress, albeit temporarily, the tendency of French commanders at all levels to sacrifice the tempo of their attacks on the altar of synchronization.[15]

Though English-language editions of *The Attack in Trench Warfare* were soon published in both Britain and the United States, the British generals seemed to have learned nothing from Laffargue. In command of men who, for the most part, lacked any sort of peacetime military training, they were even more worried than the French about the inexperience of their troops and junior leaders. It is thus not surprising (though nonetheless lamentable), that these officers took the idea of the closely synchronized, tightly controlled infantry attack to new depths.[16]

The disastrous British and French attacks of 1915 have often been blamed on the doctrine of "artillery conquers, infantry occupies." A closer look at these attacks, however, uncovers a relative paucity of artillery. Throughout the first year of trench warfare the British, who had plenty of guns and howitzers suitable for such fighting, were painfully short of the right kind of shells. The French had neither shells nor the right kind of guns. (Until the middle of 1917, the majority of French heavy batteries were equipped with pieces that had been designed in the 1870s.)[17]

The attack of two British divisions at Loos, on September 26, 1915, provides a heartbreaking case in point. Twenty minutes of bombardment, which appears to have caused the Germans no casualties, was followed by a pause of about half an hour. Then 10,000 men in twelve battalions advanced up a gentle slope toward German trenches still protected by unbroken barbed wire. At a range of 1,500 yards, the British advance met with a storm of machine-gun fire. Undaunted, the twelve battalions kept moving forward, presenting an enfilade target to a battery of field guns and a frontal target to the German riflemen and machine gunners. In roughly three and one-half hours of exposure to this cross-fire, 385 officers and 7,861 men of the twelve British battalions were killed.

As the remnants of the British infantry staggered away from what the Germans would soon christen the "field of corpses of Loos" (*das Leichenfeld von Loos*), the firing stopped. Whether this was due to the Germans having run short of ammunition or, as they were later to claim, because of compassion for the unfortunate men in their sights, is difficult to determine. What is sure is that nothing that the British did forced the Germans to stop firing. The German units opposite the attack reported no losses of their own.[18]

Needless to say, the disaster at Loos, as well as other similar, (though less one-sided) failures, attracted a great deal of high level attention in both the French and British armies. The lesson drawn from such defeats was not, unfortunately, the correct one. Instead of blaming ineffective infantry tactics, the leadership tended to use the well documented shortage of suitable artillery materièl as a scapegoat. Whether this was a function of an honest misappraisal of the situation, professional negligence, or a callous willingness to trade the lives of brave men for career advantage is beyond the scope of the study.[19] Whatever the underlying cause, the tendency of 1915 to fix blame on an insufficiency of guns and shells became the tendency of 1916 to pin hopes on a surplus of the same items.

By the time of the great Somme offensive of the summer of 1916, the British Expeditionary Force on the Western Front had become sufficiently wealthy in shells to bombard the German positions for a week. It was also sufficiently wealthy in guns to promise the infantry that their every step forward would be preceded by a moving curtain of shells known as the "creeping barrage." The preliminary bombardment was intended as a means of destroying the bulk of the German defenses, particularly the extensive barbed-wire obstacles of the type that had caused so much trouble at Loos. The creeping barrage served to protect the infantry from the handful of die-hards who were expected to survive the bombardment.

The preparatory bombardment, having changed little from the days when cannon served to tear holes in castle walls, was as old as artillery itself. The creeping barrage, however, was a more recent invention. German *Stosstruppen* often used small-scale creeping barrages to protect them during those dangerous moments between leaving the safety of their own trenches and jumping into those of the enemy. It is likely, however, that the British technique was less an imitation of German practice than an elaboration on a lesson learned during the Boer War. Infantry could cross open ground unmolested, the British had discovered in South Africa, if the enemy riflemen were kept under constant artillery fire until the very moment when the firing line made the final dash into the enemy position.

When enemy riflemen were, as they often had been in South Africa or the early months of the Great War, arrayed in a single line, such artillery fire took the form of a single row of falling shells. As the enemy riflemen began to distribute themselves over the ground, and as they were joined by machine guns, infantry guns, and trench mortars, the curtain of artillery fire had to cover more ground. The standing barrage was thus replaced by the lifting barrage and, as the lifts became more frequent and the intervals between them smaller, the lift evolved into the creep.[20]

From the point of view of the British leadership, the creeping barrage had a number of sterling characteristics. Its linear form fit in perfectly with the long, evenly dressed lines of infantry who would follow it at the prescribed distance of fifty yards. Its promise to suppress machine guns relieved the infantry of any need to provide protection. Perhaps best of all, the slow, steady, and relentless pace at which the barrage moved forward provided an excellent means of controlling the battle. Fear of running into the barrage would, to borrow Captain Laffargue's words, "restrain enthusiasts." Fear of being left behind while the barrage crept forward would encourage laggards to keep up with their comrades.

Elegant in theory, the combination of heavy preparatory bombardment with the creeping barrage proved self-defeating in practice. The heavy bombardment was generally successful in destroying German trenches and a significant proportion of their defenders. In doing so, the bombardment also destroyed the linear character of the German defense that the creeping barrage was designed to exploit. Thus, rather than serving as a line of shells protecting lines of Britons from lines of Germans, the creeping barrage became a false beacon, diverting attention from the true pattern of the German deployment.[21] In addition to making the defenders less predictable, the shell holes provided yet another obstacle to the rapid movement of the infantry. In well-drained country, the effect was bad enough. In places where the water table was high, such as Passchendaele in the aptly-named low country of Flanders, the shells could turn patches of open ground into lakes of liquid mud.[22]

Though costly, the assaults of 1915 and 1916 failed to win much ground the the Allies. Indeed, even with local superiorities of five to one, the Allies were never able to break all the way through a German trench system. What the Allies were able to do, however, was kill large numbers of Germans. These, for the most part, were the unfortunate machine gunners and riflemen of the infantry regiments stuck in the forward trenches during the great bombardments. The Germans that presented the thorniest problem for the Allies—the men of the independent machine gun units and field gun batteries posted behind the forward trenches, as well as the men of counterattack units—escaped the worst of the bombardments.

When, in August of 1916, the top leadership of the German Army passed from Falkenhayen to the team of Paul von Hindenburg and Erich Ludendorff, German defensive tactics began to adjust to this reality. Early in December of that same year, the German Supreme Army Command published a seminal pamphlet entitled, *Conduct of the Defensive Battle* (*die Führung in der Abwehrschlacht*). Written by two young officers on Hindenburg's staff, this detailed explanation of the elastic defense had an introduction signed by Ludendorff himself.[23]

The central idea of *Conduct of the Defensive Battle* was that a defensive system was less of a barrier to keep out the enemy than a trap in which to destroy him. To this end, the bulk of the infantry were to be removed from the forward trenches to the rear areas and converted from troops that held ground into counterattack troops. The forward line was to be replaced by a network of small outposts—the defensive equivalents of skirmishers—whose chief task was to repel minor attacks and warn of large ones. In between the front and the rear of the defensive zone was a network of intermediate positions, fortresses of various sizes that served to protect both heavy weapons and small counterattack forces.[24]

The fighting within this intermediate zone bore a strong resemblance to the *Stosstrupp* tactics that had been quietly spreading through the German Army since the middle of 1915. The defending artillery used barrages to isolate portions of the battlefield while heavy weapons such as machine guns, mortars, and infantry guns provided a framework within which *Stosstrupps* maneuvered. As with the offensive version of *Stosstrupp* tactics, the price of adopting the elastic defense was the repudiation of the doctrine that the laws which governed the behavior of mobs applied also to infantry units.

The elastic defense was particularly powerful when full use was made of reverse slopes. Prior to 1914, most military experts had advocated the holding of long, gentle, forward slopes. Forward slopes allowed the defenders the best fields of fire for their defender's weapons and, in an age when the maximum ranges of infantry weapons seemed to be increasing, this was an important consideration. In the aforementioned British attack at Loos, for example, the fact that the German defenses were sited on a forward slope permitted the Germans to open fire at 1,500 meters. If, however, the attacker was able to assemble a respectable artillery park, the magic of the forward slope was reversed. With greater range and considerably more destructive effect than rifles and machine guns, the attacker's artillery was often able to identify and systematically eliminate positions located on a forward slope.

Erecting defenses on a rear slope had the effect of placing an impenetrable barrier (i.e., the crest of the hill) to much of the enemy's artillery fire and most of his artillery observation. This made the small forts that made up the intermediate zone difficult for enemy artillery observers to locate and almost impossible for the big guns to knock out. An early example of this phenomenon is provided by the futile German attempt to use its heaviest artillery—the 420-millimeter "Big Bertha" and the 305-millimeter "Slender Emma" siege mortars—to destroy a handful of French pillboxes during the battle for Verdun. The pillboxes were located in the Caillette Woods on the south slope of Douaumont Ridge; the German siege artillery was located north of Douaumont Ridge. For nearly four months, the Germans fired blindly onto the reverse slope, hoping to place a giant shell on top of each pill box. Despite the extreme ballistic accuracy of the siege mortars, the Germans managed to do little more than harass the occupants of the bunkers.[25]

In addition to depriving the enemy of the full use of his artillery, distributing the bulk of the defenders behind the crest of a hill also served to break up the attacking force into smaller, more digestible pieces. The moment that the first enemy troops passed from the forward slope to the reverse slope they would find themselves alone in very unfamiliar territory. No longer under the eyes of their senior leaders (who, at this time, had gotten into the habit of observing battles through the lenses of telescopes and periscopes), cut off from their reserves and their artillery, they were forced to operate in terrain which they had never been able to study.

Having proved itself sufficiently strong to prevent any Allied breakthroughs in 1917—the year in which the British and French forces on the Western Front reached the peak of their strength—the German elastic defense was, starting in the late fall of 1917, imitated by the British and the French. Lacking the *Stosstrupp* tactics that provided one of the key pillars of the German system, however, both the French and the British succeeded in adopting the outward forms of the elastic defense without capturing all of its essential features.

The British, taking the little fortresses that dotted the landscape as a defining characteristic of the elastic defense, called their version of the elastic defense the "blob system." By focusing on the physical layout, the British missed a number of key elements. The French, who saw webs of *groupes de combat*—small squads built around a single automatic rifle—

as the essence of the new approach to the defense, were closer to the mark. They, too, however, failed to do the things necessary to make their defenses truly elastic.

British counterattack forces were often lacking. When they were available, they tended to be used improperly, either as blocking forces or as part of slow, methodical, terrain-oriented counterattacks. In neither case did the counterattack forces fulfill their definitive function of striking an attacking enemy when he was tired, confused, isolated, and overcommitted. As a result, many British soldiers began to view their little forts as "bird cages" that deprived them of the comfort of the mass without providing any compensating advantage. The fact, moreover, that the garrisons of the "bird cages" were companies rather than squads, put the British in the awkward situation of having units that were too big to hide but too weak to deliver a decisive counterstroke. Finally, as if to highlight their failure to take advantage of rear slopes, the British often placed their company "bird cages" on top of hills.[26]

The French understood the key role played by counterattack forces. They also realized the need for the defenses in the intermediate zone to keep a low profile. Instead of the ostentatious British-style company forts, the French placed individual platoons in ground-level *centres de resistance*. These centers, in turn, were broken down into three or four separate *points d'appui*, each of which was occupied by a squad. (Even though General Foch, one of the chief French exponents of the mass psychology school of combat was now the generalissimo of the French forces, the French army had finally learned to trust its squad leaders.)[27]

The French squad of 1917 bore a superficial resemblance to a *Stosstrupp*. Like a *Stosstrupp* it consisted of specialists armed with a variety of weapons—an automatic rifle or machine gun, rifles, hand grenades, and perhaps a rifle-grenade launcher. Unlike the *Stosstrupp*, the French *groupe de combat* was designed to be, at any one time, capable of either fire *or* movement, but not decisive maneuver. For while the *Stosstrupp* was capable of combining two separate actions into an integrated maneuver—using, for example, the fire of a light machine gun to enable a handful of grenade throwers to creep up within throwing range or the fire of one flamethrower to permit the advance of a second flamethrower team—the *groupe de combat* was designed to fight as an indivisible unit. The job of the French riflemen and grenadiers was to protect the automatic riflemen and machine gunners and keep them well supplied with ammunition.[28]

The French platoon was, from a structural point of view, capable of maneuver in the same way as a *Stosstrupp*. Indeed, with three or four elements, a French platoon was potentially more flexible than many varieties of *Stosstrupp*. The role of a *centre de resistance*, however, rarely required the platoon to act in this way. Rather, the chief purpose of the French platoon strongpoints was to channel the Germans into areas covered by the fire of French field guns. Given that the fire of French 75s was deadly to troops in the open but nearly harmless to troops under cover, this practice, which the British derisively referred to as "shooting at their own troops" not only reduced the need for maneuvering infantry but positively discouraged the garrisons of *centres de resistance* from leaving their trenches.

Many of the commanding generals of French armies were reluctant to adopt Pétain's version of the elastic defense. As a result, it was only tried once during the Great War. That one experiment, carried out at Reims on July 15, 1918 by the French Fourth Army, resulted in a resounding success. That the more conventional defense of a neighboring army against the western portion of the same German attack was significantly less successful supports the contention that Pétain's system was a workable one.[29]

The British version did not fare so well. Two of the five German offensives of 1918 were aimed against the British. In both, the Germans were able to break through the line of British divisions and reach open terrain. In the first (Operation Michael, 21–30 March), the Germans penetrated to a depth of 64 kilometers. In the second (Operation Georgette, 9–30 April), the penetration of fifteen kilometers was not so spectacular. The sequence of events, however, was the same. During the first two days the *Stosstruppen* infiltrated between the British bird cages to attack the British artillery. (Unlike the guns of the French Fourth Army at Reims, which had been positioned so far behind the intermediate zone that they were beyond the reach of both the German counter-battery fire and the *Stosstruppen*, the British artillery was located right behind—and, in some cases, within—the zone of bird cages.) This done, the *Stosstruppen* moved on, leaving the reduction of the bird cages to the many infantry units (many of which were not fully capable of *Stosstrupp* tactics) that followed in their wake.[30] On the third day, the Germans broke into open terrain, where their own exhaustion proved more of a hindrance than the *ad hoc* counterattack forces that were thrown in their path. In both offensives, the Germans were only stopped when the French divisions that had been rushed in by truck and train established new defensive lines.[31]

The cost to the British of the inelasticity of their copy of the elastic defense was high. Of sixty divisions available on the Western Front, nine had been deprived of their contents and a further forty-four reduced considerably. A thousand artillery pieces, 4,000 machine guns, and

300,000 men had been lost.[32] More importantly, the British forces in France and Belgium had been deprived of their power of resistance to a degree that, were it not for the speed with which the French railroads and highways brought outside help, their only salvation would have lain in sea-borne evacuation.[33]

After their second offensive ran out of steam, the Germans launched a third and fourth. On May 27, they attacked French and British forces on the Aisne River, southeast of the battlefields of the previous offensives. On June 9 they attacked French forces on the nearby Oise River. The apparent goal of these maneuvers was to soak up the French reserve divisions that had prevented victory in the previous offensives. This they accomplished by repeating, on a smaller scale, their tactical successes of March and April.[34]

The achievement of depriving the French of their reserves was a temporary one. By the time the Germans were in a position to exploit it with their fifth (and, as it turned out, final) offensive in the vicinity of Reims, the French had managed to reconstitute their reserve of truck and rail-borne infantry divisions. This triumph of French administration points out the fundamental problem faced by the Germans in 1918. They had, in their *Stosstrupp* tactics, found a reliable (though, as they discovered at Reims, less than foolproof) way of loosening the grip of Hiram Maxim. Destroying divisions, however, is not the same thing as defeating armies and, as long as the Allies could plug a gap faster than the Germans could exploit it, the Germans would be deprived of meaningful victory.

In the Allied offensives that followed hard on the heels of the failed German attack at Reims, the roles were reversed. The Allies were still largely wed to the idea that sufficient artillery could preserve infantry from the need to maneuver. Thanks to massive stocks of ammunition, and (particularly in the case of the French) the availability of large numbers of modern heavy guns and howitzers, the Allies were finally able to make this idea work. That is to say, by the middle of 1918, the British and the French were fully capable of pulverizing any German position that they chose.[35] Bringing up the guns and ammunition for such an undertaking, however, usually gave the Germans the option of withdrawing, not only their forces, but also their increasingly precious supplies.[36]

A few notable exceptions to this general trend could be seen in some corners of the Allied camp. Sometime before August 1918, for example, the Australians seem to have come up with their own version of *Stosstrupp* tactics. Whether by imitation of the Germans or coincidental invention, they had learned that a squad armed with Lewis guns (which were perhaps the best light machine guns to be used extensively in the Great War) and grenades was capable of approaching and knocking out a machine gun nest.[37] For the most part, however, even the most progressive of Allied leaders rarely advocated employing squads that were capable of independent maneuver. The Englishman Sir Ivor Maxse and the Canadian Sir Arthur Currie, for example, in criticizing contemporary British "human wave" tactics, only went as far as advocating independent maneuver by platoons.[38]

Though Sir Douglas Haig, commander of the British Expeditionary Force, argued that he had obtained a "technical knockout," the snail-like pace of the Allied offensives of the second half of 1918 permitted the German Army to escape destruction on the battlefield. That they contributed to the German collapse at the end of that year is hard to contest. That they caused the German revolution, the defection of Germany's allies, and the decision of the German leadership to sue for peace, however, is unlikely. The great stalemate of the Western Front thus ended as it began, with external forces—initially the swiftness with which defenders could move their operational reserves and finally the lethargy imposed by an over-reliance on artillery—depriving infantry of its status as the arm of decision.

While the machine gun might be made indirectly responsible for Allied over-reliance on artillery, it can hardly be blamed for the respective layouts of the French and German railroad networks or the virtuosity displayed by the French in exploiting the potential of the truck. It should thus be no surprise that solving the problem of the machine gun would not be sufficient to return to the days when great infantry armies decided the fate of nations in a handful of weeks. On the contrary, the changes made to accommodate the machine gun ensured that infantry would remain "locked in the grip of Hiram Maxim" for quite a few years to come.

NOTES

1. The ratio of machine guns to 1,000 riflemen for the following countries were as follows: Bulgaria, 1; Serbia, 1.3; Greece, 1.3 to 2 (depending on division); Ottoman Empire 1.2 to 1.6 (depending on division); Romania, 1.16. These numbers are derived from information provided by *Von Löbells Jahresberichte über das Heer- und Kriegswesen*, a military almanac published annually during the pre-war period. For the way that these machine guns were distributed, see the detailed descriptions of the various armies of the First and Second Balkan Wars in Volume II of *Tactical Notebook*.

2. The story of Falkenhayn's refusal to allow more flexible defenses is told in Graham C. Wynne's mistitled masterwork, *If Germany Attacks: The Battle in Depth in the West* (Westport, CT: Greenwood Press, 1976).

3. Largely as a result of widespread interest in the siege of Port Arthur and a fear of the delay that Belgian border fortifications might impose on the execution of the Schlieffen Plan, the decade before the outbreak of the Great War was a sort of "golden age" for German combat engineers. For a complete and detailed description, see Paul Heinrici, ed., *Das Ehrenbuch der Deutschen Pioniere* (Berlin: Verlag Tradition Wilhelm Kolk, 1932).

4. Jean Bernier, a French reserve officer, described these as "the unpardonable offensives of the first winter, including one at the Somme in December 1914 about which not a word was ever breathed and during which, from Mametz to Carnoy to La Boisselle, whole regiments charged the enemy lines every day, without a single cannon shot having been fired." Quoted by Robert Cowly in his letter to Bruce Gudmundsson, April 29, 1993.

5. For the details of these bombardments, see Bruce Gudmundsson, *On Artillery* (Westport, CT: Praeger, 1993) and the "French Offensives of 1915," *Tactical Notebook*, December 1992.

6. The details of the British offensives of this period and how they were stopped can be found in Wynne, *If Germany Attacks*. Details of the French offensives are difficult to find in English. For an excellent view of what it was like to defend against the French Champagne offensive of September 1917, see Kurt Bischoff, *Im Trommelfeuer, Die Herbstschlacht in der Champagne, 1915* (Leipzig: Gebrüder Fändrich, 1939).

7. The story of the German assault battalions is told in a number of places. Bruce Gudmundsson's *Storm Troop Tactics: Innovation in the German Army, 1914–1918* (New York: Praeger, 1989) focuses on the years 1915 and 1916. Martin Samuel's *Doctrine and Dogma, German and British Infantry Tactics in the First World War* (Westport, CT: Greenwood Press, 1992) provides a valuable comparison with contemporary British practice. Hellmuth Gruss, *Aufbau und Verwendung der deutschen Sturmbataillone im Weltkriege* (Berlin: Junker und Dunnhaupt, 1939) remains the classic overview.

8. The terms *Stosstrupps* and *Stosstruppen* are different words that are easily confused. Both come from the combination of the word *Stoss* (meaning thrust, as in the thrust of a sword) and different words derived from the French *troupe*. *Trupp* (plural *Trupps*) is the masculine version and refers specifically to a military unit of small size. *Truppe* is the feminine version and refers to a military unit of any size. The plural, *Truppen*, has an additional meaning that is the exact parallel to the English "troops." Thus, the members of a *Stosstrupp* are *Stosstruppen*. (The singular *Stosstruppe* is a grammatical possibility that the authors have yet to see in a German text.)

9. For the introduction of the squad in the Prussian Army, see Dennis Showalter, *Railroads and Rifles*, p. 102. For a description of the squad in the British Army of 1914, see R. J. Kentish, "The Case for the Eight Company Battalion," *Journal of the Royal United Service Institution*, July 1912, pp. 891–927. (Reprinted in *Tactical Notebook*, December 1993.)

10. The anecdotal evidence suggests that many of these volunteers were cavalrymen. Like *Jäger* and pioneers, cavalrymen, whose *raison d'être* was reconnaissance, had been trained to operate in squad-sized units.

11. At the beginning of the Great War, Germans referred to a raid as *Patrouillenunternehmung*—literally "patrol undertakings." By the end of the war, many Germans had switched to the term *Stosstruppunternehmung*—"storm troop undertaking."

12. André Laffargue, *The Attack in Trench Warfare: Impressions and Reflections of a Company Commander* (Washington: The United States Infantry Association, 1916).

13. It is interesting to note that Laffargue soon modified his views on the bayonet. In an article published in March of 1917, he stressed the individual use of aimed rifle fire and hand grenades. He held fast, however, to his opinion about the importance of fighting in line. André Laffargue, "Hints to the Foot Soldier in Battle," *The Marine Corps Gazette*, March 1917, pp. 37–66.

14. Letter of General André Laffargue to Bruce Gudmundsson, October 15, 1987.

15. The rationale for this unfortunate habit was the danger of exposing a flank. The reason, however, seems to be the desire of commanders to keep a tight rein on their subordinates. For an overview of French offensives in 1915, see "French Offensives in 1915," *Tactical Notebook*, December 1992.

16. The French edition of *The Attack in Trench Warfare* was published in 1915 in Paris by the Army Geographic Service Press (*Imprimerie du Service Géographique de l'Armée*). The British edition was published in August of 1915 by the General Headquarters of the British Expeditionary Force. A second British edition was published in 1916 by His Majesty's Stationery Office. Dennis Winter, *Haig's Command, A Reassessment* (London: Viking, 1991), p. 338. The U.S. edition was published by the semi-official *Infantry Journal* in 1916.

17. Gudmundsson, *On Artillery*, pp. 29–38.

18. Wynne, *If Germany Attacks*, pp. 76–77. Sir John Hackett, *The Profession of Arms* (London: Times Publishing, 1963), p. 51.

19. For a discussion of books on this subject, see Winter, *Haig's Command*, p. 323.

20. For the British side of the creeping barrage, see "Infantry Tactics, 1914–1918," *Journal of the Royal United Services Institute*, Volume 64 (1919), pp. 463–65; J. L. Jack, (John Terraine, ed.), *General Jack's Diary* (London: Eyre & Spotswoode, 1964), pp. 144–45, 225–26, and 272; Charles Edmund Carrington, *A Subaltern's War* (London: Peter Davies, 1929), pp. 63 and 137; and Guy Chapman, ed., *Vain Glory* (London: Cassell, 1937), p. 44.

21. The best short description of what happened when the British infantry attacked on the first day of the Somme offensive (July 1, 1916), can be found in Wynne, *If Germany Attacks*.

22. John Swettenham, *To Seize the Victory, the Canadian Corps in World War I* (Toronto: Ryerson, 1965), pp. 148, 181, and 197 and Carrington, *A Subaltern's War*, p. 137.

23. Wynne, *If Germany Attacks*, p. 149.

24. For a detailed description of the way this idea was translated into tactical dispositions, see Wynne, *If Germany Attacks*, pp. 153–58.

25. Hermann Wendt, *Verdun 1916, Die Angriffe Falkenhayns im Maasgebiet mit Richtung auf Verdun als strategisches Problem* (Berlin: E. S. Mittler & Sohn, 1931), pp. 160–61. For the story of how these bunkers were eventually taken, see "German Flamethrowers at Verdun," *Tactical Notebook*, April 1993.

26. Brigadier General Sir James Edmonds and Major A. F. Becke, *British Official History of the Great War: Military Operations, France and Belgium, 1918* (London: MacMillan, 1937), pp. 477–78; Sir Ernest D. Swinton, *Eyewitness* (London: Hodder and Stoughton, 1932), pp. 153; and "Infantry Tactics," *JRUSI*, pp. 466–68. For a detailed treatment of the British failure to understand the key elements of the German system of elastic defense, see Samuels, *Doctrine and Dogma*, pp. 113–36.

27. The French adoption of the elastic defense was largely the work of Phillipe Pétain. Pascal M. H. Lucas, *L'Évolution des Idées Tacticques en France et en Allemagne Pendant la Guerre de 1914–1918* (Paris: Berger-Levrault, 1923), pp. 208–9.

28. The use of *groupes de combat* seems, at this time, to be limited to the defense. For the attack, the French infantry platoon (*section*) was organized into two half-platoons (*demi-sections*), each of which consisted of two seven- to nine-man squads (*escouades*). One of these was an automatic rifle squad (with one automatic rifle and two rifles modified to launch grenades) and the other a squad of grenadier-riflemen (*grenadiers-voltigeurs*). *Note de Grand Quartier Général sur la réorganization de la compagnie d'infanterie n° 9897 de 10 septembre 1917*, quoted in Pierre Guinard et al., *Inventaire Sommaire des Archives de la Guerre, Serie N 1872–1919, Introduction: Organization de l'Armée Française, Guide des Sources, Bibliographie* (Paris: Service Historique de l'Armée de Terre, 1974), pp. 130–31. It would not have taken much imagination to convert such a half-platoon into a *Stosstrupp*. Indeed, this organization may have been an attempt to imitate contemporary German practice. The French infantry weapons—particularly the universally detested Chauchat automatic rifle—were not as well suited to *Stosstrupp* tactics as those of the Germans. After the mutinies of the spring of 1917, moreover, there was little left of the type of low-level enthusiasm for fighting so essential to *Stosstrupp* tactics.

29. For complete descriptions of the battle of Reims, see Gudmundsson, *On Artillery*, pp. 88–103 and C. Asplin, "Surprise in Defence, The Battle of Reims, 15th July, 1918," *Fighting Forces*, April 1939, pp. 2–23.

30. Even in the divisions that had been specially selected and trained for the offensives, only a portion of the infantry was trained and organized as *Stosstrupps*. Though a great deal of variety existed, the infantry training manual then in force presumes that a platoon consisting of light machine gun squads and rifle squads is the smallest unit capable of maneuver. Prussia, Kriegsministerium. *Ausbildungsvorschrift für die Fußtruppen im Kriege* (Berlin: Reichsdruckerie, 1918), pp. 108–23. The combined arms manual, on the other hand, recommends that specialists be added to rifle squads to enable them to become *Stosstrupps* and that *Stosstrupp* tactics become the standard method of attacking strongly defended enemy positions. Germany, Oberste Heeresleitung. *Der Angriff im Stellungskrieg*, paragraphs 56, 57, 60, reprinted in Erich Ludendorff, *Urkunden der Obersten Heeresleitung über ihre Tätigkeit 1916/1918* (Berlin: Ernst Siegfried Mittler und Sohn, 1920), vol. II, pp. 656–57.

31. The story of the Michael Offensive (also called the Picardy Offensive and the Kaiser's Battle) is told in a number of places. Martin Middlebrook, *The Kaiser's Battle, 21 March 1918, The First Day of the German Spring Offensive* (Harmondsworth: Penguin, 1983) is an excellent source for first hand, small unit accounts. Randal Gray, *Kaiserschlacht 1918, The Final German Offensive* (London: Osprey, 1991) presents a day-by-day account. The other offensives have received somewhat less attention. The best short treatment can be found in B. H. Liddell Hart, *The Real War, 1914–1918* (Boston: Little, Brown, 1964).

32. Lucas, *L'Évolution des Idées Tacticques*, p. 233.

33. The sorry state of the British forces in France and Flanders after the two German offensives was not entirely a matter of physical destruction. The command apparatus was in complete disarray, with many commanders (to include the Commanding General of the Fifth Army) shocked into inactivity. The British were also in danger of losing the

great supply and transportation network that enabled them to sustain their divisions. For telling descriptions of this situation, see Tim Travers, *The Killing Ground, The British Army, the Western Front, and the Emergence of Modern Warfare, 1900–1918* (Boston: Allen & Unwin, 1987), Appendix I and G. MacLeod Ross, "Death of a Division," *Infantry Journal*, April 1930, pp. 353–60.

34. Lucas, *L'Évolution des Idées Tacticques*, p. 236.

35. For a description of the French tactics of 1918, see Robert Allan Doughty, *Seeds of Disaster, The Development of French Army Doctrine, 1919–1939* (Hamden, CT: Archon, 1985), pp. 72–86.

36. Dennis Winter, *Haig's Command*, pp. 201, 214–16.

37. The Mills bomb, the standard British grenade, could either be thrown by hand or, with the help of some accessories, fired from a rifle. The Australians and Canadians used both versions.

38. Shelford Bidwell and Dominick Graham, *Firepower, British Army Weapons and Theories of War 1904–1945* (Boston: George Allen and Unwin, 1982), pp. 125–27; Herbert Fairlie Wood, *Vimy!* (London: Corgi, 1972), pp. 76, 85–87, 110–11, and 141, and Swettenham, *To Seize the Victory*, pp. 147 and 149. Sir Arthur Currie also recommended the practice, already standard among *Stosstruppen*, of putting maps in the hands of front-line troops. Wood, *Vimy!*, pp. 86 and 105.

3.

A Fork in the Road

The Western Front was not the only theater of the Great War. There are, indeed, grounds to argue that it was not even the decisive theater of that conflict. Be that as it may, there were many veterans of the Great War whose experience was not that of stalemate but of decisive maneuver by infantry armies. In Russia, Rumania, Serbia, Italy, Macedonia, and Palestine, the attacking infantry had been able to break through defensive positions, exploit those breakthroughs by hard marching, and, in many cases, deliver a blow hard enough to bring a nation to its knees, or, at the very least, the conference table.

In the little wars that followed the Great War—the Russian Civil War, the Russo-Polish War, and the Greco-Turkish War, to name only the largest of these conflicts—this pattern continued. Rifle armed infantry using tactics of the pre-war era retained its status as a strategic weapon, a direct means by which one government imposed its will on another. In both the non-Western campaigns of the Great War and post-war fighting, the reason for this continuation of pre-1914 practices was space. The infantry didn't need to learn how to deal with ground dominated by dozens of machine guns because they often had the option of going around a defended locality. Squads didn't have to learn to maneuver because regiments, brigades, and even divisions could, if well led, solve the problem with a little hard marching.

There were thus many armies—to include those of the recently formed Soviet Union, Poland, Yugoslavia, and Turkey, as well as established states such as Greece and the United States—that saw little need to introduce either *Stosstrupp* tactics of the Germans or the giant artillery parks of the Western Allies. Even the British, who had been wed so closely to the tactics of "artillery conquers, infantry occupies" had cause to retain, if only for constabulary purposes, a great deal of infantry of the pre-war style. (The dismantling of Britain's huge artillery establishment brought few protests, even from British artillerymen. They, like their comrades in the other branches, believed the Great War to have been an anomaly and were just as eager as they to "get back to real soldiering.")

For France and Germany, however, there was no going back. Both powers were well aware that the operational conditions that had created the stalemate on the Western Front were still very much intact. Neither had succumbed to the illusion (which had soon become widespread in the English speaking world) that they had the option of sitting out the next European war. Once they progressed beyond this acknowledgment of the realities of time, space, and human nature, however, the Germans and French parted company. In doing so, they created two very different approaches to infantry tactics. More precisely, both the Germans and the French continued to follow the paths that each army had laid out during the Great War.

The one word that best captures the essence of French infantry tactics as they developed in the 1920s and 1930s is *barrage*. With an original meaning of "dam" (such as a dam on a river), the military version of the French word was less specific than its English derivative. That is to say, whereas the English word refers only to a barrier made up of exploding artillery shells, a French *barrage* could be a barrier of any sort. (A line of land mines backed up by antitank guns, for example, formed a *barrage antichars*.) In the defense, various sorts of barrages, to include barriers of interlocking automatic rifle and machine gun fire established by infantry companies and battalions, kept the enemy out. In the attack, other sorts of barrages (to include a creeping barrage, or *barrage roulante*) combined to form a moving barrier that swept the enemy off a particular piece of ground.

The leitmotiv of the barrage could be seen throughout the organization and tactical dispositions of French infantry units. Three squads on the model of the *groupes de combat* of the Great War made up a platoon. As before, these platoons were designed to form defensive *points d'appui*, in which the fire of the automatic rifles interlaced to form a barrier. In the attack the disposition of these platoons resembled a moving *point d'appui*, where the men of each squad were close to one another but the squads far apart. With artillery doing the work of suppressing enemy activity to the front, the automatic rifles were given the task of covering the intervals between each squad.

In the mid-1920s, the French squad was formally divided into two teams (*equippes*), each of five men and a corporal. One team (the *fusiliers*) served the automatic rifle which was increasingly less likely to be a *Chauchat* and more likely to be the excellent *Châtellerault*. The other team was composed of a roughly equal number of riflemen (*grenadiers-voltigeurs*). Though this organization gave to the French one of the prerequisites to squads capable of decisive maneuver, the same regulations that introduced it also reiterated the doctrine that the squad was indivisible and, consequently, the platoon was the smallest unit capable of being assigned an independent task.[1]

For administrative purposes as well as for attacks, four platoons made a company and four companies (one of which was equipped with heavy machine guns) a battalion. In the defense, however, the need to reconcile the idea of the continual barrier with the irregularity of the ground turned the organization of the defense into an exercise in applied geometry. In the graphic fire plans they were required to prepare when establishing a defensive position, battalion commanders personally laid the straight "directions of fire" associated with an automatic rifle or machine gun into a crisscross pattern custom tailored to the peculiarities of the terrain being defended. This led to extensive reorganization, with machine gun squads and platoons being attached to rifle platoons and companies, and rifle squads and platoons being attached to machine gun companies.

In the course of the interwar period, the number of machine guns in the machine gun company grew steadily. The eight machine guns of 1918 grew to sixteen or twenty in 1940. At the same time, the French added light mortars (60-millimeter) to their companies, medium mortars (81-millimeter) to their battalions, and moved their 37-millimeter Puteaux infantry guns down from the regimental level. (Whether these latter guns were assigned to the companies, the battalions, or both seems to have varied widely.) These new weapons caused the name of the machine gun company to be changed to "accompanying weapons company" (*compagnie d'accompagnement*). There was, however, no appreciable effect on the way the infantry was expected to fight. Employed as single pieces, in pairs, or as groups of three, the purpose of the mortars was to cover patches of ground that could not be effectively covered by automatic rifle and machine gun fire. The Puteaux guns were also deployed to fill gaps in the wall of projectiles that the French planned to place in the path of their enemies.

As they became available, the French also added a considerable number of antitank guns to their infantry division. These were distributed in a way that might be charitably described as equitable. By 1940, the official distribution was two 25-millimeter guns for each infantry battalion, six for each regiment, and twelve for the divisional antitank company. A "battery" of six 47-millimeter antitank guns was also assigned to the division artillery. Rather than being held, as was the case with the German 37-millimeter guns, as a mobile reserve capable of forcefully reacting to a tank attack, these antitank weapons were spread throughout the division, ensuring that everybody got a little antitank defense but nobody got enough.[2]

Perhaps the most extreme expression of the idea that infantry existed to erect barriers of fire was the tendency, which became increasingly marked towards the end of the interwar period, to form independent machine gun battalions from resources that would otherwise have gone into additional infantry divisions. Composed largely of older reservists, the French machine gun battalions were organized exclusively for defensive work. The few rifle squads that were available were given a double allotment and either assigned as single squads to machine gun platoons or formed into platoons organic to the machine gun companies and the heavy weapons company.[3] This distribution ensured that the rifle squads could be used only for their intended purpose—close protection of the machine guns and filling gaps in their fire—but not for local counterattacks.

For the Germans, who explicitly rejected linear forms of warfare in the first postwar edition of their infantry training manual, the metaphor corresponding to the French idea of the barrage was the pincer.[4] At every level, from the squad up to the division, the idea underlying tactical action was trapping the enemy in both claws of the pincer. In the attack, this often took the form of fire and maneuver, with the fire of one element occupying the enemy while the other worked its way forward to a spot from which it could deliver a decisive blow. In the defense, the pincer idea underlay both the way in which counterattacks were conducted and the manner in which they fit into a larger scheme for trapping the enemy. The German willingness to give up ground so that an enemy might better expose himself to a riposte was also a reflection of this underlying concept.[5]

The French and German approaches to tactics were perfectly consistent with their respective nations' strategic plans. Throughout the interwar period, France presumed that, in the case of a war, one or more significant powers—certainly Great Britain and Poland, most likely the United States, and perhaps even the Soviet Union—would eventually come to her aid. This, combined with the belief that it would, as it had in the Great War, take years for France to make full use of her industrial potential, led France to prefer a long war over a short one. The function of the French Army of the interwar period was thus no longer the Napoleonic one of winning a decisive victory in the field. Rather, its purpose was to prolong the conflict so that other forms of pressure—variously identified as a naval blockade, diplomatic pressure, campaigns in secondary theaters, or aerial bombardment—could take effect.

For most of the interwar period the Germans also counted on eventual international intervention to save them from defeat. Denied border fortifications, heavy artillery, and, most importantly, an army large enough to provide a continuous line, the Germans chose a different method of buying time. Coining the term "delaying resistance" (*hinhaltende Widerstand*), the 100,000-man army of long-service volunteers that served Germany between 1921 and 1935 planned to carry out a more elegant version of the slow withdrawal that their predecessors had executed in the second half of 1918. As before, the key to making such an operation work was the ability to inflict a number of small but sharp defeats.

The German concept of the use of a pincer-shaped maneuver to achieve decision in battle was not a new one. The practice can be traced back at least as far as the battle of Altenzaun in 1806. There a reinforced brigade of Prussian light infantry successfully covered the retreat of a larger force by drawing a portion of their pursuers into a three-sided trap. What was different about the German tactics that emerged from the Great War was the integration of small pincer maneuvers into larger ones. That is to say, the pincer maneuvers of squads and platoons formed the arms of the pincer maneuvers of battalions and regiments and the pincer maneuvers of battalions and regiments formed the arms of pincer maneuvers of divisions.

This is not to say that the German pincer maneuvers always corresponded to a particular echelon of command. Indeed, one of the more interesting characteristics of such maneuvers was their asymmetry, the tendency of one arm of the pincer to be significantly larger than another. More evident in wartime practice than in peacetime theory, but nonetheless implicit in the German tables of organization, the general tendency was for the element doing the bulk of firing to be considerably larger than the element doing the bulk of the close combat. The experience of a German platoon in 1918 illustrates this phenomenon nicely.

On March 21, 1918—the first day of the Michael offensive—a flamethrower platoon under the command of a certain Sergeant Grund found itself faced with the task of reducing a "nest" of seven machine guns that had been holding up the German advance into the British "intermediate zone." Each one of the machine guns in the strongpoint had been so well dug in that neither the "hurricane" bombardment which had opened the day's fighting nor subsequent "special treatment" by the artillery was able to knock them out. To make matters worse, Sergeant Grund and his six back-pack flamethrowers—which could reach out to twenty-five meters or so—had to cross 1,000 meters of open ground just to get to the machine gun nest.

Grund asked a nearby infantry battalion to keep the British machine gunners under fire while he and his twenty men (divided into two *Stosstrupps* of ten men and three flamethrowers each) worked their way around what looked like an exposed flank. The suppression of the English machine gun went well—the machine gunners were so concerned with the fire to their front that they failed to notice the maneuvering flamethrower troops. Unknown to Grund, however, the route that he had chosen was dominated by the machine guns of a stranded British tank. Knocking out the tank proved costly. Two flamethrower men were hit before the two *Stosstrupps* could get close enough to fire at the tank. And although the tank's crew was soon silenced by two bursts of flame, the distinctive column of black smoke rising from the tank attracted the attention of the British machine gunners on the original objective. Grund's two *Stosstrupps* were now on their own.

The fire from the British tank had caught one of the *Stosstrupps* off guard. Two men were hit before the survivors could tumble into the shelter of a nearby shell hole. However, rather than let the fact that they were effectively pinned keep them out of the battle, the flamethrower men did whatever they could to draw every last bit of British fire. With the enemy so occupied, Grund and the remaining *Stosstrupp* used an abandoned trench to approach within flamethrower range of the British position. As long as the British didn't know they were near, the flamethrower men worked their way forward slowly and silently. Once the British opened fire on them, Grund's three remaining flamethrowers returned the compliment. Within seconds, seventy-five machine gunners were running out of their trenches with their hands in the air to surrender to Grund and his ten-man *Stosstrupp*.[6]

The first step towards institutionalizing tactics of this sort was to give the *Stosstrupp* a permanent home in the German infantry. This was first done by designing small (seven-man) rifle and light machine squads that could be combined into fourteen-man *Stosstrupps*. This arrangement, in which platoons consisting of two light machine gun squads and two rifle squads could be reorganized into two independent *Stosstrupps*, lasted until 1931 or so. At that point, the platoon was reorganized into three permanent

Stosstrupps of twelve men each. These, each consisting of a five-man light machine gun team (*leichte Maschinengewehrtrupp*) and a seven-man rifle team (*Schützentrupp*) were called the *Einheitsgruppen*. Variously translated as "single-type squad" or "all-purpose squad," the name *Einheitsgruppe* reflected the self-contained nature of this type of squad as well as the fact that it was a single pattern that replaced two previous patterns.

The light machine gun team was armed, at first, with the extremely heavy bipod version of the German Maxim machine gun. Fed by a belt and cooled with water, this model 08/15 possessed considerably more firepower than the light automatic weapons used by the British, French, or American armies of the time. Subsequent models were air-cooled and considerably lighter. They retained, however, both the belt feed and the capacity for relatively high rates of fire of their predecessor. The rifle team (*Schützentrupp*), intended to be capable of a variety of close combat tasks, was armed with rifles, bayonets, and hand grenades. As the German soldier of the interwar period was enlisted for a period of twelve years, the German army was able to simultaneously improve standards of individual marksmanship and preserve the grenade throwing skills of the *Stosstruppen*.[7]

The second step towards making *Stosstrupp* tactics a permanent part of the German infantry's way of doing business was the provision of heavy weapons to the battalion. As was the case with most armies of the time, the battalion heavy weapons initially consisted of heavy machine guns assigned to a machine gun company. In the course of the interwar period, these were increasingly supplemented by medium mortars, beginning with a handful of 75-millimeter mortars detached from the regimental mortar company and ending up with six 81-millimeter mortars that were organic to the machine gun company. When mortars were both few in number and borrowed from the regimental commander, the German machine gun companies placed a great deal of emphasis on the technique of indirect machine gun fire. As mortars became more numerous, the emphasis of heavy machine gun employment shifted to direct fire at long distance.

German machine gun companies had a lot in common with their French counterparts. Both were equipped with the same sorts of weapons. Both were trained in techniques of indirect as well as direct fire. Though both were designed to be employed as units under the direct command of their captains, they were nonetheless capable of hiving off squads and platoons for attachment to rifle platoons and companies. Both combined the fire of their weapons in similar ways—interlocking fires for the defense, concentrated fires for destroying point targets, and interdiction fires for isolating particular parts of the battlefield.

The chief difference between the two sorts of machine gun companies was their relation to other units. The French machine gun company thickened the fire of its battalion along the entire frontage of that battalion. The German machine gun company served to help the battalion commander focus his efforts against a particular vulnerability in the enemy disposition. It could do this indirectly, by isolating the area in which the battalion's other elements would maneuver and by occupying as much of the enemy as possible. The German machine gun company could also do this directly, by fixing the enemy forces most dangerous to the battalion's main effort.[8]

Because of this function, the Germans often referred to the battalion's heavy machine guns and mortars as the "main effort weapons" (*Schwerpunktwaffen*) of the battalion commander. The French machine gun company had no such status. In the defense it was absorbed into—or, more precisely formed the skeleton of—the system of platoon and company strongpoints. In the attack it was detached from the battalion to form the regimental base of fire (*base de feu*)—a grouping of three battalion machine gun companies and the regimental machine gun company. In both cases, the fire of the French machine gun company tended to be distributed rather than concentrated.[9]

To help preserve the heavy weapons of the German infantry battalion from both the Scylla of diffusion and the Charybdis of confiscation by higher authority, other echelons were increasingly provided with main effort weapons of their own. In the early part of the interwar period, infantry regiments had two companies of heavy weapons, one of mortars and the other of infantry guns. By the mid-1930s the mortars had migrated to the battalion machine gun companies and the infantry guns had become the chief main effort weapon of the regimental commander. During roughly the same period, each rifle platoon was provided with a small (50-millimeter) mortar and each company with a pair of heavy machine guns.

The infantry gun was a weapon that, while far from the exclusive possession of the German infantry, became characteristic of its style of fighting. Though often referred to by the confusing term of "infantry artillery," German infantry guns were crewed by men of the infantry and commanded by infantry officers. Their ancestry was a mixed one. One branch led back to the cut-down field pieces first used by the *Stosstruppen* of the Great War, the other to the light trench mortars that, on the eve of the spring offensives of 1918, had been placed on artillery carriages and otherwise modified for direct fire against point targets. The purpose built infantry guns of the 1920s and 1930s were of roughly the same caliber as these ancestors (75-millimeter) but, as their trajectory was flatter than that of one set of ancestors but more curved than that of the other, they might be most accurately classified as howitzers rather than guns or mortars.[10]

The relationshp between the *Einheitsgruppen* and the German battalion had an analog in the relationship between the battalions and the division. In the latter case, the role of the machine gun company was played by the division artillery. Sometimes called the division commander's main effort weapon, the German division artillery would generally be divided into two unequal segments. The larger segment cooperated directly with the infantry of the main effort. The smaller segment performed economy of force missions, to include cooperation with infantry units that were not of the main effort. In keeping with the presumption that Germany would be fighting a highly mobile campaign, the barrage fire of the Great War (to include the elaborate German version of the creeping barrage, the *Feuerwaltz*) was largely replaced by short but intense concentrations of fire.[11]

Commanded by officers who considered personal observation of the battlefield and rapid adaption to changing battlefield conditions among the higher military virtues, the German machine gun companies and artillery batteries were able to perform their functions without excessive expenditure of ammunition. The chief service they provided to maneuver units, after all, was not so much to protect by fire but to prevent surprises. This was done by keeping the battlefield under continuous observation and, to prevent the enemy from taking the full measure of German strength, keeping a portion of the heavy weapons and artillery batteries silent until a truly lucrative target appeared. This, in turn, allowed enemy units that showed themselves to be fired upon as soon as they appeared rather than sometime after fire support had been requested.[12]

In sharp contrast to French and German theories, much of the British thought on the subject of infantry that appeared in the interwar period was a reaction against, rather than an elaboration of, their characteristic practices of the Great War. This was given a jump start by Sir Ivor Maxse, the general in charge of training the large numbers of British troops that arrived on the Western Front in the late spring and summer of 1918. Maxse introduced practices that, though old hat to the Germans and even the French, were revolutionary for the British Army. These included platoons *à la Française*, with two Lewis gun squads and two rifle squads (and thus the capability for independent maneuver) and the use of individual field guns for direct cooperation with the infantry.[13]

The period between the end of the Great War and the beginning of the Second World War was an extremely fertile one for British military thought. Specialized journals such as *Army Quarterly*, the *Journal of the Royal United Service Institution*, and the iconoclastic *Fighting Forces* published articles that reflected a spectrum of ideas far wider than the range of views presented in contemporary German or French journals. Insofar as the future of infantry was concerned, the extreme ends of this spectrum were staked out by the two military writers of the period whose fame has lasted until today, B. H. Liddell Hart and J.F.C. Fuller.

Like the French, Fuller thought that infantry had lost its capacity to maneuver at both the operational and the tactical levels. He did not, however, share the French belief that the Great War had proved the futility of all operational maneuvers. Rather, he pinned his hopes for a restoration of mobile warfare on great armies of armored vehicles—to include what we would now call self-propelled artillery, armored reconnaissance vehicles, and armored engineer vehicles, as well as main battle tanks—that he simply referred to as tanks.

In May 1918, in a military "novelette" entitled "Plan 1919," Fuller laid the foundation stone of his theories of mechanized warfare.[14] This revolutionary plan had as its objective the moral deterioration or psychological dislocation of the German high command. The means was to be a surprise stroke by some 5,000 medium and heavy tanks driving deep into the enemy rear to capture, destroy, or paralyze the enemy's apparatus for command and control. To better effect the desired disorganization, Fuller even suggested that the means of communication should be left intact, as it was "important that the confusion resulting . . . should be circulated by the enemy. Bad news confuses, confusion stimulates panic."[15] The immediate inspiration for Fuller's notion of paralyzing the enemy command structure came from his direct experience on a staff of a British formation on the receiving end of the German offensive of March 21. The idea of using tanks for this purpose was derived from his low opinion of the capabilities of infantry.

Thinking in terms of tactical elements or functions—protection, offensive action, and movement ("guarding, hitting, and moving")—Fuller believed that the tank combined within itself these three tactical elements to a higher degree than any other arm. Armor having "completely defeated the rifle bullet," Fuller deduced that infantry would be reduced to "playing the game of interested spectators." Rather than "queen of battle," infantry would become "queen of fortresses" responsible for "holding by fire and occupying by movement." For the French slogan that "artillery conquers, infantry occupies," Fuller substituted "tanks conquer, infantry holds."[16]

Fuller's many proposals for reorganizing land armies reflected this basic dichotomy. In his *Lectures on F.S.R. III*, for example, he divided the ideal field army into two classes of troops, one mechanized and the other motorized. Fuller saw the first as being the "protective sword" of the second and the second as being the "protective shield" of the first. Each of these classes would likewise be divided into two subclasses. The mechanized force would consist of both a tank and an antitank wing, with the latter consisting largely of antitank gunners and engineers. The motorized force would consist of two types of "second line" troops. "Field pioneers," armed with antitank weapons and transported in cross-country vehicles would establish the defenses of the army of occupation, "the base of the mechanized and motorized troops." The field police, armed with machine guns, rifles, and possibly nonlethal gas, would occupy and organize conquered areas and territories.[17]

Liddell Hart approached the "riddle of the trenches" from a completely different angle. In place of Fuller's belief in the obsolescence of infantry, Liddell Hart devised schemes that would permit infantry to thrive on the modern battlefield. Some of these, like his emphasis on the use of smoke and artificial moonlight, were external to the infantry. Most of his early work, however, was focused on changing the way that infantry performed its fundamental tasks.

A subaltern in the King's Own Yorkshire Light Infantry, Liddell Hart had participated in the 1916 Somme offensive, during which struggle his battalion was destroyed and he was badly gassed. His experience in this and previous actions prompted him to seek, like the Germans, a tactical rather than technical solution to the trench impasse. Eventually invalided to the half-pay list and finally out of the army, Liddell Hart was in the interim to make himself an expert on infantry small-unit tactics and training. In fact, his entire professional reputation as a military critic was founded on his writings and lectures on infantry tactics.[18]

While serving as adjutant to volunteer units in Stroud and Cambridge during the last two years of the war, Liddell Hart published numerous pamphlets on discipline, training, and tactics. Of particular importance was "The 'Ten Commandments' of the Combat Unit—Suggestions on its Theory and Training," in which he stressed that the platoon had now become a "combat unit" in the sense that it contained "several subdivisions, each capable of separate manoeuvre."[19] He also developed a "battle drill," a new and simplified method designed to facilitate movement and to exercise formations that could be applied in battle and practiced on the parade square. However, it was in attempting to devise a new tactical training system for the defense, attack, and counterattack that he came to doubt the validity of tactical precepts and practices that had been taught before and during the Great War.

In 1920, encouraged by General Maxse, Liddell Hart published his "Man in the Dark" theory of war and "A New Theory of Infantry Tactics."

These articles were so well received that he asked to assist in the preparation of the postwar *Infantry Training* manual. In the course of doing so, he devised his "expanding torrent" system of attack for breaking through a defense in depth. He presented his expanded theories in lectures to the Royal United Service Institution (RUSI) and Royal Engineers, and they were subsequently published in several journals and books. This was indeed fortunate because by the time the army manual was circulated through the War Office and Staff College for comment, "the basic ideas had been watered down."[20]

Like Fuller, Liddell Hart thought in terms of tactical functions, and he used the example of a man fighting another in the dark as his model for framing fundamental principles. The analogy of personal combat was to be the "soldier's pillar of fire by night," a framework of elementary tactical principles on which the junior officer and NCO could base their battlefield actions.[21] Hoping to work "upwards from the elementary, instead of downwards from the complexities of large operations," he described the fighter's actions as follows:

> In the first place . . . the man stretches out one arm to grope for his enemy, keeping it supple and ready to guard himself from surprise (principle of protective formation). When his outstretched arm touches his enemy, he would rapidly feel his way to a highly vulnerable spot such as the . . . throat (reconnaissance). The man will then seize his adversary firmly by the throat, holding him at arm's length so that the latter can neither strike back effectively, nor wriggle away to avoid or parry the decisive blow (fixing). Then while his enemy's whole attention is absorbed by the menacing hand at his throat, with his other fist the man strikes his opponent from an unexpected direction in an unguarded spot, delivering out of the dark a decisive knock-out blow (decisive manoeuvre). Before his enemy can recover the man instantly follows up his advantage by taking steps to render him finally powerless (exploitation).[22]

Noting that the actions of the "man in the dark" could be simplified to two, guarding and hitting, Liddell Hart extracted from the five foregoing "battle principles" two "supreme governing" principles: security and economy of force. In applying these to deployment of infantry platoons, companies, battalions, and brigades (all of which were "square" at the time) he deduced that only three dispositions were possible: one fixing, three striking; two fixing, two striking, or three fixing, one striking. Stressing that striking "is useless unless the enemy is first fixed in another direction," he at the same time intimated that the striking body, though not necessarily the largest, is often "the last straw which breaks the camel's back."[23]

In order to train soldiers in these new tactics, Liddell Hart saw the need to get rid of the terminology of linear warfare:

The recognized terms "firing line" and "supports". . . are no longer applicable to modern infantry tactics. In order to instill a correct doctrine into the minds of the average officer and NCO it is advisable to eschew misleading terms, and not try to reconcile modern ideas with out-of-date phraseology. The term "firing line" does not convey the idea of the outstretched arm or of distribution in depth. It suggests a broad frontal attack with no attempt to make use of covered ways of approach or to find the soft spots. In the case of "supports" both the word and the idea are dangerous. It does not inculcate the essential idea of manoeuvre, but rather the obsolete and unsound idea of reinforcing frontally troops who are held up, which means piling the dead in front of the enemy's strongest points.[24]

In developing his argument for fixing and maneuvering "right down to the scale of the smallest combat unit," Liddell Hart emphasized that weight of force in modern war was related to weight of fire and not merely numbers of men. He further stressed that though in large actions it might appear that infantry units have been confined to a purely frontal role, the wider dispersion forced on combatants by the increased effectiveness of modern weapons made it possible for small but well armed groups to infiltrate between enemy strongpoints. The role of the squad, platoon, and company commander in such circumstances should be to exploit "their penetration to change their sector of the battle from a mere bludgeon fight into a manoeuvre combat."[25]

Liddell Hart likened the infantry in attack to a "human tank, comprising both offensive power and protective armour," the former in its weapons and legs and the latter in its field formation, "which prevents more than one of the sub-units being surprised by the enemy." To ensure the efficient operation of sub-units, he recommended adoption of sensible open formations such as diamond, square, and section arrowhead—and the use of field signals. He further recommended the use of section scouts moving ahead by bounds. Maneuver groups and fixing (forward) groups at all levels were to move in the same manner. He finally stipulated that though attacking battalions should be divided into maneuver, forward, and reserve bodies, companies and platoons need only be distributed in the first two.[26]

For breaking through a series of enemy positions, such as the elastic defense used by the Germans in the Great War, Liddell Hart devised the "expanding torrent" method of attack. Again, he based his tactics on the "intelligent manoeuvre of firepower," likening them to the flow of a strong water current exploiting a breach in an earthen dam. The essence of his "scientific system of attack" was to be a combination of "speed with security." Rejecting as a "sheer waste of force" the notion that an attack should be pressed equally at all points, he advocated feeling and testing an enemy position everywhere to find or make a weak spot, and then exploiting that weak spot to the fullest with the use of reserves.[27]

As for method, the first forward (fixing) sub-unit to effect a breach was to continue to advance straight ahead so long as it was still backed up by the maneuver element of its parent unit. Forward units held up on the flanks of the breach would then dispatch their respective maneuver elements through the breach to attack the enemy in the flanks and so widen the gap. Meanwhile, units in the rear would pass through the gap and take over the frontage and lead in place of the units engaged in fighting. With the reduction of the enemy, the latter units would then follow on as maneuver units to support the new forward units. This flowing system of attack was, in Liddell Hart's opinion, universally applicable to all units and formations from the platoon upwards. He cautioned platoon commanders, however, that squads were not tactical units "composed of interdependent fighting parts." Therefore, if a forward squad of a platoon was held up, the platoon commander would have to use his other squads to extricate it before continuing the platoon advance.[28]

The keynote of Liddell Hart's system was simplicity. The maintenance of the pressure of the advance rested with the "immediately superior commander," thus preventing "an unorganized dogfight to get forward, with each unit playing for its own hand." He also foresaw the battle tactics of the infantry becoming more automatic and less dependent on receiving fresh orders from superiors in the rear. In fact, he wanted to drill his framework into junior leaders until they acted on it instinctively.[29]

In the defense, Liddell Hart's "expanding torrent" became the "contracting funnel." Platoons, companies, and battalions would still be broken down into two fixing (forward) and two maneuver (reserve) elements each. These elements would be given an area in which to fight rather than a point to defend. Thus, "if the enemy takes a defense post at a disadvantage, by crushing shell fire, smoke or manoeuvre, the commander should use his initiative to quit the post and take up a fresh position on the flanks of the post so he can outmanoeuvre the attacking infantry." This option was to be available to NCOs leading squads as well as the officers commanding platoons and companies.[30]

While he affirmed the reigning orthodoxy that the defense could not lead to victory, Liddell Hart nonetheless argued that the best way to blunt an attack was to strike one of its flanks. This was to be done generally by moving troops into positions from which the enemy could be taken under enfilade fire but sometimes by assault, by the commanders of the reserve elements. One great advantage of the defense was that reserve elements could be positioned beforehand in critical areas or rehearsed in movement to those areas. Liddell Hart nonetheless emphasized the "sheer waste of force" of a counterassault that fails, and declined to recommend counterattacks by "any unit smaller than platoons." He also placed great stress on mutually supporting fire and active patrolling, with the ultimate aim of all actions being to draw the enemy into a funnel raked by flanking fire.[31]

How much Liddell Hart was influenced by others in developing his theory is difficult to establish. He admitted in his *Memoirs* that he had examined the infiltration techniques evolved by the Germans and imitated by the Allies in the Great War. However, in 1925 he argued that his "expanding torrent" idea differed from the *Stosstrupp* tactics in the important respect that it spelled out a controlled system for expanding the penetration and maintaining the original breadth and pace of the advance. In other words, Liddell Hart permitted far less freedom in the execution of his scheme.[32]

Liddell Hart's system differed from *Stosstrupp* tactics in a number of other important respects. He placed far less emphasis on heavy weapons than the Germans did: the heavy machine gun was still a defensive weapon, the mortar an artifact of trench warfare, and the infantry gun an alien concept. With less faith than the Germans in either the Lewis gun or the squad leader, Liddell Hart declined to design a squad capable of independent maneuver. Most importantly, at a time when German military writers still emblazoned explanatory diagrams with the phrase "Nicht ein Schema!" ("Not a formula!") and stressed the importance of teaching soldiers to think for themselves, Liddell Hart was peddling an all-purpose solution.

Despite these differences, Liddell Hart's writings were well received in Germany. General Fuller, recently returned from observing German army maneuvers in 1935, told Liddell Hart that one German military spokesman had ordered 5,000 copies of Liddell Hart's *The Future of Infantry*—a book, first published in 1933, that explained the expanding torrent in some detail. Heinz Guderian admitted to reading *The Future of Infantry*, as well as many others of Liddell Hart's many books and articles.[33] To argue, however, as Liddell Hart himself later did, that the Germans borrowed their ideas about the *Blitzkrieg* from the Englishman's writings, is to take what was, at most, confirmation of existing ideas for the importation of new ones. Likewise, even if Liddell Hart's claim that *The Future of Infantry* was used as a textbook by the Waffen S.S. and the rifle regiments of some *Panzer* divisions is true, this may have been as much as tribute to the clarity of Liddell Hart's exposition than the originality of his ideas.[34]

Liddell Hart's influence on the British Army was somewhat more pronounced. Though he would later falsely identify himself as the chief pre-war apostle of the *Blitzkrieg* and did, in fact, pass through a short period of nearly complete agreement with Fuller, Liddell Hart's writings on tactics dealt mostly with the infantry.[35] It's not surprising, therefore, that many of Liddell Hart's ideas found their way into the training manuals, organization, and tactics of the British infantry of the late 1930s. As is often the case with the history of ideas, it is difficult to trace the exact route between Liddell Hart's writings and British practice. The circumstantial evidence for such a link is nonetheless considerable.

Those aspects of Liddell Hart's teachings that found the most favor with the British Army were precisely those which were original to it or, at least, in keeping with its prejudices. Thus, the fact that the platoon was, on the very eve of the Atomic Age, the smallest unit of British infantry capable of maneuver was in perfect consonance with Liddell Hart's preference for indivisible squads. Likewise, Liddell Hart's advocacy of battle drill found a permanent place in the hearts of officers who preferred soldiers who reacted to soldiers who thought. Finally, Liddell Hart's lack of interest in infantry heavy weapons fits in nicely with the longstanding inability of the British infantry to make full use of their Vickers heavy machine guns.

Thus, the British infantry battalions that went to war in 1939 did so without a single heavy machine gun. If needed, heavy machine guns would have to be detached from the machine gun battalion attached to most corps and a few fortunate divisions. Despite the availability of a suitable weapon (the 3.7 inch howitzer) there was no evidence that infantry guns had even been considered for a place in the infantry battalion or even brigade organization. Similarly, the British battalion of 1939 had but two medium (3 inch) mortars and no explosive shells for its light (2 inch) mortars. (The latter were conceived of as a means of giving platoon commanders the means of firing smoke shells. Though not directly attributable to Liddell Hart's writings, this was in keeping with his emphasis on the importance of night, mist, and artificial smoke as a means of permitting infantry to close with the enemy.)[36]

There were, however, areas where Liddell Hart's ideas did more than confirm existing prejudices. His proposal that the platoon be simplified by equipping all squads with a light machine gun was adopted at roughly the same time (1936) that the venerable Lewis gun was replaced by the much lighter Bren gun. In place of two rifle squads and two Lewis gun squads there were now three seven-man Bren gun squads. Liddell Hart's insistence that the infantryman be freed of the baggage that turned him into a "human Christmas tree" found its way into the *Infantry Training* regulations published in 1937.

Perhaps the most curious fruit of Liddell Hart's writings was the uniquely British institution of the lightly armored "carrier." Built on the chassis of a midget tank, the carrier was an open-topped armored vehicle capable of carrying its driver, the lighter sort of infantry weapons (Bren gun, antitank rifle, light mortar), and one or two men. Though far from a true tank and even less capable of fighting than the tankettes from which it derived, the carrier came close to fulfilling Liddell Hart's vision, presented in *The Remaking of Modern Armies*, of a small armored vehicle that would protect the infantryman without depriving him of his essential character as an individual combatant.[37] The silly way that these vehicles were used, however, cannot be blamed on Liddell Hart. For, instead of being used to form carrier battalions, the little armored vehicles were parceled out to the walking infantry at a rate of ten or twenty per batallion. This all but guaranteed their use as an aid in battlefield housekeeping—moving weapons and ammunition within the battalion sector—rather than as a means of making the battalion as a whole more mobile.

The harnessing of the carrier to conventional infantry battalions was typical of the kind of compromise that characterized the British infantry of the late 1930s. Additional compromises—indicative of the practice of having committees write manuals—could be seen in the 1937 edition of the official infantry handbook, *Infantry Training: Training and War*. Recommending fire and maneuver and explicitly condemning the reinforcement of troops "held up in the hopes of carrying a position by weight of numbers," it nonetheless prescribed set piece, stereotyped frontal attacks in which the infantry followed a timed barrage. While alluding to the need for depth and flexibility in the defense, *Infantry Training* was full of diagrams that depicted linear dispositions exclusively oriented towards keeping the enemy out of the defensive system rather than destroying him within it.[38]

The Germans, French, and British were, of course, not the only soldiers to think about infantry in the interwar period. The paths taken by each of these armies, however, are indicative of the options that were available to the infantrymen of the interwar period. The Germans followed the route laid by the *Stosstruppen*, who thus became "the trailblazers of the army" in more ways than one. The French also followed a road whose broad outlines could be seen by 1917. Though this was entirely different from the German route, at least it had the virtue of being consistent. Between these two well defined approaches lay the half-measures of the British.

Indeed, it might be said that when presented with a fork in the road, the British turned neither left nor right but forged straight ahead.

To be fair to the British, their reluctance to commit themselves to any logically consistent path was imitated by most other armies of the day. The Italians and Czechoslovaks were caught between senior officers who had been taught by the French and younger ones who practiced tactics on the model of the *Arditi* and *Stosstruppen* of the Great War as well as the *Bersaglieri* and *Jäger* of the previous century. The Americans and the Poles were likewise split between formal doctrine taught by the French and indigenous traditions that placed more trust in the rifle than the automatic rifle.[39]

The war that began in 1939 would give the infantrymen of various countries a chance to see which approach was best. As had been the case with the Great War, however, the infantry debates of the interwar period would soon be overshadowed by the *Blitzkrieg*—a phenomenon so powerful that it surprised even its creators. The job of the thinking infantrymen was now made even more difficult. Not only did he have to evaluate the different approaches to infantry tactics, but he had to find a way of integrating the approach he decided upon into a world turned upside down.

NOTES

1. "French Regulations for the Infantry," *Infantry Journal*, January 1927, pp. 51–59; "The French Infantry Regulations," *Infantry Journal*, February 1926, pp. 187–90; "Military Notes on Foreign Armies," *Infantry Journal*, 1925, pp. 594–99.

2. Stéphane Ferrard, ed., *L'Armement de l'Infanterie Française 1918–1940* (Paris: Gazette des Armes, 1979), p. 13 and "Mass," *Tactical Notebook*, February 1992.

3. Ferrard, ed., *L'Armement de l'Infanterie Française 1918–1940*, p. 13 and "The French Army Machine Gun Battalion, 1940," *Tactical Notebook*, February 1940.

4. Osterroht, "Über Kampfweise der Infanterie, Betrachtungen zu Heft 1 der A. V. I.," *Wissen und Wehr*, 1923, pp. 201–2.

5. The term "pincer tactics" (*Zangentaktik*) was first applied to small unit tactics by Bernhard Reddemann, the reserve combat engineer officer who also coined the term *Stosstrupp*. Bernhard Reddemann, "Die Totenkopf-Pioniere," in Paul Heinrici, ed., *Ehrenbuch des Deutschen Pioniere* (Berlin: Verlag Tradition Wilhelm Kolk, 1932), p. 519.

6. Reddemann, "Die Totenkopf-Pioniere," pp. 521–22.

7. The strong connection with hand grenades often led to *Schützentrupp* being called the *Stosstrupp*. This second meaning of the term *Stosstrupp* was sufficiently confusing to convince a number of German soldiers to favor the term *Kampfgruppe* for a small unit capable of decisive maneuver and reserve *Stosstrupp* for a small team armed primarily with hand grenades. Indeed, many manuals from 1920s referred to the unit formed by combining a rifle squad and a light machine gun squad as a *Kampfgruppe*.

As the term *Kampfgruppe* would soon be applied to larger combined arms units, the attempt met the fate of most attempts to standardize German military terminology and the expression *Stosstrupp* retained both of its meanings. Germany, Generalstab. (7. Abteilung), "Die Entwickelung der deutschen Infanterie im Weltkrieg 1914–1918," *Militärwissenschaftliche Rundschau*, 1938, Vol. 3, pp. 381–82.

8. The German idea of the main effort has been explored in a number of articles that have appeared in the *Tactical Notebook*. These include: "The Main Effort," October and November 1991; "Amiens, 1940: The Schwerpunkt in Action," December 1991, and "78th Assault Division: A Paper Battle," July 1992. The idea of the main effort has been adopted by the United States Marine Corps, and is explained in Fleet Marine Force Manual 1, *Warfighting* and Fleet Marine Force Manual 1–3, *Tactics* as well as the Marine Corps Institute course on *Warfighting Skills*.

9. The regimental machine gun company later became known as the *compagnie regimentaire d'engins* (C.R.E.).

10. Augustin, "Die Minenwerfer des deutschen Heeres (Fortsetzung)," *Technik und Wehrmacht*, 1920, Volume 5/6, pp. 81–85, and Siegfried Westphal, "Von der 'Bombenkanone' zum Infanteriegeschütz," Wehrtechnische Monatshefte, July 1938, pp. 306–12.

11. Osterroht, "Über Kampfweise der Infanterie, Betrachtungen zu Heft 1 der A. V. I.," p. 207.

12. For detailed descriptions of how this worked in practice see Josef Remold, *Tagebuch eines Bataillons Kommandeurs. Das III./Gebirgsjäger Regiment 99 im Frankreichfeldzug* (Munich: Schild Verlag, 1967). A number of Remold's battles have inspired tactical decision games that have been published in October, November, and December 1991; April, August, September, November, December 1992, and January and March 1993 issues of *Tactical Notebook*.

13. For examples of how these worked in practice, see C. E. Hudson, "Flanking Machine-Gun Fire," *The Infantry Journal*, February 1925, pp. 177–82. The French look of these platoons was not accidental. Maxse had been a close observer of French tactical developments since late 1916. See Winter, *Haig's Command*, pp. 338 and 344.

14. This was originally entitled "The Tactics of the Attack as Affected by the Speed and Circuit of the Medium D Tank" and later as "Strategical Paralysis and the Object of the Decisive Attack."

15. J.F.C. Fuller, *Memoirs of an Unconventional Soldier* (London: Ivor Nicholson and Watson, 1936), pp. 322–36.

16. J.F.C. Fuller, *Armored Warfare: An Annotated Edition of Lectures on F.S.R. III (Operations Between Mechanized Forces)* (Harrisburg: The Military Service Publishing Company, 1943), pp. 12, 16–17 and 106–7 and *The Reformation of War* (London: Hutchinson, 1923), pp. 158 and 161–64.

17. Fuller, *Armored Warfare*, pp. 16–17, 70, and 106–7; and *Machine Warfare* (London: Hutchinson, 1941), p. 93. Fuller also noted that "guerilla wars may run concurrently with great ones, wars of the first magnitude, as happened in the Franco-Prussian war." *Armored Warfare*, p. 3.

18. Brian Bond, *Liddell Hart, A Study of His Military Thought* (London: Cassel, 1977), pp. 16–17, 23, and 32–33. On the first day of the Somme the British Army suffered 60,000 casualties, the heaviest day's toll in British military history. Liddell Hart's battalion was practically wiped out; he was one of but two surviving officers. He

had seen enough action by this time, however, to make him reflect that something was wrong with the system of tactics.

19. B. H. Liddell Hart, "The 'Ten Commandments' of the Combat Unit—Suggestions on Its Theory and Training," *Journal of the Royal United Services Institution*, 1919, p. 288.

20. Liddell Hart, " 'Man-in-the-Dark' Theory," pp. 1–22; B. H. Liddell Hart, *Memoirs* (London: Cassell, 1965), vol. 1, pp. 28–29, 31–32, 34–35, and 37–48; Bond, *Liddell Hart*, pp. 10 and 23–24; and Jay Luvaas, *Education of an Army, British Military Thought, 1815–1940* (Chicago: University Press, 1964), pp. 378–79. The 1932 revision of *Infantry Training* was done by General Montgomery, and some restorations were made. Liddell Hart, *Memoirs*, vol. 1, p. 48.

21. B. H. Liddell Hart, "The Soldier's Pillar of Fire by Night; The Need for a Framework of Tactics," *Journal of the Royal United Services Institution*, 66 (1921): 619–20 and 623–25.

22. Liddell Hart, " 'Man-in-the-Dark' Theory," pp. 2–3 and "A Science of Infantry Tactics," *The Royal Engineers Journal* 33 (1921), pp. 169–70. The same material later appeared in *A Science of Infantry Tactics Simplified* (London: William Clowes, 1923).

23. The term "striking body" as used in this paragraph corresponds closely to the German idea of the "*Stoss*" element and exactly to Liddell Hart's use of the word "manoeuvre." The latter word has been avoided in this discussion because it is used differently from the way that "maneuver" is used in the rest of this work. For Liddell Hart, maneuver was a strike, albeit an elegant one. For the purposes of this work, maneuver is a complete action aimed at decisive results and thus includes both fixing and striking.

24. Liddell Hart, "A Science of Infantry Tactics," pp. 170–73; and *Thoughts on War* (London: Faber and Faber, 1944), p. 128.

25. Liddell Hart, "A Science of Infantry Tactics," pp. 173–77; and *Memoirs*, Vol. 1, pp. 44–45.

26. Liddell Hart, "A Science of Infantry Tactics," pp. 171–78 and 181–82. In Liddell Hart's lexicon, "bounds" are tactically defensible features from which one fire element can cover the movement of another. Liddell Hart advocated a pair of scouts from each section, moving individually by bounds, the last signaling the section to come forward or not. He later changed his mind on the use of section scouts, claiming them to be "more nuisance than protection—a source of continual delay, masking fire and breaking up the fighting unit and fire-readiness of the section" (Liddell Hart, *Thoughts on War*, p. 185).

27. Liddell Hart, "A Science of Infantry Tactics," pp. 215–16; and Bond, *Liddell Hart*, p. 27.

28. Liddell Hart, "A Science of Infantry Tactics," p. 216; and Luvaas, *Education of an Army*, p. 380.

29. Liddell Hart, "A Science of Infantry Tactics," pp. 217–18, and "The Soldier's Pillar of Fire By Night," p. 610; and Luvaas, *Education of an Army*, p. 381.

30. Liddell Hart, "A Science of Infantry Tactics," pp. 218–19 and 222; and *Memoirs*, Vol. 1, p. 45.

31. Liddell Hart, "A Science of Infantry Tactics," pp. 219–23; and *Memoirs*, Vol. 1, p. 45.

32. Bond, *Liddell Hart*, pp. 25–27; and Liddell Hart, *Memoirs*, Vol. 1, pp. 43–44.

33. Bond, *Liddell Hart*, pp. 216, 219–21; and 229.

34. This claim is made in Liddell Hart, *Memoirs*, Vol. 1, p. 222.

35. Liddell Hart's most Fulleresque book is an overgrown pamphlet called *Paris, or the Future of War* (London: Kega, Paul, Trench, Trubner, 1926).

36. Chris Ellis and Peter Chamberlain, *Handbook on the British Army, 1943* (New York: Hippocrene, 1976), pp. 22–25.

37. Liddell Hart, *The Remaking of Modern Armies*, pp. 61–79 and 115–16.

38. Great Britain, War Office, *Infantry Training: Training and War* (London: H. M. Stationery Office, 1937), pp. 107, 116–26, 144–71.

39. The characterization of the various armies is drawn from a variety of sources, to include: "Czechoslovakian Infantry, 1923," *Tactical Notebook*, August 1992; the reports of the various U.S. military attachés in Vienna and Warsaw filed at the U.S. National Archives, Record Group 165; after action reports of the various German divisions that served in the Polish Campaign of 1939, U.S. National Archives, Series T-78, Roll 861; Steven Zaloga and Victor Madej, *The Polish Campaign, 1939* (New York: Hippocrene, 1985); Italy, Esercito, Corpo di Stato Maggiore, *Manuale di Regolamenti Per i Corsi Allievi Ufficiali di Complemento* (Rome: Edizioni delle Forze Armate, 1942), pp. 476–94; K. Urban, pseud., *Kurze Zusammenstellung über die Polnische Armee* (Berlin: Eisenschmidt, 1939), pp. 27–30; and Jack Greene, *Mare Nostrum, The War in the Mediterranean* (Watsonville, CA: Jack Greene, 1990).

4.

Fair Weather War

Once France fell, a small army of authors immediately set about the task of explaining the disaster. Some of these, like the great French medievalist Marc Bloch, blamed the defeat on a breakdown in morale. Some claimed that the Germans had simply overwhelmed France and her allies with superior numbers. Others, unwittingly repeating German propaganda, described giant tanks, whole armies of parachutists, and a fifth columnist under every bed. More recent studies of the fall of France have stressed the role of the German armored divisions, the clumsiness of French command and control, and, what is of most interest to this work, the role played by the infantry.[1]

Contrary to the reports that immediately followed the catastrophe, the Germans of 1940 did not outnumber the Allies present for duty on the continent that spring. Together with the British Expeditionary Force, the French, Dutch, and Belgian armies could muster about three million men. The Germans had two and a half million. In the rough calculus of divisions (which omits the large numbers of men in World War II armies that fought in non-divisional units), the Allies had 156 divisions with which to oppose the 136 divisions available to the Germans. The Allies also outnumbered the Germans in terms of tanks, with 3,600 British and French tanks to 2,574 German tanks.[2]

The Germans compensated for their relative inferiority in both men and tanks by the ruthless application of the idea of the main effort. Tanks, motorized infantry, artillery, and combat engineers, as well as motorized services, were concentrated into ten *Panzer* divisions. These *Panzer* divisions were, in turn, formed into *Panzer* corps of (at least) two *Panzer* divisions plus additional motorized infantry, heavy artillery, and specialized assault engineers. So organized, each *Panzer* corps had sufficient strength, mobility, and staying power to both make and effectively exploit a breach in the Allied defenses.

The first three *Panzer* divisions had been created in October 1935. Three more had been added in time for the invasion of Poland in 1939 and four more in the winter of 1939–1940. Though the details of their organization varied considerably—most *Panzer* divisions of 1940 had unique tables of organization and equipment—the basic structure was the same: one *Panzer* brigade, one brigade of motorized infantry, a small artillery regiment, a reconnaissance battalion, a combat engineer battalion, and a small antitank battalion. The *Panzer* brigades consisted of between 273 and 402 tanks organized into three or four battalions. The motorized infantry brigades consisted of four or five infantry battalions, with 75 to 80 percent of the men mounted in trucks, a relative handful in half-tracked armored personnel carriers, and the rest riding motorcycles.[3]

Though many units had a strong cavalry tradition and all of them belonged to the autonomous "army within an army" that provided most of the components of the *Panzer* divisions and corps, there was no doubt that the men of the German motorized infantry were infantrymen in every sense of the word. They were trained to fight on foot using the same basic tactics as the walking infantry. They were provided with the full panoply (and, in some cases, an extra ration) of infantry heavy weapons. In keeping with this method of employment, the German motorized infantrymen were generally referred to as *Schützen*. Literally translated as "riflemen," the term had originally applied to the sharpshooters assigned to line regiments at the end of the eighteenth century and to certain elite light infantry battalions of the early nineteenth century.[4]

In both the 1939 and 1940 campaigns, the *Schützen* and *Panzer* brigades tended to fight separate battles. As a rule, the *Schützen* brigades, working closely with the artillery and engineers, would break through the defensive position. Once this was done, the *Panzer* brigades would exploit the breach by punching through into the "green fields beyond." Sometimes a few tanks would assist the *Schützen* by serving as mobile gun platforms. As a general rule, this service was provided by the heavy weapons organic to the *Schützen* units as well as antitank and antiaircraft units pressed into service as direct-fire artillery. By cooperating with these units and practicing *Stosstrupp* tactics, the *Schützen* were generally able to break through most of the field fortifications that stood in the way.

For attacking particularly difficult defenses, such as those of permanent fortifications, the German Army of 1940 had a number of units that might best be described as updated versions of the elite assault battalions of the Great War. Belonging to the Pioneer Corps, these "assault engineers" (*Sturmpioniere*), practiced *Stosstrupp* tactics with flamethrowers and satchel charges. Their achievements in the 1940 campaign include the siezure of the Belgian Fort Eben-Emael and the capture of the only part of the Maginot Line to fall in battle, the work at La Ferté.[5] The former was an achievement of great importance to the German victory—Eben-Emael blocked one of the more important routes used by the Germans in their invasion of the Low Countries.[6]

The techniques used by the German tank units, combat engineers, and infantry (motorized and walking) differed considerably. Their tactics—the ideas that brought these techniques to life and applied them within the context of a larger plan—were remarkably similar. In the intellectually fertile years of the interwar period, a number of ideas that had long been present in the German military culture were combined with the experience of the Great War to create a new approach to fighting. More precisely, a number of classic military concepts were employed to explain what had been observed and practiced in the Great War.

German soldiers, who were part of an army that had a common understanding of the nature of war but no single way of expressing it, explained this new synthesis in a number of different ways. General Waldemar Erfurth, for example, used the idea of surprise as a means of unifying the various threads of the German approach to tactics. Quoting the German infantry manual which stated that "every action ought to be based on surprise," Erfurth argued that surprise was as important at the lowest level: to machine-gun bursts and mortar fire, the making of a sound, and even the sudden shot of a rifleman—as it was at the highest. Positions of the smallest defending groups were to be changed at intervals so that the enemy was constantly faced with new problems. Mobility, Erfurth reminded his readers, was valuable because, among other things, it was a means of creating surprise.[7]

An alternate way of explaining German tactics in the *Blitzkrieg* campaigns was offered by Friedrich Otto Miksche, a Czechoslovak officer who had served in the Spanish Civil War as well as World War II. Miksche saw the idea of the *Schwerpunkt* as the most frequently repeated motif of the complex tapestry of the *Blitzkrieg*. First applied to warfare by Clausewitz, *Schwerpunkt*, has been variously translated as "center of gravity," "main effort," or "focus of efforts." Trying to capture the idea of a concentration of force aimed at seeking out the weakest point of enemy resistance, Miksche preferred to translate *Schwerpunkt* as "thrust point." This avoided confusion with the French *effort principal*, which referred to that portion of the attack to which the larger portion of the force had been allocated. As Miksche saw it, the *Schwerpunkt* was further distinguished from the effort principal by its flexibility and universal applicability. The French considered the *effort principal* as mainly associated with grand tactics. Miksche saw the *Schwerpunkt* as equally relevant to the movement of a section of infantry as to the maneuvering of an army corps. The *effort principal* was fixed at the beginning of an attack and never altered. The *Schwerpunkt* was subject to change.[8]

At its most prosaic, the idea of the *Schwerpunkt* represented the German willingness to gamble. Forces concentrated where victory was most likely were, after all, no longer available as an insurance policy against disaster. At a more sublime level, the designation of a *Schwerpunkt* allowed the German commander to quickly communicate the essence of his plan. Leaders of units at the *Schwerpunkt* were told that their mission was paramount, that, in effect, overall success or failure rested on their shoulders. All other leaders were provided with a simple criterion for judging their actions—they succeeded to the degree that they supported the units at the *Schwerpunkt*. The designation of a *Schwerpunkt* thus described the most important aspects of a maneuver. This was the point that Field Marshall Paul von Hindenburg was trying to express in his famous dictum that "An attack without a *Schwerpunkt* is like a man without character."[9]

The handmaiden of the *Schwerpunkt* was the *Aufrollen*. Translated literally as "rolling up," it described the lateral exploitation of a breach formed by the *Schwerpunkt*. *Stosstruppen* of the Great War had used the term to portray the action of *Stosstrupps* that had broken into a trench and were clearing it from one side to another. Miksche described the *Aufrollen* as the "immediate and methodical exploiting of each local thrust by side thrusts." These side thrusts served to protect flanks, widen the gap created, and, most importantly, offer new opportunities for decisive action.[10]

An attack organized according to the ideas of *Schwerpunkt* and *Aufrollen* thus searched constantly for a weak point in the enemy's position. This accomplished, the attacker continually used this very point as a launch pad for flank attacks and attacks against the enemy's rear. Such an attack bore a certain resemblance to Liddell Hart's expanding torrent.[11] In contrast to Liddell Hart, who seems to have been content with a tactical success, many German theorists stressed the dangers of spending too much time and energy on widening the gap. To the Germans, the important thing was the rapidity with which a gap was exploited, and not, as both Liddell Hart and Fuller seem to have thought, in its width.[12]

Yet another way of describing the approach used by the Germans during the *Blitzkrieg* years is *Flachen und Luckentaktik*, the "tactics of the surfaces and gap." The message implicit in this designation was simple: areas where the enemy resisted ("surfaces") should be avoided and areas where the enemy was weak ("gaps") should be exploited. The implications were, at least to most British and French officers, radical. Units which encountered resistance, for example, were expected to leave their own assigned sector and follow in the wake of whatever neighbor was making better progress.[13]

This behavior, which in other armies might result in a court martial, required leaders with an unusual degree of intelligence and that peculiar character trait that the Germans called *Verantwortungsfreudigkeit*—a certain willingness to accept, or, more particularly, enjoy responsibility. At least in the early days of the Second World War, the Germans had little trouble finding officers and NCOs like this. This was largely due to the fact that these traits had been valued by the German Army for such a long time that leaders were expected to possess them.[14]

That such leaders required considerable latitude in the performance of their duties soon became obvious. Whether this attitude started with Frederick the Great, with Scharnhorst and Gneisenau during the Napoleonic Wars, or with Moltke during the Austro-Prussian War of 1866, is a matter for scholarly debate.[15] What was clear was that, to a degree unheard of in other armies, the German soldier was expected to do whatever the situation required. Failure to act when the situation demanded action was considered worse than a wrong choice of method. In extreme cases, this philosophy required that a soldier disobey orders that were inconsistent with the situation. Hellmuth von Moltke, the chief of the general staff who did so much to shape the German Army of the late nineteenth century, was fond of recounting the tale of a young major who, on receiving a reprimand from Prince Frederick Charles, offered the excuse that he was only obeying orders; the prince's prompt retort was "His Majesty made you a major because he believed you would know when *not* to obey orders."[16]

During the Great War the latitude traditionally granted to German officers was gradually extended to NCOs, particularly those who served as squad leaders. Indeed, it was the German confidence in their sergeants and corporals that led them to place so much emphasis on the squad: to give it a capability for decisive maneuver and to practice tactics that often left squads alone in the "emptiness of the battlefield." To prepare them for this responsibility, NCOs received training that, in other armies, was usually associated with junior officers. This included the playing of tactical decision games, short scenarios that forced the player to quickly assess the situation, make a decision, and promulgate that decision in the form of orders.[17]

How these traditions and tactical concepts worked to the benefit of the German Army, and, more specifically, to the German infantry, can be seen in the operation that made the subsequent *Blitzkrieg* possible—the crossing, on May 13, 1940, of the Meuse River. This waterway, which ran north from the northern terminus of the Maginot Line through Belgium to join the Rhine just short of the North Sea, formed a natural antitank ditch separating the bulk of the German forces from the Allied field armies. Unless they were to break through the Maginot Line, the German *Panzer* divisions would have to secure crossing points across the Meuse. This, for the most part, was a job left to the German infantry. More specifically, it was a job left for the *Schützen* of the *Panzer* divisions.

The *Schwerpunkt* of the whole German campaign in the west lay with Panzer Group Kleist, an army-level formation consisting largely of five *Panzer* divisions divided into two *Panzer* corps. This great concentration of tanks and motorized infantry, the Germans hoped, would be able to cross the Meuse in force and, racing to the sea, cut the long lines of communication of the Allied armies in the Low Countries. The *Schwerpunkt* of Panzer Group Kleist lay with Heinz Guderian's XIX *Panzer* Corps, a formation of three *Panzer* divisions that was assigned the task of breaking through the French defenses on both sides of the city of Sedan.

The *Schwerpunkt* of the XIX *Panzer* Corps lay with the 1st *Panzer* Division. The most concrete manifestation of this could be found in the way artillery units were assigned to cooperate with each division. The other two *Panzer* divisions of Guderian's XIX *Panzer* Corps, the 2nd and 10th *Panzer* Divisions, were each deprived of their heavy artillery battalion—a unit that, in each case, represented all of the heavy artillery and a third of all of the artillery normally available. These two batallions, plus all of the independent artillery battalions belonging to the XIX *Panzer* Corps were placed under a single artillery commander and ordered to cooperate directly with the 1st *Panzer* Division. This gave the 1st *Panzer* Division a total of 236 artillery pieces, nearly ten times as many as the twenty-four pieces belonging to each of the other two divisions.[18]

Guderian's plan for the operation was a simple one. The divisions would make simultaneous crossings of the Meuse, with their *Schützen* units eliminating the French forces on the south side of the river so that the tanks could cross safely. Once the tanks were on the French side of the river, they would be able to attack due west, and commence their race to the sea. The *Schützen* regiments thus formed the initial main efforts (*Schwerpunkte*) of their respective divisions. This made the 1st *Schützen* Regiment, comprising three of the four *Schützen* battalions of the 1st *Panzer* Division, the main effort of the division that formed the main effort of the corps that formed the main effort of the army that formed the main effort of the whole German campaign.[19]

The French defenses on the south bank of the Meuse were an adaptation of the French doctrine of defense in depth to the particular problem of defending a river line. The now traditional placement of platoon-sized *points d'appui* into company *centres de resistance* was modified to place a greater number of automatic weapons along the bank of the river. A second modification was the use of concrete bunkers, pillboxes, and blockhouses rather than field fortifications to shelter the defenders of these positions. The French division that occupied these positions was a mediocre one. Composed largely of reservists in their thirties it was, nonetheless, well equipped. It had plenty of machine guns, a full measure of antitank guns, and enough extra batteries to double the strength of the divisional field artillery.[20]

When the Germans struck on May 13, the French artillery reacted vigorously. This response was relatively short-lived, for the rear areas of the French position at Sedan were to be the object of continuous bombing and strafing by the dive bombers of an entire German aviation corps. While these attacks inflicted remarkably few casualties on the French artillerymen, they greatly aided the German cause by inciting panic. As some gunners began to move to the rear others used their radio and telephone links to spread the panic to most of the thirty or so batteries belonging to the division. From there, it spread to other arms.[21]

The panic of the division opposite the German main effort at Sedan was of great help to the attackers. In addition to depriving the French of much of their field artillery, the constant flow of refugees moving to the south greatly hampered French efforts to organize counterattacks. The German breakthroughs at Sedan cannot, however, be dismissed as a contest between those who had the will to win and those who had no stomach for a fight. There were cases at Sedan where German probing attacks ran into serious resistance and were called off.[22]

Even at those points where the Germans managed to break in to the French position, success was often hard won. Hard won or not, German success was, in keeping with *Lücken und Flachentaktik*, exploited. French success, on the other hand, was not. Too far to the rear to be even aware of the minor victories of their troops in the front lines, the French generals at Sedan husbanded their reserves. By the time these had been assembled and the counterattacks properly synchronized, the Germans were well disposed to defend their gains.[23]

The relatively small overall role played by panic in the German victory of 1940 can be seen in those breakthroughs where the French did not panic. The German breakthrough at Monthermé, a town overlooking a deep gorge cut by the Meuse west of Sedan, for example, benefited from no such breakdown in morale. The "one resolute and well-equipped battalion" which Liddell Hart believed should have been able to hold the gorge against an army corps was available in the form of a reinforced French machine gun battalion. This battalion was part of a division that had been assembled from machine gun battalions—a division rich in firepower but incapable of maneuver.[24]

The German infantry battalion that attacked at Monthermé was the main effort of an armored corps. The main effort of this battalion was a handful of *Stosstrupps* that had crossed the Meuse in rubber boats at the one place where the French machine gun fire didn't reach. (The fault was not with the original fire plan. The "dead ground" was created by the wreckage of a bridge that the French had recently blown up.) Once across, the *Stosstrupps* began to reduce the French bunkers one by one as the rest of the German infantry battalion crossed the river on an improvised foot bridge.

French artillery fire on the crossing point was, in keeping with the high technical standards of the French gunners of the era, extremely accurate. Had it not been for the quick action of a German sergeant, this fire would have prevented the Germans from reinforcing their *Stosstrupps* on the French side of the river. The NCO, a member of the engineer unit responsible for the footbridge, noticed that the French volleys aimed at the crossing point were fired at intervals of exactly three minutes. Stopwatch in hand, he brought his countrymen through the barrage in relays.[25]

The French counterattack was unusually prompt—two infantry battalions from the division reserve arrived within twenty-four hours. Instead of being used to drive the Germans back across the river, these battalions were used to bolster a secondary line of defense. As a result, the Germans were able to build up their forces on the French side of the river and, a few hours later, break out in force. The fact that French machine gunners were still holding out on the outskirts of Monthermé was of no consequence to the two armored divisions racing towards Dunkirk.

In the 1940 campaign, moreover, panic was hardly a French monopoly. There were at least two cases where German regiments responded to Allied tank attacks by abandoning their positions in an undisciplined manner. At

Abbéville on the Somme, for example, many units of the German 57th Infantry Division responded to the attack of General De Gaulle's 4th Armored Division by running away. At Arras, portions of the *SS. Totenkopf* Division responded to British tanks in the same way. In both cases, the failure of the Allies to exploit their initial victories allowed the leaders of these units to restore order before the next blow fell.[26]

The fact that it was German infantry that made all of the breakthroughs across the Meuse is underscored by what happened when, in the second phase of the campaign, some German divisions attempted to do things differently.[27] While the French had suffered serious defeat in the preceding phase of the campaign—the meeting engagement in the Low Countries and the German breakthrough in the Ardennes—their position was not hopeless. They retained sufficient forces to establish a line of forty divisions along the "Weygand Line"—a meandering, 360-kilometer long front that connected the left wing of the Maginot Line with the English Channel.

For most of its length the French front was located on the south bank of the Somme River. This gave the French a considerable advantage. In most spots a German attack would have to begin with a river crossing under fire. As their success at Sedan and Monthermé had proven, the Germans were adept at such operations. Nonetheless, the Germans were not so foolhardy as to base the outcome of the war on their ability to paddle rubber boats across well-defended water obstacles.

For this reason the Germans had striven, with some success, to establish bridgeheads over the Somme. By June 5, four were firmly established. Two of these—at St. Valery-sur-Somme and Abbéville—were near the Channel Coast and thus formed less than optimal avenues for rapid exploitation. The one near Peronne was far enough inland. Attackers trying to break out of it, however, would soon run into the Avre River. As the Avre ran parallel to the Somme, it would form a convenient "stop line" for any French attempt to contain a German breakout from the Peronne bridgehead. The fourth bridgehead lay just south of the city of Amiens. The two rivers (the Selle and the Noye) on the French (south) side of that bridgehead ran south to north into the Somme. This meant that they would form an obstacle in the path of French forces trying to attack a German breakout while leaving the way clear for the Germans themselves. In short, the Amiens bridgehead provided a first-class jumping-off point for the kind of deep attack that the Germans were so fond of.

For the campaign against France in 1940 the German Army had been broken up into three army groups. Army Group "C" faced the Maginot Line. Army Group "A" faced the northwestern portion of the Maginot Line and the eastern portion of the Weygand Line. Army Group "B" faced the bulk of the Weygand Line, starting at the western boundary of Army Group "A" and ending at the mouth of the Somme on the Channel Coast. In the first week of June, the overall German plan was to break through the Weygand Line and put significant forces *behind* the Maginot Line before making any attempt to take the permanent fortifications. They therefore designated the attack of Army Groups "A" and "B" as the "main operation" (*Hauptoperation*) and left Army Group "C" in a subsidiary role. Of the two army groups of the main operation, Army Group "B"—in whose sector all the bridgeheads were located—was responsible for the main attack. The attacks of Army Group "A" would serve to divert enemy attention and resources from the big push.

Within Army Group "B" the main effort (*Schwerpunkt*) lay with the 6th Army, the formation responsible for the Amiens bridgehead and its immediate vicinity. The most tangible proof of this status came in the form of *Gruppe von Kleist*, a fully gasoline-powered formation consisting of two armored corps of two armored divisions each. General von Reichenau, the commanding general of the 6th Army, expressed his concept of operations as "breaking through the enemy in selected places so that the entire structure and cohesion of his defense is brought to collapse." The two places that Reichenau chose for his breakthroughs were the Peronne and Amiens bridgeheads.

Reichenau believed that the walking infantry and horse-drawn artillery units which made up the bulk of his army were too weak to carry out these breakthroughs by themselves. For that reason, he decided to violate Guderian's concept of concentrating armored troops in large formations. So rather than using four quick-moving divisions of *Gruppe von Kleist* as a single "operational maneuver group," Reichenau planned to split his armored forces between the bridgeheads. This way, when the 6th Army as a whole started to push south, there would be two simultaneous breakouts.

General von Kleist, the commanding general of the temporary formation that carried his name, disagreed with Reichenau's concept. A true disciple of Guderian, Kleist wanted his two armored corps used as a single entity to exploit a single breakthrough at a single location. Instead of scattered objectives on the south bank of the Somme, Kleist wanted to be assigned one objective of operational significance deep in the French rear. Reichenau's response to Kleist's objection was to combine features of both plans. During the first phase of the operation, each bridgehead would still get its armored corps. Once the French line had been pierced, the armored corps would be returned to Kleist's direct control and given the mission of penetrating seventy-five kilometers into the French rear in order to secure crossings on the Oise River and then pushing another sixty kilometers or so to establish bridgeheads over the Marne.

Until this reunion happened south of Amiens, General von Kleist was to occupy himself with breaking out of the Amiens bridgehead. For that purpose, he was given, in addition to two of his armored divisions (the 9th and the 10th *Panzer* Divisions, of XIV *Panzer* Corps), one infantry (the 9th Infantry Division) and one motorized infantry (the 13th) division as well as the elite, overstrength infantry regiment *Großdeutschland.* Even more telling were the orders to the VIII Aviation Corps. This Air Force unit consisting largely of ground attack aircraft was ordered to attack command posts, lines of communication, and known artillery positions in the area between the Amiens and Peronne bridgeheads (centered on the town of Montdidier) where *Gruppe von Kleist* was to reassemble and begin to exploit the breakthrough.

Although his immediate superior seemed to be playing fast and loose with the concept of the *Schwerpunkt*, Kleist himself remained faithful to the traditional interpretation. In his planned breakout of the Amiens bridgehead, he designated one of his two armored divisions, the 10th *Panzer* Division, as the *Schwerpunkt* of the operation. As a reinforcement for its already strong tank and infantry brigades, this division received the services of the *Großdeutschland* regiment.[28] Kleist's other armored division, the 9th *Panzer* Division, was cast in a supporting role on the west end of the penetration. The purpose of the 9th *Panzer* Division's attack was to protect the right (from the point of view of a German facing south) flank of both the local breakout at Amiens and the larger operation.

The artillery of Kleist's task force was to support this operation by focusing on the French artillery on the heights on either side of the German line of advance. Because of their favorable position, the French guns threatened to enfilade any German attack to the south. Their suppression during the attack was thus critical to the success of the entire operation. To ensure that all of the artillery pieces of Kleist's force took part in the counter-battery battle, he put the artillery of all his divisions under the direct control of his corps artillery commander. Only when the battle was underway would Kleist release these guns back to the division. This was a classic German technique, making an artillery *Schwerpunkt* to support the *Schwerpunkt* of the maneuver forces.

On May 30, General Mordant, the commanding general of the 16th Infantry Division, received orders to take over defensive positions south of the German-held city of Amiens. The mission of the 16th Infantry Division was to hold the ground south of Amiens between the Selle River in the west and the Avre and Noye rivers in the east. Because this was the natural route that the Germans would take to break out of their bridgehead, the task of the 16th Infantry Division was, in fact, to prevent such a breakout.

The French position, though not ideal, was defensible. Its major feature was the Dury Plateau, a feature formed by the three valleys—that of the Somme to the north, that of the Selle to the west, and that of the Avre to the east. (The latter two streams are tributaries of the Somme.) To the south, the Dury Plateau had no similar border. Instead, from a level that was about the same as the city of Amiens, it sloped gently until it ran into features belonging, no longer to the Somme, but to the next major river of the region, the Oise. The main features of the Dury Plateau were long, irregular north-to-south meadows, sizable copses and small woods, and small villages whose brick bungalows served mainly as summer homes for well-to-do citizens of Amiens.

The flanks of the 16th Infantry Division were well protected. On the left and the right stood infantry divisions that, although they had seen some fighting, were still very capable of inflicting damage on the Germans. The strength of these flank guards was considerably increased by the terrain: before the Germans could begin their attack against them, they would have had to make an opposed river crossing. To the rear was another infantry division, ready to serve as a second line of defense in case of a German breakthrough.[29] Having spent the month of May in Alsace, far from the fighting in the Low Countries, the 16th Infantry Division was a fresh formation. It was, moreover, at full strength in terms of both men and equipment, with three infantry regiments (of three battalions and a regimental weapons company each), two field artillery regiments, and the usual assortment of combat support and service units. (The only shortage, that of 25-millimeter antitank guns, was partially compensated for by a surplus of the more powerful 47-millimeter antitank guns.) Because of the importance of its position, the 16th Infantry Division was provided with an extra division's worth of field artillery, 120 field pieces in calibers ranging from 75-millimeter to 155-millimeter.[30]

General Mordant had divided his sector (*secteur*) into three regimental sub-sectors (*sous-secteurs*). Designated "West," "Center," and "East," these sub-sectors were placed astride each of the three main roads leading to Amiens from the south (see Figure 2). Each sub-sector was, in turn, divided into three battalion areas, with two battalions (the first and the third of each regiment) in the front line and one battalion (the second of each regiment) in position some six kilometers to the rear. The latter battalions did not, as might be assumed, serve as the reserve battalions of each regiment. Rather, they formed a second, independent line of defense

Figure 2
Dispositions of the French 16th Infantry Division South of Amiens, June 5, 1940

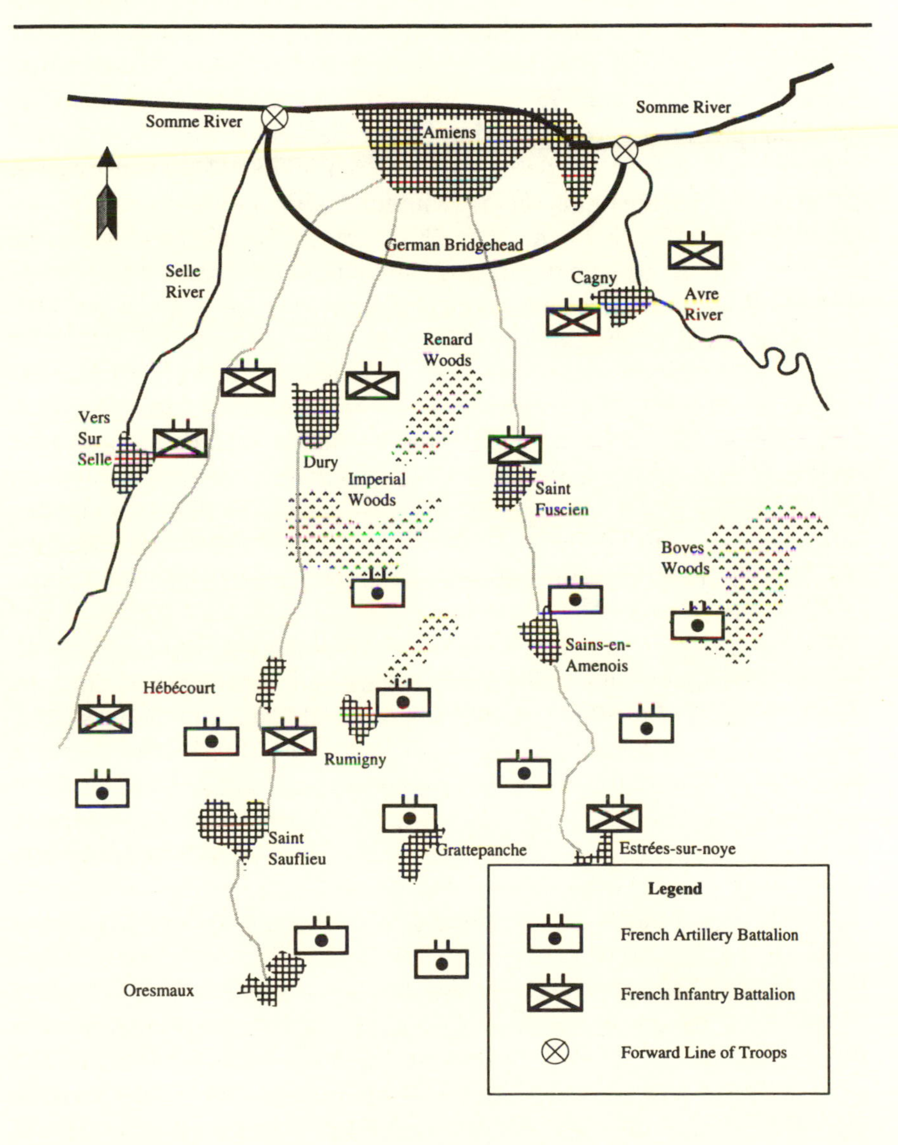

directly subordinate to the division commander. Its chief purpose was indicated by its doctrinal title of "antitank barrier" (*barrage antichars*).[31] Both of the defensive lines—the infantry regiments and the antitank barrier—were further divided into a number of *centres de resistance*. These, which were located in either villages or woods, were each defended by one or two rifle companies reinforced with machine guns, 81-millimeter mortars, and antitank guns. Most of the latter were 25-millimeter and 47-millimeter antitank guns from regimental and division antitank units. Fourteen, however, were 75-millimeter guns which had been taken, as individual pieces or two-gun sections, from the field artillery.[32]

The French plan for the defense of the 16th Infantry Division's sector called for the holding of the sector "without thought of withdrawal" (*sans esprit de recul*). To that end, the bulk of French fire planning seems to have been concerned with organizing "stopping fires" (*tirs d'arrêt*), thick barrages designed to prevent the enemy from entering a given position during the crisis of the defense.[33] This job of coming to the rescue of infantry units in trouble was made more important by a paucity of reserves. Neither infantry battalions nor infantry regiments formed reserves, either for counterattack purposes or to fill the inevitable gaps that would take place once the fighting started.[34] The only reserve worth mentioning, that of the division, was a Mulligan stew of odd units—the divisional reconnaissance group, the divisional schools and replacement unit, the divisional combat engineer company, and two companies (thirteen tanks each) of Renault R-35 tanks.[35]

The German plan called for the armored regiments of the two available armored divisions to attack side by side. The single armored regiment (two tank battalions) of the 9th *Panzer* Division would attack in the west. The two armored regiments (four tank battalions) of the 10th *Panzer* Division would attack in the east, where the ground was more open, the roads more numerous, and thus, the opportunities for a successful breakthrough greater. In keeping with previous practice, the armored regiments planned to attack in waves of battalions. The latter would be massed in tight "wedges" of between five and forty-five tanks that maximized chances to make use of suitable avenues while minimizing the odds that a single barrier might stop the forward momentum of the attack.

The initial breach in the French position was to be facilitated by two infantry task forces (*Gefechtsgruppen*), one of which was to be attached to each of the armored divisions for the purpose of taking the forward strongpoints (the villages of Dury and Saint Fuscien) that posed the greatest danger to advancing tanks. Both task forces were composed of two infantry battalions, a pioneer company, and lots of antitank and infantry guns. The task force attached to the 9th *Panzer* Division was relatively weak in these weapons—it had twelve 37-millimeter antitank guns and part of a regimental infantry gun company. The task force working for the 10th *Panzer* Division, on the other hand, was relatively strong. It had the same heavy weapons as the other task group, plus an additional infantry gun company.[36]

At 4:00 A.M. a portion of the artillery fire shifted onto the forward French positions. Ten minutes later the German infantry task forces, as well as the first tank battalions, had crossed over into the low ground that separated the southernmost German outposts from the first line of French strongpoints. In the west, the first wave of attackers from the 9th *Panzer* Division were stopped by a combination of mines and direct fire (machine guns and antitank guns) coming primarily from the French positions around Dury. In the east, similar means, to which was added long range fire from a battalion of 75-millimeter guns, caused losses to the forward tank units of the 10th *Panzer* Division, but failed to stop them.[37]

At 4:15, in accordance with the original German plan for the attack, thirty or so Stukas struck Saint Fuscien, the northernmost village which straddled the main north-south road in the attack sector of the 10th *Panzer* Division.[38] About the same time, the French 75-millimeter gun battalion which had fired on the German tanks was itself made the object of German artillery fire.[39] At 4:45 the first German tanks reached Saint Fuscien. After a brief skirmish with a French platoon on the north edge of town, they changed their route. At 4:53, the German tank commander reported a successful bypass of Saint Fuscien.[40] Less than ten minutes later, these same tanks were among the French batteries that were arrayed in a rough circle around the village of Rumigny.[41]

In terms of actual destruction, the French guns got the better of the German attackers. For each French gun knocked out, the Germans lost one or two tanks to fire from their intended victims. German losses were particularly heavy when they attacked, without support, French 75-millimeter batteries. German casualties also increased as they progressed further into the French position and began to take fire from the guns of the anti-tank barrier. (Of the latter weapons, the 75-millimeter gun mounted on the turntable platform proved especially deadly. A single one of these managed to destroy six German tanks.)[42]

The German tanks, eager to break through the French defensive system, rarely tarried to complete the work they had begun. Once or twice tanks would try to overrun a battery, destroying with their treads what they could not wreck with their cannon and machine guns. Occasionally, one or two tanks would be left in position to cover a route useful to the artillery. In most cases, however, the German tanks were satisfied with making a pass at a battery in the manner of an eighteenth century warship and leaving the rest of the job to successive waves of tanks. The French batteries were thus in the unenviable position of being attacked by a fresh group of tanks every hour or so.

As if this were not enough, the tanks traveling through the intervals between batteries cut many of the telephone cables that provided the chief form of communication within the 16th Infantry Division. Easily jammed radio communications provided an unsatisfactory replacement. Remarkably, the French gunners used the intervals between the tank attacks to reestablish liaison, repair the damage, and get back to the job of firing on the Germans. Though each tank attack made this more difficult, the French guns were efficient enough to make the German attackers howl (with some justice) that their own artillery had failed to do an effective job of suppressing its opposite number.[43]

From the point of view of the commanding generals of the armored divisions and the XIV *Panzer* Corps, the chief problem presented by the French artillery on the morning of June 5 was its domination of the intervals between the fortified villages. This fire could do little to prevent the tanks of the 10th *Panzer* Division from penetrating as far as the antitank barrier. What it did do, however, was prevent the "soft-skinned" vehicles from following in the wake of the tanks.[44] The damage done to the French batteries in the wake of the tanks, moreover, did little to solve this problem.[45]

Because of this, the overall success of the German attack became dependent upon the seizure of the French strongpoints that stood between the German infantry and the French batteries, as well as upon the progress of the infantry divisions which were attacking the divisions on both sides of the 16th Infantry Division. Unfortunately for the Germans, neither the short preparatory bombardment nor the initial attacks of the German infantry had done more than drive in outposts and cause random casualties to the French defenders of these villages. This failure became apparent to the German corps commander when, around 6:00 A.M., he arrived at the command post of the 10th *Panzer* Division in the bell tower of the cathedral at Amiens. From that vantage point, he noticed that the German infantry in front of Saint Fuscien was making no progress.

The commanding general of the 10th *Panzer* Division, no doubt aware that Saint Fuscien was the biggest obstacle in the path of the unarmored portion of his command, responded to this revelation by putting the full weight of his divisional artillery behind the task force attacking the village. At 7:00 A.M., forward observers from this artillery regiment reported that

German infantry had entered Saint Fuscien. At 7:30 they started to call in fire "in accordance with the wishes of the infantry."[46] By 10:00, the Germans had captured the north half of the village, as well as a number of nearby platoon strongpoints.[47]

German attacks against other portions of the French forward line were even less successful than the block by block capture of part of Saint Fuscien. The attack against the other pillar of the French forward line, the village of Dury in the sector of the German 9th *Panzer* Division, failed miserably. The attack of a single battalion of the 9th Infantry Division against the overlying town of Cagny also resulted in nothing more than German losses.[48] If the intensity of the bombardment is any indication, the attack against Dury was supported, from the very beginning, by both of the artillery battalions belonging to the 9th *Panzer* Division, as well as by some of the corps artillery. This all-day affair, which was interrupted ten times for breaks of ten to fifteen minutes, set both houses and granaries ablaze and resulted in the nearly total destruction of the village. The artillery fire that fell precisely on the village, however, molested neither the cows grazing in the nearby fields nor the French infantrymen ambushing German patrols in the nearby woods.[49]

While the infantrymen and gunners were fighting for the villages, the tank brigade of the German 10th *Panzer* Division was making steady progress towards the south. At 7:00 A.M., it had run into a portion of the French antitank barrier near the village of Grattepanche. By 9:00, the German tanks had penetrated that barrier, apparently with little trouble, and began the process of regrouping. In less than five hours, they had broken through the French lines to a depth of eight kilometers, annihilated a handful of French batteries, interrupted the work of others, and even caused a few to retreat from their positions. At the same time, they were running out of both fuel and ammunition, had no contact with friendly infantry, and had stopped moving forward.[50]

The commander of the XIV *Panzer* Corps responded to this halt by renewing the attack. Once again, the main effort was with the 10th *Panzer* Division. It attacked, along the same route that its two armored regiments had used, with its own *Schützen* brigade, as well as one of the *Schützen* regiments and the single armored regiment of the 9th *Panzer* Division. The *Schützen* of the 10th *Panzer* Division were to attack along an axis east of Saint Fuscien, with the objective of making contact with the isolated tanks. The elements detached from the 9th *Panzer* Division were to swing west, and take the French strongpoints of Dury, Rumigny, and Hébécourt, as well as the artillery units which lay in their path from the flank and in the rear. Other infantry units—the remaining *Schützen* regiment of the 9th

Panzer Division as well as those of the 9th Infantry Division, were to continue attacking the strongpoints of the first line, to include such hard nuts to crack as Dury and Cagny.[51]

This attack, which was launched at 1:00 in the afternoon of June 5, soon ran into trouble. Before they were able to get past Saint Fuscien, the two *Schützen* regiments ran into machine gun, antitank gun, and artillery fire. Unable to move forward, the *Schützen*, already dismounted, turned on their tormentors. For the rest of the afternoon, the two regiments were involved in the fighting for Saint Fuscien and nearby strongpoints.[52] Once again, the French artillery's ability to control the main avenues into the 16th Infantry Division's position had deprived the Germans of their ability to exploit the success of their tanks.

The afternoon attack of the German tanks, like that of the morning, was not without success. The tanks of the 9th *Panzer* Division managed to wipe out two batteries of 155-millimeter howitzers by attacking them from the flank. Nonetheless, the French batteries that remained continued to fire, both in support of the infantry defending their positions and against German troops trying to move in the open ground. The German infantry that had been engaged were still in the business of fighting fierce and costly battles for the control of the villages. The German reserves of motorized infantry were still unable to rush through the gap created by the tanks because that gap was still covered by fire—from both the French artillery and the French machine gunners in the villages. As night fell, it became clear to the Germans that they were in for a second day of combat.

The German plan for the sixth of June reversed the roles that the tanks and *Schützen* had played the day before. This time, the *Schützen* brigades were to lead the attack aimed at clearing a path through the French position, while the tanks were to be held in reserve to exploit success. Though this involved a great deal of hard fighting, this method, which was in accord with the approach used so successfully in crossing the Meuse, worked. By midnight, all of the elements of the 16th Division that had survived death or capture were in the sectors of other divisions.[53]

After two days and five major attacks, three German divisions, heavily reinforced, had managed to push a single French division off the Dury Plateau. Before the German motorized divisions were free to roam in the French rear areas, the Germans would have to spend another two days knocking a second French division out of the way. From the point of view of the larger German attempt to get across the Somme in force, the battle of Amiens must be counted as a German defeat. By the time the XIV Army Corps broke through the French position, the *Schwerpunkt* of the campaign had been shifted to Abbéville, where another *Panzer* Corps had been able to achieve a much faster breakthrough. The German attack had not even contributed to this breakthrough by attracting significant French reserves. The French mechanized divisions which might have caused a great deal of trouble for the isolated German tanks were employed elsewhere.[54]

The battle south of Amiens showed the French Army of 1940 at its best. The men of the 16th Infantry Division did not want for courage, tenacity, skill, or self-reliance. The French infantry made the Germans pay dearly for every block of every village that they took. The French artillery, likewise, made movement in the open a very expensive proposition for the men of the XIV *Panzer* Corps. The fight for the Dury Plateau also uncovered an underlying weakness in the outlook of much of the German leadership, an underestimation of what good infantry could accomplish.

NOTES

1. In addition to the works cited below, the most important recent contributions to our understanding of the Battle of France are R.H.S. Stolfi, "Equipment for Victory in France," *History*, Volume 55 (1970), pp. 1–20; and Robert Allan Doughty, *The Seeds of Disaster, The Development of French Army Doctrine 1919–1939* (Hamden, CT: Archon, 1985).

2. Trevor N. Dupuy, *A Genius for War: The German Army and General Staff 1807–1945* (London: Macdonald and Janes, 1977), p. 267.

3. Leo W. G. Niehorster, *German World War II Organizational Series, Vol 2/I, Mechanized Army Divisions (10th May, 1940)* (Hannover: Niehorster, 1990), pp. 12–21. The exact location of the motorcyclists varied from unit to unit. Many divisions had full motorcycle battalions, others distributed motorcycle companies among the truck-mounted battalions. In most *Panzer* divisions, only one of the *Schützen* companies was equipped with armored personnel carriers.

4. For a complete account, see Peter Hofschröer, *Prussian Light Infantry, 1792–1815* (London: Osprey, 1984).

5. Rudolf Berdach and Erich Dethleffsen, *Der Artillerie gewidmet* (Vienna: Berdach, 1975), pp. 14–16 and appendix III.B.1.; and Roger Bruge, *Faites Sauter La Ligne Maginot* (Paris: Fayard, 1973), pp. 211–69. The latter work contains the definitive account of the fall of the *ouvrage* at La Ferté.

6. The myth that Eban-Emael was captured by paratroops, a myth started by German propaganda, is still very much alive today. The combat engineers landed by glider on top of the fort and blinded the observation cupola that served the guns that covered the bridge used by the bulk of the German forces that eventually took the fort. However, the actual work of reducing each Belgian strongpoint was carried out by a battalion of assault engineers (*Pionier Bataillon 51*) and a battalion of ordinary infantry (*II./Infanterie Regiment 151*). Karl Rossmann, *Kampf der Pioniere* (Berlin: Zentralverlag der NSDAP, 1943), pp. 23–24; Walther Melzer, *Albert-Kanal und Eben-Emael* (Heidelberg, Scharnhorst Buchkameradschaft, 1957), pp. 46–47; S. J. Lewis, *Forgotten Legions, German Army Infantry Policy, 1918–1941* (New York: Praeger, 1985), p. 23.

7. Waldemar Erfurth, *Surprise*, trans. Stephan Possony (Harrisburg: Military Service Publishing Company, 1943). A complete survey of German tactical thought on the eve of World War II is beyond the scope of this chapter.

8. Friedrich Otto Miksche, *Blitzkrieg* (London: Faber and Faber, 1941), pp. 17–18, 39, and 51–55.

9. Herbert Rosinski, *The German Army* (Washington, D.C.: The Infantry Journal, 1944), pp. 187–188.

10. F. O. Miksche, *Blitzkrieg*, pp. 17, 39, and 53–55.

11. Liddell Hart, "The Soldier's Pillar of Fire by Night," pp. 618–22.

12. For a particularly strong statement to this effect, see Hermann von Witzleben, *Taktik-Fibel* (Berlin: Verlag Offene Worte, 1935), p. 34.

13. Witzleben, *Taktik-Fibel*, pp. 25–26.

14. For an interesting view of the roots of these attitudes, see Colonel Lonsdale Hale, "Glimpses of German Military Life," *Colburn's United Service Magazine*, No. 715, June 1888. This article was reprinted in the September 1992, December 1992, and January 1993 issues of *Tactical Notebook*.

15. For attempts to trace the origins of this attitude, see Bruce I. Gudmundsson, "The German Tradition of Maneuver Warfare," in Richard Hooker, ed., *Maneuver Warfare, An Anthology* (Novato, CA: Presidio, 1993).

16. Miksche, *Blitzkrieg*, p. 8; Depuy, *A Genius for War*, p. 116.

17. The magazine *Kriegskunst im Wort und Bild*, published by the military publisher "Offene Wort" from 1924 until the end of World War II, if full of such problems.

18. Florian Rothbrust, *Guderian's XIXth Panzer Corps and the Battle of France, Breakthrough in the Ardennes, May, 1940* (New York: Praeger, 1990), pp. 146–47.

19. The 1st *Schützen* Regiment consisted of three battalions, as did the 2nd *Schützen* Regiment (of the 2nd *Panzer* Division). The 10th *Panzer* Division had two *Schützen* Regiments (the 69th and the 86th), of two battalions each. Niehorster, *German World War II Organizational Series, Vol 2/I, Mechanized Army Divisions (10th May, 1940)*, pp. 12–13 and 21.

20. Robert Allan Doughty, *The Breaking Point, Sedan and the Fall of France* (Hamden: Archon, 1990), pp. 101–30.

21. Doughty, *The Breaking Point*, pp. 166–201.

22. Rothbrust, *Guderian's XIXth Panzer Corps*, pp. 75–78.

23. Doughty, *The Breaking Point*, pp. 239–93.

24. R. H. Liddell Hart, *Defense of the West* (London: Cassell, 1950), pp. 9–10. The French battalion defending Monthermé was the 2nd Battalion of the *52ème Demibrigade de Mitrailleurs Coloniales*, of three companies of twelve heavy machine guns each plus a weapons company of six 81-millimeter mortars and three 25-millimeter antitank guns. It was reinforced by three more machine gun companies drawn from other units. Guy Chapman, *Why France Fell, The Defeat of the French Army in 1940* (New York: Holt, Rinehart and Winston, 1968), pp. 124–26 and "The French Army Machine Gun Battalion," *Tactical Notebook*, February 1992.

25. Heinz Maasen, *Par-Dessus la Meuse, Comment fut forcé le passage à Monthermé*, trans. J. Jamin (Paris: Payot, 1943), pp. 43–47; and "Einzelschilderungen aus dem Kriege an der Westfront," *Militärwissenschaftliche Rundschau*, 1940, Heft 4, pp. 358–64.

26. Yves Buffetaut, *De Gaulle Chef de Guerre* (Bayeux: Editions Heimdal, 1990), pp. 49–50 and 66.

27. The third crossing of the Meuse by an armored corps, at Dinant, was led by the five *Schützen* battalions of General Erwin Rommel's 7th *Panzer* Division. R.H.S. Stolfi, *A Bias for Action, The German 7th Panzer Division in France and Russia 1940–1941* (Quantico, VA: Marine Corps Association, 1991), pp. 6–7.

28. The 10th *Panzer* Division was a full strength armored division with two full tank regiments of two battalions each. The 9th, on the other hand, was a converted Austrian "quick" division with only one tank regiment, also of two battalions. Both divisions had a full *Schützen* brigade of two regiments of two battalions each.

29. Heinz Volkmar Regling, *Amiens, 1940, Die Deutsche Durchbruch Südlich von Amiens, 5 Bis 8 Juni, 1940* (Freiburg im Breisgau: Verlag Rombach, 1968), pp. 26–27.

30. Pierre Vasselle, *La Bataille au Sud D'Amiens, 20 Mai–8 Juin 1940* (Abbéville: Imprimerie F. Paillart, 1963), pp. 95–97 and 100–1.

31. For more on this, see Robert Allan Doughty, "French Antitank Doctrine, 1940: The Antidote that Failed," *Military Review*, May 1976, pp. 36–48.

32. The heavier antitank weapons—the 47-millimeter and 75-millimeter guns—tended to be concentrated in the antitank barrier, leaving many of the forward companies with nothing more powerful than 25-millimeter guns. *Historique du 89e Régiment d'Infanterie* (Paris: Charles Lavauzelle & Cie, 1943), p. 14 and *Historique du 56e Régiment d'Infanterie pendant la Campagne 1939–1940* (Macon: X. Perroux et Fils, 1947), pp. 40–44.

33. Armee Oberkommando 6 Ic/40, "Feindnachrichtenblatt von 3.6. 1940," U.S. National Archives microfilm series T-312, Roll 1379.

34. The sole exception to this rule was the 1st Battalion of the 29th Infantry Regiment, which kept one company in reserve. Vasselle, *La Bataille au Sud D'Amiens*, p. 96.

35. Vasselle, *La Bataille au Sud D'Amiens*, pp. 100–1.

36. *Gefechtsgruppe Oberstleutant Wiese* was attached to the 9th Armored Division. *Gefechtsgruppe Oberstl Herrlein* was attached to the 10th Armored Division. All units for these task forces, as well as the commanders, were taken from the 9th Infantry Division. An infantry gun company had two 150-millimeter infantry guns and six 75-millimeter infantry guns. 9. Infanterie Division, Ia, Nr. 300/40 *geheim* dated 4.6.40, U.S. National Archives microfilm series T315, Roll 508.

37. "Rapport du Chef d'Escadron Brock," S.H.A.T. carton 34N672, p. 2; and Vasselle, *La Bataille au Sud D'Amiens*, pp. 118–19.

38. 10. *Panzer* Division, Ia, "Kriegstagbuch."

39. "Rapport du Chef d'Escadron Brock," p. 3.

40. 10. *Panzer* Division, Ia, "Kriegstagbuch."

41. "Rapport du Chef d'Escadron Brock," p. 3.

42. "Rapport du Chef d'Escadron Brock," p. 3; and "Essai de Reconstitution du J.M.O. du 37ème R.A.D. du 5 Janvier au 16 Juin 1940," S.H.A.T. carton 34N568, pp. 17–18.

43. "Rapport du Chef d'Escadron Brock," p. 3; and 9. Infanterie Division, Ia, "Tagesmeldung, den Generalkommando XIV. AK," U.S. National Archives microfilm series T315, roll 508. (Note: The edges of this document were burned, making it impossible to read the normal document identifying codes.)

44. Regling, *Amiens, 1940*, pp. 39–40.

45. XIV. Armee Korps, Ia, "Fernspruch von HVZ+39," included as appendix 127 to XIV. Armee Korps, "Kriegstagbuch," U.S. National Archives, microfilm series T-314, Roll 528. Although undated, this message clearly refers to the June 5, 1940.

46. 10. *Panzer* Division, Ia, "Kriegstagbuch."

47. Vasselle, *La Bataille au Sud D'Amiens*, pp. 114–15.

48. Vasselle, *La Bataille au Sud D'Amiens*, pp. 114–15 and 183–84.

49. Vasselle, *La Bataille au Sud D'Amiens*, pp. 112–13 and 183–84.

50. Regling, *Amiens, 1940*, p. 36.

51. Regling, *Amiens, 1940*, pp. 40–41.

52. 10. *Panzer* Division, Ia, "Kriegstagbuch."

53. Vasselle, *La Bataille au Sud D'Amiens*, pp. 149–51.

54. Robert Altmayer, *La Xème Armée sur la Basse-Somme en Normandie et vers "le réduit breton" Mai–Juin 1940* (Paris: Editions Défense de la France, 1944), pp. 64–78, provides the details of the movement of French reserves during this period.

5.

Stalin's Hammer, Hitler's Anvil

In war, as in sports, the immediate reward of victory in one's neighborhood is the right to represent that neighborhood in a larger contest. This was certainly the case in the summer of 1941, when an ill-prepared Germany found itself locked in a life-and-death struggle with the Soviet Union, a power that could only be described as "out of its league."

When, in the early morning of June 22, 1941, the German and Soviet forces first exchanged shots, the actual strength of the Red Army was approximately five million men, 24,000 tanks, and 7,000 aircraft.[1] Against this array, and the nations behind it, the Germans and their allies hurled 108 infantry, 19 *Panzer* (now comprising 150 to 200 tanks each), and 14 motorized infantry divisions. Better than three million soldiers, 2,000 aircraft, and 3,350 tanks—about half again as many as had been needed to defeat the roughly fifty million people of France, Belgium, and the Netherlands—were put up against an empire of some 170 million. Against a state that had recently demonstrated the ability to produce 12,000 tanks and 21,000 aircraft a year, the Germans pitted an industry that would, in 1941, produce about 2,800 tanks. At the time of the invasion, however, only one German general, Field Marshal Fedor von Bock, registered the opinion that German resources were inadequate for the task.[2]

The initial moves of the offensive that the Germans called *Barbarossa* achieved surprise at every level. Nearly everybody in the Soviet Union, from the border guards to Marshal Stalin, was caught off guard. Within sixteen hours, the two Soviet army groups (or "fronts," as the Soviets called them) in the border region were no longer functioning as military organizations. In a very short time, three German army groups were pushing into Russia. Army Group North, under Field Marshal von Leeb, was aimed at Leningrad. Army Group Center, under the aforementioned von Bock, struck out for Moscow while Army Group South, under Field Marshal von Rundstedt, cut into the Ukraine.[3]

From the beginning, the pattern of fighting was different. In the West, the Germans had sealed their victories by trapping their enemies between their armies and the English Channel. In the East, such obstacles were not available. The Germans therefore revived the old tactic of encircling their enemies and, as a consequence, forcing them to attack infantry in prepared positions. The Germans called such a pocket a *Kessel*, a term that evoked images of a witches' cauldron (*Hexenkessel*) as well as the old hunter's technique in which game was driven into a killing zone (*Jagdkessel*).[4]

Though the initial trace of each encirclement was formed by the *Panzer* corps, the chief means of forming these pockets were the "ordinary" infantry divisions that formed the bulk of the German land forces throughout the Second World War. Having been stripped of most of their organic motor transport in order to provide the *Panzer* and fully motorized divisions with a full complement of vehicles, these divisions were almost entirely muscle powered. Scouts rode horses or bicycles, the big guns of the artillery were pulled by Clydesdales and Percherons, the lighter guns and infantry heavy weapons were pulled by smaller horses, and the riflemen walked. The few motor vehicles that were available were reserved for those elements which had to move quickly from one part of the division to another—commanders and antitank companies.

By June 28, the Soviet western front had in effect been broken up and smashed. In the battle of the Bialystok-Minsk pocket, the Germans claimed the destruction of 2,585 Soviet tanks and the capture of 290,000 prisoners. A further 350,000 prisoners and 3,000 tanks fell into German hands with the closure of the Smolensk pocket in August. At the end of September, the German encirclement tactics yielded an even greater victory (450,000 Soviet prisoners) in the area of Kiev. The encirclement of Leningrad was also completed in the meantime, though Hitler forbade direct attack on that city. The biggest pocket of all, that of Vyazma-Bryansk, was formed in October and produced, according to German records, a staggering 650,000 prisoners. These same German records report that, between the start of the campaign and November 1, 1941, the day that Hitler rather prematurely announced the annihilation of the Red Army, a total of 2,053,000 prisoners had been captured and 17,000 tanks destroyed.[5]

Why the Soviets were caught so completely off balance remains a mystery. The most convincing explanation was that the Red Army, which had already displayed considerable interest in, and would soon display a certain talent for, the defense in depth, was caught in the middle of preparations for an offensive of their own. This would explain why, among other things, the Germans ran into so few prepared defenses, why so many Soviet units were caught with their heavy equipment loaded aboard trains, and why Soviet supply dumps were located so near to the frontier.[6] Such a disposition for the offensive would also explain why the initial contacts had the character of encounter battles—a type of fighting in which the German Army, with its emphasis on rapid decision making and initiative at all levels, excelled.

A more traditional, albeit partial, alternative explanation is the long term effects of the purge of 1937–38. In that period, the head literally was chopped off the Red Army. Marshal Mikail Tukhachevskii, reputedly the most gifted general officer in the Soviet hierarchy, was executed along with about 60 percent of all Soviet general officers; some 30 to 40 percent of officers between the ranks of colonel and captain were either liquidated or imprisoned. The ever-suspicious Stalin had quite clearly judged Tukhachevskii—who combined extreme ruthlessness with a first-class intellect—to be a political threat. The political commissar system, which had fallen into disuse, was consequently reinstituted in 1937.[7]

The decapitation of the Red Army left the Soviet land forces weak in basic leadership and without the dynamic doctrine postulated by Tukhachevskii. Under the influence of this officer, Chief of Staff since 1926, the Soviet army had become a pace setter in its own right, surging ahead of all other countries in the development of mechanized forces. Arguing that the Red Army should be a highly mobile professional force, Tukhachevskii stressed encirclement and maneuver. New infantry regulations, published in 1927 to replace the provisional Frunze manual, consequently stated that firepower and mobility were the cardinal principles for success in infantry combat, the aim of all maneuver being to envelop, or turn, one or both enemy flanks.[8]

Though the Soviets were aware of the writings of Liddell Hart, de Gaulle, and Guderian, they displayed more interest in the theories of J.F.C. Fuller. Over 100,000 copies of a Soviet edition of *On Future Warfare* were sold in the Soviet Union. *Lectures on F.S.R. III* was also supposedly made a military "table book" around the same time. It should be noted, however, that many Soviet officers regarded Fuller as much too extreme; they therefore continued to exercise their own distinct brand of combined arms doctrine. The 1936 *Field Service Regulations*, which reflected Tukhachevskii's tactical ideas, saw a ground offensive developing in a manner reminiscent of the German practice of 1941. A number of assault groups (of infantry, tanks, and artillery) would probe suspected weak points in the enemy's line. Those assault groups that made the most progress would be heavily reinforced by mobile support groups and artillery. The gaps made by these units would be exploited by tanks, cavalry, and motorized infantry formed into highly mobile units whose rapid advance would trap enemy forces in pockets. The pockets would then be reduced by infantry, artillery, and air attacks.[9]

Though Tukhachevskii's ideas were written into the 1936 Field Service Regulations, there were indications that further refinements were necessary; infantry tactical methods, for example, left room for improvement, as did tank-infantry cooperation. It was also arguable whether the progressive doctrine contained in the regulations had filtered down to all levels of the Red Army. Tukhachevskii had, for example, stressed and encouraged maximum initiative and "nerve" at all levels. The Red Army, and, indeed, the entire Soviet society, on the other hand, was governed by extremely specific and ostensibly "scientific" plans and norms. Adherence to the letter of these plans and norms was the only excuse for failure. Divergence from them left an officer open to a frequently fatal accusation of "sabotage."[10]

As might have been expected, the men who followed Tukhachevskii were unable to comprehend, let alone implement, the style of warfare described in the 1936 regulations. Though many were combat veterans, the fighting that concerned them most was of the bureaucratic kind. Courtiers rather than warriors, poseurs rather than professionals, they "mouthed slogans but understood nothing of principles, paraded statistics about firepower without grasping the implications of the new weapons their own designers were developing. They were martial in a swaggering sense without the least grasp of the professionalism necessary to the military." And though generally devoid of intellect they were painfully aware that, while the Germans were a potential danger to their country, the secret police were an immediate danger to their lives.[11]

It is thus not surprising that, after the death of Tukhachevskii, the Red Army tended towards a more linear, less flexible, and more stereotyped approach. Far from the centers of power, on the border between Mongolia and Manchuria, there was, however, enough of Tukhachevskii left in the Red Army to bring swift victory in an undeclared war with Japan. Though the Soviet infantry paid heavily for deficiencies in platoon and company training in the engagements around Lake Khasan, Soviet forces under

General Zhukov applied Tukhachevskii's teachings with brilliant success in the 1939 Battle of Khalkhin Gol. Attacking on a broad front of some forty-eight miles with infantry supported by tanks and aircraft, Zhukov completed the encirlement of the Japanese with a maneuver group of tanks and motorized infantry. Over 18,000 Japanese were killed and 25,000 wounded; total Soviet casualties were but 10,000. More importantly, Japan was convinced to drop its plans to make full-scale war on the Soviet Union.[12]

For the Soviets, this victory provided a false sense of security, leading many to believe their own propaganda that German armies could never pierce the western frontier. A year later, the German *Blitzkrieg* in Poland may have shaken this faith a bit, but it really took the Finnish experience to confirm Red Army inadequacies. In the fall of 1939, following the German defeat of Poland and benefiting from his pact with Hitler, Stalin demanded the readjustment of the border around and in the Gulf of Finland (with Finland to be compensated with parts of Soviet Eastern Karelia). The Finnish government refused Stalin's offer, and on November 30, 1939, four Soviet army groups attacked along a line stretching from Leningrad to the Arctic Ocean.

The Finnish Army of 1939 consisted of ten infantry divisions, three infantry regiments, and thirty-six light artillery pieces. Though most of the men who filled these divisions were reservists, their standard of individual and small unit training was extremely high. Camouflage and the use of terrain were practiced until they became second nature, and rifle marksmanship was stressed. These skills were complemented by an ebullient morale and junior leaders who were both competent and full of initiative. Though certain aspects of the Finnish national character—particularly a fondness for winter sports and a tradition of extreme self-reliance—played an important role, the Finnish approach to infantry tactics was largely the legacy of the German *Jäger* who trained the infant Finnish Army during the Great War.[13]

The main Soviet thrust was launched by the 350,000-man Seventh Army Group against the Mannerheim Line, a fortified zone of fire points, "dragon's teeth" tank traps, and trenches that protected both the population centers and the agricultural heartland of Finland. Frontal attacks were the order of the day: first, with tanks preceding infantry; then, when the light and medium tanks fell easy prey to the Finns, by massed infantry sent forward to create breaches for massed tanks held in reserve. When daylight attacks failed, the Soviets began to attack at night. The enterprising Finns responded by installing searchlights and the Soviet attacks continued to fall apart in the face of Finnish machine gun fire.[14]

The other Soviet attacks had a more mobile character. Aimed at using the sparsely populated north of Finland as a means of avoiding Finland's fixed defenses, these attacks were initially unopposed. As the long columns of men, horses, and motor vehicles moved into the pine forests and across the frozen lakes, they encountered something far less impressive, but ultimately, far more effective than the Mannerheim Line—a minature version of the *Blitzkrieg* that the Finns called *motti* tactics. The idea behind *motti* tactics was to strike so rapidly and at so many places that the enemy was deprived of his ability to effectively react. The means of doing this were small teams of infantrymen, often on skis and sometimes even using reindeer sleighs to carry heavy weapons. The chief techniques were the ambush, the hit-and-run raid, and maneuvers that make use of the peculiarities of the environment. These included such things as the destruction of field kitchens (to deprive the Soviets of warm food) and the use of well-placed howitzer shells to crack the ice that supported Soviet troops who were moving over a frozen lake.[15]

In the area of Suomussalmi on the waist of Finland, the Finnish army scored its greatest success, wiping out at least one Soviet division and badly mauling another. However, on February 2, 1940, a new offensive under the direction of Marshal S. K. Timoshenko was renewed against the Mannerheim Line. Although Soviet troops had been put through a winter indoctrination course and an intensive training program in the storming of fixed fortifications, the Finns were, on the whole, bludgeoned into submission by an enemy able to deploy 1.2 million Soviet soldiers to defeat a nation of some 3.7 million.[16]

Many shortcomings of the Red Army came to light in Finland. Divisional organization was considered too rigid and the army generally far too road bound. Though the Soviet soldier's doggedness and ability to withstand severe hardships had shown through, there was no denying that his standard of training was low and his marksmanship particularly poor. Soviet infantry were not properly trained for close-quarter fighting, and all arms cooperation was lacking. Neither *Stosstrupp* tactics nor platoon tactics of the type advocated by Liddell Hart had managed to find a home in the Red Army, as many officers were concerned about the adverse effect these might have on command and control. The result was that Soviet batallions in Finland initially attacked in tightly packed formations. Later assaults on the Mannerheim Line did, of course, prove that maneuver by small units was essential to the task.[17]

Reforms were not long in coming, however, as the man of the hour, Timoshenko, was made Defense Commissar. Infantry manuals again were amended, and although the mass infantry attack was still recommended as the ultimate method of annihilating the enemy, infantry tactics were made more flexible with greater initiative allowed to junior leaders. Winter equipment was improved and production of the T-34 tank was given the go-ahead. No longer were submachine guns dismissed as "police weapons." Combat training was intensified and made more realistic, with special emphasis placed on fighting under "difficult conditions." Programs were set in motion to exercise troops by day and night in all weathers, with rigorous physical exertions, so that sections, units, and formations could maneuver on any terrain. The infantryman was taught how to dig in quickly and how to deal with surprise attacks. Equally important, a new disciplinary code was introduced: whereas before troops had been exempted from fulfilling "criminal" (i.e., anti-Soviet) orders open to wide interpretation, they were henceforth to obey all orders unconditionally. Commanders' prerogatives were also buttressed in other areas, though the word "officer" was still banned as being essentially repugnant to a socialist army. Significantly, in August 1940, the powers of political commissars were restricted to advising on political matters and troop indoctrination. All military and political training became the responsibility of the commander.[18]

Though these and many other badly needed reforms had been fully implemented by the time that Germany attacked, they seem to have had a salutory effect on Soviet performance. Though many Soviet formations disintegrated and hundreds of thousands of Soviet soldiers surrendered as soon as the opportunity presented itself, many other Red Army soldiers bitterly contested the German advance, hanging on tenaciously in pockets of resistance and, as early as August, launching local counterattacks. As a result of this ferocious fighting, German casualties began to mount. From June 22 to July 16, 102,000 German soldiers had been reported killed, missing, or seriously wounded on the Eastern Front. By the end of August, this number had risen to 440,000, of which 94,000 had been killed. By September 26, the total was 534,000. (This represented 15 percent of the overall German strength on the Eastern Front and 30 percent of German infantry strength in that theater.) By the end of November, total casualties had reached 743,000, of which 200,000—including 8,000 officers—were dead or missing. By comparison, total German casualties in Poland and France had been, respectively, 44,000 and 156,000.[19]

The main reason for these substantially higher casualty rates must largely be ascribed to the fighting qualities of the Soviet troops. The combat characteristics and military effectiveness of Soviet units did not, of course, adhere to any common pattern, as the Red Army was a multinational and somewhat polyglot organization. However, it was noticeable that in broken or close country such as mountain waste, forest, or marsh, the Red Army soldier generally fought better than in the open. Thus while the fighting performance of Soviet formations and units in the Ukraine often varied from high to low, Soviet resistance in the wooded swamps near Leningrad was uniformly bitter. Around Moscow, there were occasional variations, a case in point being the LVII *Panzer* Corps rounding up the drunken remnants of the Soviet Forty-third Army while nearby the German 98th Division fought for its life against the elite V Airborne Corps.[20]

As the advancing *Panzers* outflanked and pierced Soviet positions, skirting swamps and bypassing large forested areas in their rush to seek decision in the open, Red Army units retired laterally into the depths of the bypassed areas. In the early stages of *Barbarossa*, the Germans considered this to be a desirable result, and there were numerous occasions when the Germans deliberately drove the Soviets into swamps. While this sometimes had the desired result of causing the Soviet units to melt away by desertion, starvation, and surrender, the policy often backfired. Soviet forces that had been pushed into marginal terrain by the *Panzer* corps often emerged from their hiding places once the armored and motorized units had left the area. This resulted in a large number of infantry battles between the revised Soviet forces and the German infantry divisions that were marching in the wake of the tanks.[21]

The work of the German infantry was rendered difficult by the speed and skill with which Soviet units constructed and defended field fortifications. Great believers in overhead protection, the Soviets often laid logs as thick as telegraph poles, five layers deep, over their trenches, thereby making them proof against a direct hit by all but the heaviest of German howitzers. To ensure that their position remained undetected for as long as possible, Soviet infantrymen normally held their fire until the enemy closed to the very shortest of ranges. Then, to gain maximum psychological effect, the fire was delivered as a volley. Perhaps as a consequence of the Russo-Finnish War, the Soviets placed a great deal of stress on sharpshooting. Interunit competitions were commonplace and snipers were treated with great respect. Interestingly, the Soviets were never satisfied with being able merely to dominate an area by fire; it had to be occupied by infantry. Like the French before them in the Great War, they never voluntarily abandoned ground they had gained by attack.[22]

When fully dug in, the Soviet infantryman was particularly dangerous to tanks, often allowing them to pass over his almost invisible trench so that he could take them in the rear. This tactic also aimed at separating enemy tanks from their infantry, in which regard it proved exceedingly effective. Once isolated, the German tanks could be dealt with by any one of a variety of infantry antitank weapons. The massed fire of 14.5-millimeter antitank rifles, for example, was a part of the Soviet antitank repertoire long after other armies had declared their antitank rifles obsolete while the hand-placed antitank grenade seems to have been the chief antitank weapon of companies and platoons. In addition, the Soviet infantryman used improvised weapons of foreign design but local manufacture. The "Molotov cocktail" was copied from the Finns of the Winter War of 1939–1940 while the satchel charge was borrowed from the Asturian miners of the Spanish Civil War.[23]

The areas in which Soviet infantrymen best applied their defensive skills, however, were the swamps and forests. One particularly effective technique was the placement of field fortifications deep within a forest, preferably behind swampy ground. The bulk of the firing positions of such works were oriented towards the rear, so that Germans who had penetrated could be conveniently shot in the back. To hide the fortification as a whole as well as this particular feature, the Soviets refrained from clearing the vegetation from their fields of fire. Instead, they cut waist-high tunnels in the undergrowth.[24]

The organization of the Soviet infantry was in concert with such tactics, which would depend for their success on extensive use of infantry heavy weapons. Platoons were well provided with *Degtyarev* light machine guns, which were distributed at a rate of one or two per squad. Companies had 50-millimeter mortars and one or two heavy machine guns. Battalions had heavy machine guns, 81-millimeter mortars, antitank rifles, and a pair of antitank guns. Regiments were provided with 76-millimeter infantry guns, 120-millimeter mortars, additional antitank guns, and the uniquely Soviet institution of an entire company armed exclusively with submachine guns and another company of antitank rifle teams.[25]

Though such organization was also consistent with flexible offensive tactics, the Soviet infantry attacks were often anything but flexible. Red Army small-unit tactics in the offense were officially based on the idea of taking enemy strongpoints by double envelopment. Units were to penetrate the weaker portions of the enemy defense on each side of the objective and then overrun it from the rear and flanks. For this reason, attacking Soviet infantry units tended to fight with subordinate elements abreast. Though battalions were generally expected to keep about a third of their forces in a second echelon, the desire to reach around both flanks of an objective sometimes led to situations where all of the rifle platoons in a battalion were placed in line.[26]

A natural consequence of this antiquated approach—which resembled the firing line tactics of periods before the Great War—were actions such as that reported near Zelva in June 1941 and described in lucid detail by German observers:

> Again and again they swept up against the German positions with their unnerving cries of "Urra"—companies, battalions, regiments. The picture was one that made the German troops' imagination boggle. The Soviets were charging on a broad front, in an almost endless-seeming solid line, their arms linked. Behind them a second, a third, and a fourth line abreast.[27]

The frequency of such attacks notwithstanding, there were occasions where Soviet small unit tactics displayed a great deal of skill on the part of the individual soldier. One of these was the short-distance raid. Where possible, the Soviet infantrymen crawled silently and without firing to a starting position or "jumping-off" spot. (For more deliberate attacks, troops in contact would dig to within 200 yards of the enemy and prepare jumping-off positions for assault units in depth.) There they would wait, often in the cold, until the hour of attack, which would normally be launched under cover of darkness. At other times, the Soviets would assault in a driving snowstorm or under cover of a howling wind. Moving by night and disappearing by day, hiding in villages and woods, the Soviet infantryman could be expected to strike at unexpected times under the most adverse conditions. The Germans paid a backhanded compliment to the stalking ability of Soviet infantry by adopting the policy of holding their fire until the last minute; they knew that the sooner they opened fire, the sooner the Soviets would go to ground and merely creep up under cover.[28]

Perhaps the most impressive characteristic of Soviet infantry in the offense was its unmatched ability to infiltrate enemy positions. According to General von Mellenthin, practically every Soviet attack was preceded by large-scale infiltrations of small units and individual men. The Soviet methods, described by Liddell Hart as an "ant strategy," usually followed the same pattern. During the first night, a few men would infiltrate German positions and vanish in the forest. During the second night, reinforcments would bring the force up to platoon strength. In this manner, provided no countermeasures were taken, a whole battalion could be lodged in the rear of German lines within one week. Such infiltration tactics forced German troops in the northern and central parts of the Soviet Union to attempt to form continuous fronts. This involved considerable strain—additional patrolling, digging, watchstanding, and, what was most important of all, frequent counterattacks.[29]

An important variation on this theme was the use of infiltration as a means of forming bridgeheads on the German side of rivers and streams. That these "bridgehead tactics" were taken seriously by the Germans is clearly illustrated in an appreciation by the chief of staff of the XLVIII *Panzer* Corps.

Bridgeheads in the hands of the Russians are a grave danger indeed. It is quite wrong not to worry about bridgeheads and postpone their elimination. Russian bridgeheads, however small and harmless they appear, are bound to grow into formidable-danger points in a very brief time and soon become insuperable strongpoints. A Russian bridgehead, occupied by a company in the evening, is sure to be occupied by a regiment on the following morning and during the night will become a formidable fortress, well equipped with heavy weapons and everything necessary to make it impregnable. No artillery fire, however violent and well concentrated, will wipe out a Russian bridgehead which had grown overnight. Nothing less than a well planned attack will avail. The Russian principle of "bridgeheads everywhere" constitutes a more serious danger, and can not be over-rated. There is again only one sure remedy which must become a principle: . . . Attack when the Russians are still above ground, when they can be seen and tackled, when they have no time to organize their defense, when there are no heavy weapons available.[30]

The paradox of Soviet soldiers who were clever in the defense, skilled at infiltration, and yet clumsy in the attack requires some elaboration. The fact that many of the soldiers who participated in the "human wave" assaults were recently conscripted peasants, inmates of labor camps, members of penal units, or even drunk does not explain how the same sort of troops behaved differently at different times. Similarly, a look at Soviet regulations issued both before and during the war indicates frequent attempts by the Soviet hierarchy to induce the infantry to adopt more fluid offensive tactics. The blame cannot therefore be placed on military leaders who had failed to learn the lessons of the Great War.[31] The cause, rather, seems to lie with the very nature of Soviet society.

The chief work of the Soviet government during the 1920s and 1930s was the attempted destruction of those mediating institutions—churches, villages, associations of any kind, the family, and private property—that stood between the individual and the state. The chief achievement of these years was the creation of a generation of "new Soviet men" who had learned to exist on two separate levels. As individuals, they had learned how to live in conditions of permanent scarcity punctuated by frequent famine and permanent class warfare punctuated by various terror campaigns. As members of large groups, they had learned to perform simple tasks within the context of complex "scientific plans" as well as to cheer on command. It is thus not surprising that the average Soviet soldier was good at hiding himself and that he knew how to play his role within an intricate plan of defense drawn up by an expert. It is also not surprising that the same soldier did not take naturally to the type of small group cooperation so essential to tactics based on the independent and, from the point of view of the higher leadership, largely unobserved maneuver of squads and platoons.

The exception that proves this rule is provided by the offensive tactics perfected within the city limits of Stalingrad by troops under the command of General Vasili I. Chuikov. To employ these tactics, Chuikov authorized the reorganization of his infantry into "storm groups" that bore a strong, but not complete resemblance to some of the German *Stosstrupps* of the Great War. Like a *Stosstrupp*, the storm group consisted of close combat specialists backed up by infantry heavy weapons. Unlike most German *Stosstrupps*, which rarely exceeded the size of a small platoon, Chuikov's storm groups were about as large as a small company.[32] Similarly, while the Germans were able to convert *Stosstrupp* tactics into a flexible system of tactics for ordinary infantry, the Soviets were unable to do the same with their storm group tactics.

The Soviet storm group consisted of three distinct elements: assault, reinforcement, and reserve. Together, they constituted one whole designed to carry out a single task. The strength and constitution of each storm group depended on the objective it was to attack. The special features of the operations of each group were worked out on the basis of reconnaissance information about the nature of the objective and the size of its garrison. These special features were naturally crucial, for without clarifying them, it was normally impossible to come to grips with the tactics of the battle for a fortified building. In an actual engagement, the spearhead of the storm group was the assault element, composed of several subgroups of between six to eight men in each. The task of this element, under one commander, was to break in swiftly to a building and wage battle independently inside it. Assault-element members were lightly armed with submachine guns, grenades, daggers, and spades (the edges sharply honed for hand-to-hand fighting).

The reinforcement element was usually divided into separate parties that entered the building simultaneously from different directions once the assault element fired off signal rockets or flares indicating a successful break-in. Armed with heavier weapons (heavy machine guns, mortars, antitank rifles and guns, picks, crowbars, and explosive charges), the reinforcement element included sappers, snipers, and soldiers of various trades. Commanded by the storm-group commander, its task was to quickly seize firing positions and create a defensive network against the enemy to prevent the latter from coming to the aid of his beleaguered garrison. The reserve element supplemented and strengthened the assault element, securing the flanks as necessary or taking up blocking positions.[33]

The offensive tactics of the storm group were based on rapid action and boldness on the part of every soldier. Since city fighting generally consisted of an endless series of assaults on well-fortified houses, buildings, and other objects, attacks by storm groups had to be short and sharp, their execution marked by swiftness and daring. Timing and surprise were the two most important ingredients required for success. The timing of an attack was usually fixed in accordance with the enemy's behavior, his sleeping and eating habits as well as relief times receiving constant and particularly detailed scrutiny. Launched almost always by night or under cover of smoke screens, storm group attacks were frequently made without any preliminary artillery bombardment. In fact, it became a rule that when enemy weapons were concentrated solely inside a building or other object transformed into a strongpoint, an attack would be carried out without prior artillery preparation, relying for its success on the surprise factor alone. Experience, recorded Chuikov, had taught the Soviet that both timing and surprise were always attainable.

> Get close up to the enemy's position; move on all fours making use of craters and ruins; dig your trenches by night, camouflage them by day; make your build-up for the attack stealthily, without any noise; carry your tommy-gun on your shoulder; take ten to twelve grenades. Timing and surprise will then be on your side.[34]

The storm group also played a key role in the occupation of Soviet strongpoints and centers of resistance during the battle for Stalingrad. A classic example of the former occupation was the defense of "Pavlov's house," a four-storied edifice into which Sergeant Jacob Pavlov of the 13th Guards Division managed to cram sixty men, mortars, heavy machine guns, antitank weapons and a full complement of skilled snipers. The antitank weapons were deployed on the ground floor, machine guns on the higher stories, and infantry at all levels, including the basement. This virtual fortress covered the approaches to a square in which Pavlov had skillfully mined all the open ground leading to his "house." From the third story, his observers detected German ground movement, while tank attacks came to grief on mines. Bombing and artillery and mortar fire finally wrecked most of "Pavlov's house," but for fifty-eight days it beat off every German assault.

The key to moving storm group tactics work was detailed planning. The conditions of urban warfare, where each building was a battlefield in miniature, allowed a storm group leader both the time and the information to work out his attack or defense in exquisite detail and to assign each individual his place in the plan. Adherence to a plan and individual accountability to the leader thus provided a substitute for the improvisation and social relationships that formed the basis for small unit tactics in other armies.

One area in which the extreme individualism taught by Soviet life paid off was in sniping. Characterized as much by his ability to kill in cold blood as his marksmanship, the sniper has, in Western armies at least, often suffered ostracism at the hands of soldiers who fight in squads and platoons. Whether such ostracism existed in the Red Army is unknown. What is known, however, is both the high quality and considerable quantity of their snipers. During the fighting at Stalingrad, the ascendancy of the Soviet sniper became so marked that the head of the German sniper school at Zossen was reportedly sent in to help redress the balance. He was subsequently shot and killed by the famous Soviet sniper Vasili Zaitsev.[35]

Though extremes of weather, the lack of roads, and the poverty caused by twenty years of socialism played a role, the capability of the Soviet soldier to fight as an individual as well as a member of an impersonal mass made the service on the Eastern Front particularly difficult for the German infantry. This is underscored by a catechism issued to units headed East:

The soldier in Russia must be a hunter. The Bolshevist's greatest advantage over the German is his highly developed instinct and his lack of sensitivity to the weather and to the terrain. One must be able to stalk and creep like a huntsman.

The soldier in Russia must be able to improvise. The Bolshevist is a master of improvisation.

The soldier in Russia must be constantly on the move. Hardly a day passes on which the Soviets however weak they may be, do not attempt to push against our lines. Day after day they work to improve their positions.

The soldier in Russia must be suspicious.

The soldier in Russia must be wide awake. The Soviet practically always attacks during the night and in foggy weather. In the front line there is nothing to be done but to remain awake at night and to rest during the day. But in Russia there is no

> front line or hinterland in the military sense of the word. Anyone who lays down his arms east of the old Reich frontier may greatly regret this a moment later.
>
> The soldier in Russia must reconnoiter. Reconnoitering is the main component of all fighting in Russia.
>
> The soldier in Russia must be hard. Real men are needed to make war in forty degrees of frost or in great heat, in knee-deep mud or in thick dust. The victims of the Bolshevist mass attacks often present a sight against which the young soldier must harden his heart. He must reckon with the possibility of losing his life. Only men who do not lose their nerve when death threatens them are fit to be fighters against Bolshevism. Weak characters must realize that the leadership is sufficiently hard to punish cowardice by death.[36]

Although his march performance in Russia was from the beginning even more unbelievable than that in France (normally twenty-five miles per day over atrocious roads, all good ones being reserved for motorized movement), the German infantryman, in comparison with his Soviet counterpart, was much too spoiled. He had become accustomed to barracks with central heating and running water, to beds with sheets and mattresses. It was not, therefore, easy for him to adapt to the extremely primitive conditions of the Soviet Union. As a first adjustment to local conditions, the German Army revised the standards for selecting small-unit commanders; their average age was lowered, and the physical-fitness requirements were raised. It was said that the studious kind of officer who relied chiefly on maps was out of place in Russia. Excess personal baggage and staff cars were also left behind and impedimenta generally reduced to a minimum.

One measure specifically introduced for warfare in the East was the organization of light infantry (*Jäger*) divisions. Raised after the Germans discovered that their mountain infantry (*Gebirgsjäger*) divisions were the most effective type of unit for sustained combat in forests and swamps, these formations borrowed most of their defining characteristics from the mountain troops. These included extensive use of mules for carrying supplies and heavy weapons; providing battalions with an extra measure of independence by adding a fifth company of infantry guns, antitank guns, and infantry pioneers; and elimination of the third infantry regiment. At the same time, the light infantry divisions were provided with conventional divisional artillery, which was of heavier caliber than the pack artillery of the mountain divisions.[37]

Though the vast majority of German infantry divisions were not officially converted into *Jäger* divisions, conditions on the Eastern front caused them to acquire many of the same characteristics. The scale of motor transport was repeatedly reduced, both by combat action and by the transfer of the increasingly scarce trucks and motorcycles to the *Panzer* and motorized divisions. In the place of both motor vehicles and the grain-fed European horses that pulled both the infantry baggage wagons and the bulk of the divisional artillery, the Germans made increasing use of Russian ponies and Russian peasant carts. More significantly, as casualties mounted, the three infantry regiments in most divisions were often reduced to two.[38]

In the case of the *Jäger* divisions, the elimination of the third infantry regiment was a matter of design. Its purpose was to reduce the length of the marching column and thus increase the flexibility of the unit in broken terrain. In the case of the ordinary infantry divisions, the elimination of the third regiment was an attempt to make a virtue of necessity. Even when the third regiments were used to form new infantry divisions, the effect was to greatly reduce the number of infantry battalions available on the Eastern Front. This shortage of infantry battalions, in turn, made it difficult for the Germans to conduct the kind of elastic defense that all of their regulations published after 1917 had called for.[39]

The shortage of infantry battalions was exacerbated by Hitler's refusal to allow the German Army to rationalize its position on the Eastern Front. During the Great War, deliberate withdrawals from "bulges" in the line had brought a number of benefits. These included the reduction in the frontage that had to be manned, the use of terrain that was easier to defend, the ability to build stronger installations, and the shortening of supply lines. Because he was, like Falkenhayn before him, a devotee of the doctrine of mass psychology, Hitler only gave his generals permission to repeat such maneuvers after losses compelled him to. The result was the widespread adoption of what soon became known as the "hedgehog" (*Igelstellung*) defense.

Instead of spreading squad positions over the terrain to create a continuous belt, the hedgehog defense was characterized by the conversion of villages into company and battalion strongpoints. Though this system had one of the great disadvantages of the British bird cage system of 1918—the ease with which enemy infantry could infiltrate between positions—the hedgehog defense retained some of the advantages of the old elastic defense. The hedgehog itself, for example, was a series of well dispersed squad positions. Extensive use was made of rear slopes. And, within each hedgehog, as much of the infantry as possible was kept out of the trenches for use in local counterattacks.[40]

The same lack of infantry that had led to the adoption of the hedgehog system also prevented the formation of divisional counterattack reserves.

In such a situation, the field artillery took over the role of providing the "glue" that kept the hedgehogs together. This was done in two ways. First, the fire of the field artillery served to break up large-scale attacks that might otherwise overwhelm a hedgehog. Second, the artillery positions, as well as the areas occupied by service units, were converted into hedgehogs in their own right.[41]

The acute shortage of infantry on the Eastern Front forced the German army forces to adopt desperate expedients. In moments of crisis, when the Soviets had broken through the thin crust of hedgehogs and there were no proper reserves available, "alarm units" (*Alarmeinheiten*) would be formed from whatever human material was available in the rear areas. Men going on leave, men returning from leave, men attending courses, school personnel, and men from service units were all susceptible to being drafted into such units, armed with whatever was available, and sent forward into battle. As might be expected, the fighting quality of alarm units, in which squads were filled with men who were strangers to one another, was generally low.[42]

The Germans seem to have had better luck with the deliberate formation of fighting units from rear-echelon organizations. The trick was to take an intact unit led, if possible, by its own leaders, and give it a series of progressively more difficult combat tasks. Once it had proved itself capable of holding a defensive line or position, for example, such a unit might be given easily obtainable objectives to seize. In this way, the men gained confidence in themselves and each other as they learned the many skills of the modern infantryman.[43]

As the Soviets recovered from the disastrous summer of 1941, they began to have more resources to devote to their counterattacks. Though massed infantry attacks and infiltration continued throughout the war, large scale tank attacks and increasingly heavy artillery bombardments had, as early as the spring of 1942, become a major part of the Soviet repertoire. Defending against Soviet artillery was relatively easy—the German soldier just dug a little deeper. Defending against the tanks would prove more difficult.[44]

The most immediate problem of the German infantry was obtaining sufficient numbers of antitank weapons capable of destroying the heavily armored tanks that, thanks to the sacrifices of the Soviet population as well as Anglo-American aid, began to appear in large numbers in 1942. As purpose-built antitank weapons were slow to arrive at the front, the name of the game was close combat.[45] The methods—extensive use of mines, Molotov cocktails, antitank grenades, and satchel charges—were similar to those already adopted by the Soviets.[46] The first step in learning how to employ these methods was getting used to the particular type of fear engendered by the iron monsters.

The remarks of a member of the *Grossdeutschland* division show one technique for teaching infantrymen how to deal with "tank terror":

> As we had already been taught to dig foxholes in record time, we had no trouble opening a trench 150 yards long, 20 inches wide, and a yard deep. We were ordered into the trench in close ranks, and forbidden to leave it, no matter what happened. Then four or five Mark-IIIs [tanks] rolled forward at right angles to us, and crossed the trench at different speeds. The weight of these machines alone made them sink four or five inches into the crumbling ground. When their monstrous treads ploughed into the rim of the trench only a few inches from our heads, cries of terror broke from almost all of us. . . . We were also taught how to handle the dangerous *Panzerfaust*, and how to attack tanks with magnetic mines. One had to hide in a hole and wait until the tank came close enough. Then one ran, and dropped an explosive device—unprimed during practice—between the body and the turret of the machine. We weren't allowed to leave our holes until the tank was within five yards of us. Then, with the speed of desperation we had to run straight at the terrifying monster, grab the tow hook and pull ourselves onto the hood, place the mine at the joint of the body and turret, and drop off the tank to the right, with a decisive rolling motion.[47]

The German reliance on infantry close combat as a means of dealing with tanks was a microcosm of the larger German experience on the Eastern Front. Outnumbered, outgunned, and, for the most part, provided with weapons that were not up to the job, the German infantryman managed to hold on for nearly four years. That it managed to achieve what it did is a credit to its leadership, particularly those entrusted with the command of platoons and squads. That it managed to hang on at all is a function of the particular way that the German Army was put together.

Social scientists would later call this sense of belonging and the strange bonds of affection that linked members of a squad to each other a "high degree of primary group integrity."[48] The Germans called the phenomenon "comradeship" (*Kameradschaft*) and cultivated it at every opportunity. The methods for doing this included, but were not limited to, linking units to particular recruiting districts so that men would go to war alongside their neighbors; keeping men in the same squad, platoon, or company for long periods of time; returning convalescents, trained specialists, and recently promoted junior officers and NCOs to the units in which they had previously served; and forming new units by expanding existing ones.[49] "We are beginning to understand," concluded the perceptive Lord Moran, "that the secret of the awful power of the German army is not in tanks and aircraft, but in a certain attitude of mind of her manhood."[50]

NOTES

1. Albert Seaton, *The Russo-German War, 1942–45* (New York: Praeger, 1970), pp. 17–18, 46, and 60–62, and Larry Addington, *The Blitzkrieg Era and the German General Staff* (New Brunswick, NJ: Rutgers University Press, 1971), p. 183. According to Marshal Zhukov, 149 Red Army divisions—including thirty-six armored, eighteen motorized rifle, and eight cavalry divisions—were stationed in the Soviet western frontier districts when the Germans attacked. Georgy Konstantinovich Zhukov, *Memoirs* (London: Jonathan Cape, 1971), p. 250.

2. Albert Seaton, *The Battle for Moscow* (London: Jonathan Cape, 1971), pp. 30 and 38–39, and *The Russo-German War*, pp. 61–62, 74–75, and 95; Wladyslaw Anders, *Hitler's Defeat in Russia* (Chicago: Henry Regnery, 1953), p. 18; John Erickson, *The Road to Stalingrad* (London: Weidenfeld and Nicholson, 1975), pp. 98; Addington, *The Blitzkrieg Era*, p. 187, and B. H. Liddell Hart, *The Other Side of the Hill* (London: Pan, 1978), pp. 255–57.

3. Seaton, *The Russo-German War, 1941–45*, p. 61.

4. "Wedge and Kessel," *Military Review*, August 1941, p. 811.

5. Malcolm Mackintosh, *Juggernault: A History of the Soviet Armed Forces* (New York: Macmillan, 1967), pp. 133, 143–46, and 156; John Erickson, *The Soviet High Command* (London: Macmillan, 1962), p. 625, and *The Road the Stalingrad*, pp. 210–19; Seaton, *The Russo-German War, 1941–45*, pp. 130–84, and *The Battle for Moscow*, pp. 45, 47–48, 65, 74, and 83; and Anders, *Hitler's Defeat in Russia*, p. 58. German claims of Soviet prisoners taken may be exaggerated. Alan Clark, *Barbarossa: The Russian-German Conflict, 1941–1945* (London: Hutchinson, 1965), p. 137.

6. This argument is admirably presented in Viktor Suvorov, *Icebreaker, Who Started the Second World War?*, trans. Thomas Beatie (London: Hamish Hamilton, 1990).

7. Erickson, *The Soviet High Command*, pp. 463–64 and 506.

8. Charles Messenger, *The Art of Blitzkrieg* (London: Ian Allen, 1976), pp. 60–63 and 83–87; Mackintosh, *Juggernaut*, pp. 80–81; and Erickson, *The Soviet High Command*, p. 317.

9. Messenger, *The Art of Blitzkrieg*, pp. 60–63 and 83–87; Mackintosh, *Juggernaut*, pp. 80–81; Erickson, *The Soviet High Command*, p. 317; and Luvaas, *Education of an Army*, p. 374.

10. Erickson, *The Soviet High Command*, pp. 317, 444, 507, 537, and 567.

11. Erickson, *The Road to Stalingrad*, p. 7.

12. Mackintosh, *Juggernaut*, pp. 108–10; and Erickson, *The Soviet High Command*, pp. 499, 502, 518–22 and 532–37.

13. The role played by the German *Jäger* in the training of the Finnish Army is described in Heinz Halter, *Jäger im Freiheitskampf, Finnlands Jugend im Weltkrieg* (Leipzig: Schwarzhäupter-Verlag, 1941).

14. Erickson, *The Soviet High Command*, pp. 541–44.

15. Journi Keravouri, *The Russo-Finnish War 1939–1940: A Study in Leadership, Training, and Esprit de Corps* (Unpublished study project, U.S. Army War College, 1985), pp. V-8 through V-14.

16. Liddell Hart, *The Soviet Army* (London: Weidenfeld and Nicolson, 1956), pp. 83–85 and 89–91; O'Ballance, *The Red Army* (London: Faber and Faber, 1964), pp. 144–52; and Mackintosh, *Juggernaut*, pp. 119–23.

17. O'Ballance, *The Red Army*, p. 154; Mackintosh, *Juggernaut*, pp. 122–24; Erickson, *The Soviet High Command*, p. 206, and *The Road to Stalingrad*, p. 30.

18. Liddell Hart, *The Soviet Army*, p. 86; O'Ballance, *The Red Army*, pp. 154–55; Erickson, *The Soviet High Command*, pp. 554–55; and Mackintosh, *Juggernaut*, p. 127.

19. George E. Blau, *The German Campaign in Russia: Planning and Operations (1940–1942)*, Department of the Army Pamphlet 20–261A (Washington, D.C.: U.S. Government Printing Office, 1955), pp. 65 and 88.

20. Seaton, *The Battle for Moscow*, p. 84.

21. Seaton, *The Battle for Moscow*, p. 109.

22. *Small Unit Actions During the German Campaign in Russia*, Department of the Army Pamphlet 20–269A (Washington, D.C.: U.S. Government Printing Office, 1955), pp. 4, 33, 42, and 60.

23. John Weeks, *Men Against Tanks* (New York: Mason Charter, 1975), pp. 30–31 and 65; Paul Carell, *Hitler Moves East, 1941–1943* trans. Ewald Osers (Boston: Little, Brown and Company, 1964), p. 80; A. Yekimovskiy, "Tactics of the Soviet Army During the Great Patriotic War," *Voyenni Vestnik*, No. 4 (April 1967), translated and reprinted in Combat Studies Institute, *Selected Readings in Military History: Soviet Military History, Volume I, The Red Army, 1918–1945* (Fort Leavenworth, KS: U.S. Army Command and General Staff College, 1984), p. 19.

24. Carell, *Hitler Moves East*, pp. 69, 105, and 243.

25. Jac Weller, *Weapons and Tactics* (London: Nicholas Vane, 1966), p. 151. "The First Polish Division in 1942" and "A Soviet Motorized-Mechanized Brigade in September 1943," *Tactical Notebook*, July 1992.

26. Louis B. Ely, *The Red Army Today* (Harrisburg, PA: The Military Service Publishing Company, 1949), pp. 24–26.

27. Carell, *Hitler Moves East*, pp. 49–50.

28. *Small Unit Actions During the German Campaign in Russia*, pp. 6, 15, and 32; *German Defense Tactics Against Russian Breakthroughs*, Department of the Army Pamphlet No. 20–233 (Washington, D.C.: U.S. Government Printing Office, 1951), pp. 32 and 37; Liddell Hart, *The Soviet Army*, p. 34; and Carell, *Hitler Moves East*, p. 95.

29. These "infiltration tactics" should not be confused with the German "infiltration tactics" of the Great War. The latter term is derived from an early French attempt to characterize the *Stosstrupp* tactics described in Chapter 2.

30. F. W. von Mellenthin, *Panzer Battles, 1939–1945* (London: Cassell, 1955), p. 181.

31. A. Yekimovskiy and N. Makarov, "The Tactics of the Red Army in the 1920 and 1930s," *Voyenni Vestnik*, No. 3, (March 1967), translated and reprinted in Combat Studies Institute, *Selected Readings in Military History: Soviet Military History, Volume I, The Red Army, 1918–1945* (Fort Leavenworth, KS: U.S. Army Command and General Staff College, 1984), p. 91.

32. Vasili I. Chuikov, *The Beginning of the Road*, trans. Harold Silver (London: MacGibbon and Kee, 1963), pp. 109, 146–47, 150, 205, 284–98, and 302.

33. Chuikov, *The Beginning of the Road*, p. 294.

34. Chuikov, *The Beginning of the Road*, p. 292–98.

35. For a detailed account of the duel between Major Konings, the head of the German sniper school, and Zaitzev, see *The Beginning of the Road*, pp. 142–45.

36. *The Red Army Today*, pp. 20–21.

37. Ernst Ott, *Jäger am Feind, Geschichte und Ofergang der 97. Jäger-Division, 1940–1945* (Munich: Selbstverlag Kameradschaft der Spielhahnjäger E. V., 1966), pp. 14–15 and appendices. Care must be taken not to confuse the light infantry divisions of 1942–1945 with the four German light divisions of 1936–1939 (which were motorized cavalry formations) and the light divisions sent to Africa (the 5th, 90th, 164th, and 999th, which were custom-tailored desert formations). For a discussion of the organization and employment of a German *Jäger* division of World War II, see "Depicting a German Division," *Tactical Notebook*, January and February 1992.

38. Normalgliederung Inf. Division (Ost), table included in folder marked "Ia, KTB, Akte D, Band 2, Kriegsgliederungen," U.S. National Archives, Captured German Documents, Series T-312, Roll 783, Frame 785.

39. Various reports from infantry division and corps commanders contained in the folder "Hebung der Kampfkraft und Befehl Nr. 15," U.S. National Archives, Captured German Documents, Series T-78, Roll, 759.

40. Timothy A. Wray, *Standing Fast: German Defensive Doctrine on the Russian Front During World War II* (Fort Leavenworth, KS: U.S. Army Command and General Staff College, 1986), pp. 68–69.

41. For diagrams of such artillery hedgehogs, see "The German 18th Artillery Division—(1943–1944)," *Tactical Notebook*, February 1993. For more on the role of German artillery on the Eastern Front, see Gudmundsson, *On Artillery*, Chapter 7.

42. Edward N. Luttwak, "Urban Warfare Task Forces (*Kampfgruppen*) and Emergency *ad hoc* Forces (*Alarmeinheiten*)," unpublished report for U.S. Army TRADOC, 1 March 1983 (DTIC AD-B085 081).

43. Wray, *German Defense Tactics Against Russian Breakthroughs*, pp. 21 and 34.

44. Blau, *The German Campaign in Russia*, p. 56. Though numbers lightly armored "fast tanks" had survived 1941, the tendency within the Soviet armored forces was towards heavier tanks—to include British Matildas, American Lees, and Soviet-built T-34s and KVs.

45. As late as October of 1943, German infantry divisions on the Eastern Front had an average of only nine heavy (75-millimeter or larger) antitank guns each. General der Infanterie beim Chef Generalstab des Heeres IV Nr. 2886/43 geh. dated October 20, 1943. U.S. National Archives, Captured German Records, Series T-78, Roll 759. This was enough to equip but one of the four to six antitank companies rated by each infantry division at the time. The rest of the antitank companies had to make do with obsolescent 50-millimeter guns, converted French 75-millimeter field pieces, or even the obsolete 37-millimeter gun.

46. The German Army training film, "Männer gegen Panzer" is the best way to get a thorough view of German antitank training and methods during the last three years of World War II. It is available on videotape from International Historic Films, PO Box 29035, Chicago, IL 60629.

47. Guy Sajer, *The Forgotten Soldier*, trans. Lily Emmet (London: Weidenfeld and Nicholson, 1967), p. 166.

48. Morris Janowitz and Edward A. Shils, "Cohesion and Disintegration in the Wehrmacht in World War II," in Morris Janowitz, ed., *Military Conflict: Essays in the*

Institutional Analysis of War and Peace (Beverly Hills: Sage, 1975), pp. 178–82, 197, 216, and 218.

49. "Forming New Units," *Tactical Notebook*, October 1992; "Ersatz Divisions in 1914" and "The Many Meanings of Ersatz," *Tactical Notebook*, July 1993.

50. Lord Moran, *The Anatomy of Courage* (London: Constable, 1967), pp. 171–72.

6.

The Cutting Edge of Battle

The English-speaking world emerged from the Great War with a powerful consensus that the "war to end all wars" should never happen again. Civilians embraced pacifism to a degree unthinkable in countries which shared borders with powerful neighbors. Thinking soldiers looked for means of fighting—such as the terror bombing of civilians or the formation of great fleets of tanks—that spared them the need to fight on the ground. And all but a few agreed that infantry, though useful for "small wars," was not worth a great deal of attention.

During the Battle of France, the infantry of the British Expeditionary Force (B.E.F.) gave a reasonable, though not spectacular, account of itself. According to a report prepared by the German IV Army Corps, which had fought the B.E.F. from the Dyle River to the coast, "The English soldier was in excellent physical condition . . . [and in] battle he was tough and dogged . . . a fighter of high value . . . In defence . . . [he] took any punishment that came his way."[1] Coordination between infantry and the other arms was, however, poor. The British counterattack at Arras, for example, was marred by the failure of tanks, infantry, and artillery to work closely with each other.[2] This deficiency was highlighted by knowledge that the German infantry which had done so much to defeat the B.E.F., "supported by weapons subordinated to a single purpose," had gone forward in a resistless combination of fire-power and rapid movement, infiltrating every position, making full use of strategem and cover, and constantly seeking to close and destroy."[3]

After the Dunkirk evacuation, a number of British officers made serious attempts to inculcate their rapidly expanding army with new tactical ideas. The appointment of a group of veterans of the Battle of France—General Sir Alan Brooke as Commander in Chief, Home Forces, with General Sir Bernard Paget his Chief of Staff—to positions of influence did much to accelerate change. Assisted by veteran generals like Sir Harold Alexander and Bernard Law Montgomery, Brooke and Paget began the process of regeneration. For the British infantry, it represented an attempt to restore to that arm a truly offensive capability, only this time one based on small-unit fire and movement. A director of infantry was accordingly appointed at the War Office with a staff in every theater of war to study the special requirements of infantry and ensure it proper weapons. Divisional and general headquarters "battle schools" were also established to set the new standard of infantry training. The infantry, to quote General Paget, was to become "the cutting-edge of battle."[4]

Though the 1936 reorganization of companies and platoons was accepted as a starting point, the revitalized tactical training of the British army was presented as a totally "new look." "Battle drills," the stereotyped responses to particular situations that Liddell Hart had so long advocated, were devised, standardized, and taught at "battle schools." The idea was to infuse soldiers with the will to win, to make their actions in battle instinctive, to save time by streamlining procedures, and to provide the entire infantry with a uniform way of doing business. Thus, while individual fieldcraft skills continued to be stressed, every basic military action that could be was taught as a drill. There were drills for advancing, reacting to enemy fire, launching assaults, and breaching obstacles as well as drills for giving orders, cooperating with tanks, and organizing a defense or patrol.[5]

Significantly, all British infantry battle drills began with the squad, or, to use the term in use in the British Army since 1914, the section. Though it was emphasized that the section could rarely expect to operate by itself, the idea was nonetheless fostered that if a section happened to be left on its own, it should continue to fight independently. This was in accord with Liddell Hart's theory that the platoon, not the section, was the basic maneuver unit:

> The fact that the section is the unit of command presupposes it to represent the largest number of men who can be controlled in action by a *single* leader. This in turn means that it is incapable of tactical sub-division and therefore is limited to frontal action.[6]

While the platoon was considered to be the maneuver unit, the rifle company was judged to be the smallest unit capable of conducting independent operations for short periods of time. At this level, and that of the battalion to which it belonged, the contradictory demands for speed of reaction and time for reconnaissance, planning, orders, coordination of fire support, movement, and assault were felt acutely. Company commanders had to learn, therefore, how to make decisions on the move. Rather than trying to find ways of giving these officers experience in rapid decision making, however, the British Army provided them with battle drills of their own. Time would be saved, for example, if company commanders made a habit of always taking their artillery and mortar advisers with them when they went forward to reconnoiter and plan. Such new methods were not always readily acceptable, however, as a conservative element with a decided bias toward deliberate methods of tactical preparation remained strong and influential within the British Army. The difference between these competing philosophies, however, was not a great one. Both placed a great deal of emphasis on teaching officers to follow a set routine.

Battle drill was not the only method used by the British Army to train its infantry. Some of these, like the ritual shouting of "blood, blood, blood" and "kill, kill, kill," bordered on the juvenile. Others, such as the splashing of animal blood and the visiting of slaughter houses to "inoculate" men against the sights and smells of the battlefield, bordered on the ridiculous. General allowances of training ammunition permitted men to experience near misses from rifles, tommy guns, Bren guns, light mortars, and field artillery while the wide availability of armored vehicles made it possible for infantrymen to learn the feel of sheltering in a slit trench that was being run over by tank. Whatever their intrinsic value, most of these supplementary exercises served to train the body and the involuntary nervous system. They thus shared the essential defect of the battle drill approach—a failure to require infantrymen to think about what they were doing.[7]

The result of this quite deliberately "mindless" training program, as described by the German generals after the war, was an "unwieldy and rigidly methodical technique of command . . . [and an] over-systematic issuing of orders, down to the last detail, leaving little latitude to the junior commander."[8] While praising the courage and toughness of the individual British soldier, one official German manual stated that: "The British . . . [had] not yet succeeded in casting off . . . [their] congenitally schematic methods of working, and the clumsiness thereby entailed. This clumsiness continues down the scale of command by reason of the method of issuing orders, which go into the smallest detail."[9]

If basic British tactics were sometimes lackluster and uninspired, tank-infantry cooperation was to remain one of the Commonwealth forces' major coordination problems. Within the Eighth Army, this was so serious as to be described as "a most intense distrust, almost hatred" of friendly armor.[10] To remedy this problem, the British Army introduced an additional set of squad and platoon battle drills. The aim of these drills was to teach the infantry how to take advantage of tank firepower and mobility and, in turn, how best to support tank troops. As with other sorts of drills, however, these "second echelon" battle drills failed to teach the infantryman the essential habits of battlefield cooperation—understanding the strengths and weaknesses of the other unit so that its needs can be anticipated and its action exploited.[11]

In the immediate aftermath of Dunkirk, the major source of combat experience for British soldiers was the Western Desert. To a degree even greater than had been the case with the lessons of the Battle of France, however, the lessons of the desert war were misinterpreted. The initial victories over the Italians in Libya were largely credited to the superior British tanks. Subsequent defeats at the hand of the same enemy, by that time reinforced with a sprinking of German units, were blamed on German tanks.

This perception fit in nicely with the then current myth that the fall of France was entirely the work of German tanks, with a hurried familiarity with the works of J.F.C. Fuller, and the desire of the Royal Tank Corps to run its own show. That more subtle forces were at work was harder to see. The British were largely unaware of the paralysis imposed upon Italian units by the practice of writing long and detailed operation orders.[12] They could not see the pernicious effect of the huge gap that separated Italian officers from their men or the benefits achieved by the German emphasis on comradeship and leadership by example.[13] Similarly, the close cooperation between German units—such as the ruse by which a handful of German tanks drew much larger British tank units into the kill zones of invisible antitank guns—was often interpreted as a superiority in numbers or quality of tanks.[14]

Despite this perception, much of the fighting in the Western Desert was infantry combat. Five Axis infantry divisions—four Italian and one German—were, for example, involved in the siege of Tobruk. When the Axis attacked on May 6, 1941, they suffered about 1,200 men killed. In Rommel's opinion, this engagement made it "only too evident that the training of . . . [the German and Italian] infantry in position warfare was nowhere near up to the standard of the British and Australians." Being a firm believer that even "in the smallest action there are tactical tricks which can be used to save casualties" and that these "must be made known to the men," he instituted a crash training program in positional warfare for his infantry. In the small-scale infantry tactics that were subsequently prescribed, Rommel stressed "a maximum of caution, combined with supreme dash at the right moment."[15]

Apart from sieges, which even J.F.C. Fuller recognized as a proper task for infantry, the reign of the tank as "Queen of the Desert" left plenty of work for the infantry to do. As Rommel saw it, the primary role of infantry in desert warfare was "to occupy and hold positions designed either to prevent the enemy from [conducting] particular operations or to force him into other ones." In his attack on the heavily mined Gazala Line in May 1942, Rommel used his unmotorized infantry divisions to fix the opposing British forces. This allowed him to use his mechanized elements for an "end run" into the British rear.[16]

Because of the marked British superiority in both numbers of tanks and thickness of armor plating on those tanks, Rommel's infantry was provided with antitank guns on an unprecedented scale. During the summer of 1942, for example, Rommel's 90th Light Division consisted of four infantry battalions, two antitank battalions, and one field artillery battalion. The four infantry battalions, described by the commanding general of the 90th Light Division as "entire arsenals," were expected to serve either as conventional motorized infantry or as antitank troops. For the former task they had a full complement of light machine guns, heavy machine guns, mortars, and infantry guns. For the latter duty, each *squad* was provided with one of the many 76.2-millimeter field guns captured from the Russians in 1941.[17] This same weapon equipped one of the antitank battalions and the field artillery battalion. Given that the second antitank battalion was equipped with 50-millimeter antitank guns, it can be said that every one of the seven combatant battalions of 90th Light Division was an antitank battalion.[18]

The same could not be said for the British. Cursed with the notion that each arm ought to have a monopoly on a particular class of weapons, the British kept the infantry out of the business of manning first-rate antitank weapons. Instead, the job was given to the antitank battalions of the division artillery. (The infantry was allowed to use the obsolete two-pounders that the artillery had cast off.) The damage caused by this arrangement could have been mitigated if the British had adopted the German notion of the antitank battalion as a "fire brigade"—a reserve held in readiness to respond to a tank breakthrough by establishing an "instant tank ambush." Instead, the British adopted an approach that was nearly as bad as the one the French had used in 1940.

The premise of the British antitank philosophy was a sound one. Since tanks were the main danger, the "backbone" of the defense was no longer the machine gun but the antitank gun. However, when executed according to the bureaucratic staff procedures that plagued the British Army of the Second World War, the result was a major limitation on the freedom of maneuver of the British infantry. In particular, antitank plans laid out by the division staff (more precisely, the staff of the commander of the division artillery) determined the disposition of the division as a whole. With three layers of command (the infantry brigade, the infantry division, and the division artillery) between an infantry battalion commander and the antitank plan, the effect on an infantry battalion commander's options can be imagined.[19]

It was largely as a result of the experience in the Western Desert that the British increased, in 1942, the infantry component of their armored divisions. Instead of two armored brigades, each of which had a single infantry battalion and three tank battalions, the new pattern of armored divisions had one armored brigade and one infantry brigade. The new armored brigade retained its organic infantry battalion. The infantry brigade, of three battalions, consisted entirely of infantry. As a result of this action, infantry battalions in a British armored division now outnumbered armored battalions while the total number of tanks dropped from 368 to 188. Such a proportion would prove useful when the scene of the North African fighting shifted from the deserts of Libya and Egypt to the much more compartmentalized terrain of Tunisia.[20]

The same pattern of hills and valleys that made infantry so important to the British effort in Tunisia presented particular problems for that infantry. Part of the problem lay with organization. The British rifle battalion was, true to its name, composed largely of men armed with rifles. Though the allowance of three-inch mortars had, since 1939, been raised from two to six, and the Bren gun was generally recognized as the principal infantry weapon, neither the battalion commander nor the company commander was provided with any tripod-mounted machine guns. The result was platoons and companies that were often forced to operate without the heavy weapons "framework" that their German counterparts took for granted.[21] These heavy weapons were particularly missed when the Germans defended from rear slope positions that hindered British use of their excellent field artillery.[22]

This deficiency was exacerbated by the twin experiences of desert warfare and training based on battle drills. Desert warfare, with its emphasis on long range fire and large unit maneuver, had prevented the British infantry from developing a taste for small unit maneuver. Battle drills had prevented the development of the skills necessary to the effective maneuver of squads and platoons. As a consequence of this, the British infantry that fought in Tunisia in late 1942 and early 1943 had to relearn much of what their fathers had learned in the last six months of 1918.

As might be expected from such "reinvention of the wheel," the elements that had been central to sound infantry tactics since the middle of the Great War were given new names. The idea that every engagement was a unique problem whose solution required a custom-tailored maneuver was reborn under the heading of reconnaissance. The notion that the movement of infantry under fire required the suppression of all enemy firing positions was hailed as a great invention and christened with the term "pepper pot." As in 1918, ability of the British infantry to solve its own problems was limited by bureaucratic methods of command and control. In particular, the insistence that each infantry unit keep within its own boundaries sector prevented the timely elimination of enemy weapons positioned in a neighboring sector.[23]

The same forces also caused a vacuum in defensive tactics. In this case, however, the sin of the Battle Schools was largely one of omission. (The choreography of defensive actions had been neglected in favor of more offensive drills to the point where British "lessons learned" memoranda from Tunisia had to remind leaders of the importance of digging in.) As had been the case with offensive tactics, the methods invented to fill this vacuum bore a strong resemblance to German methods that were already a generation old:

However huge an area of country you are given, in placing your troops imagine you have only three-quarters of your platoon. Put your spare quarter aside as a mobile reserve; then forget all the books and put the rest wherever your common sense and your knowledge of Boche habits tells you. Whenever possible, you want to be on reverse slopes—any movement on forward slopes brings the shells down, and it is not easy to stay still all day. If the ground forces you to take up forward slope positions, keep the absolute smallest number at battle posts to observe, and the rest in cover until you are attacked. It is then that your fire control comes in. The first time, unless you drum it in daily, everyone will blaze off at any range at the first Boche to appear, giving all your positions away. It is much more satisfying to let the Jerries come up a bit and catch them in numbers on some open patch. If by chance they knock out one of your posts and start getting in among you then you thank God for that quarter you kept in reserve and nip in the counter-attack straight away. If you have got a counter-attack properly rehearsed with supporting fire, etc., for each of your posts, you should be able to get it in almost as soon as they arrive, or better still, get them in a flank as they advance.[24]

British small-unit defense in Tunisia also had to deal with the German fondness for fighting at night. German patrols had a habit of lashing positions with indiscriminate automatic fire, hoping to draw British return fire. The correct training response was to condition the soldier to hold off until a positive target could be identified and then aim to kill. The writer of the previously quoted paragraph on the defense considered it foolish to pursue German patrols, as the latter normally retired under cover of mortars specifically registered to engage pursuers.[25] (These latter weapons were so feared that they accounted for 43 percent of the psychiatric casualties suffered by the British forces in Tunisia.)[26]

The German virtuosity with the infantry mortar continued to be a problem in the next phase of the struggle for control of the Mediterranean, the landings on Sicily, and subsequent invasion of the Italian mainland.

> The German mortar is the greatest modern pest on the battlefield. . . . They are cordially disliked by all since they give no indication of their arrival and make a great noise. We have tried all possible means to pick them up, such as Sound Ranging, Air OPs [observation posts], and Ground OPs, but no proper solution has yet been reached. Constant watch and knowledge of the enemy's habits are of great assistance, but usually it becomes necessary to fire a great many shells, most of which hit nothing, in order to silence one or two mortars. The expenditure is justified.[27]

The fight for possession of the long boot of Italy was to be an even more wearisome slugging match than either the campaign for Tunisia or the battle for Sicily. The "soft under-belly" of Europe turned out to be anything but soft geographically, and the struggle became a matter of "one more river, one more mountain." It was also a struggle in which a force composed largely of North African and French mountain troops under the French General A. P. Juin, using only a few vehicles and pack animals, actually moved faster in difficult terrain than vehicle-clogged British divisions closer to the coast. Contrary to common expectation, modern equipment had not necessarily made an army more mobile. Road and weather conditions underscored the difference between physical and tactical mobility. In Italy, the unceasing winter rains turned the countryside of "sunny Italy" into a quagmire that restricted even tracked vehicles to the roads. Most offensive action, therefore, had to be effected by infantry, sappers, and artillery, not always in sufficient numerical superiority. The battlefields of Italy soon began to bear a striking resemblance to those of the Western Front of the Great War, the conditions of the Somme, Verdun, and Passchendaele being in large part recreated in the battles of Anzio and Cassino.[28]

Savage city fighting, though on a lesser scale than that of the Eastern Front, also marked the Italian campaign. At Ortona, the 1st Canadian Division became locked in a costly "street-fighting" battle with the German 1st Parachute Division. Choosing to defend only the north part of the town but leaving the southern half a nightmare of trapped and mined houses, the Germans made its defense into a miniature Stalingrad of interconnected and heavily mined strongpoints. Here the *Panzerfaust*, an expendable infantry antitank weapon, made its appearance. Here, also, the Canadians adopted the German technique of "mouseholing," using demolition charges to blow holes in walls so that troops could clear rows of houses without having to appear in the fire-swept streets. However, as the Germans often attempted to recapture houses by infiltrating through "mouseholes" of their own, captured buildings consequently had to be occupied in strength. Such practices naturally resulted in extremely close quarter combat, a condition amply attested to by the fact that the frontage of 2nd Canadian Infantry Brigade was not more than 250 yards.[29]

The amphibious landing at Anzio in January 1944 was intended to provide a tactical alternative to the tedious and costly advance of the Allied armies. Unfortunately, the Anzio bridgehead with its 70,000 men and 18,000 vehicles (one for every four soldiers) became hostage to German arms. Often likened to a beached whale, this "army of chauffeurs" had to be rescued by the very force it had been landed to aid—the Allied armies in southern Italy. This rescue, in turn, required the taking of the ancient monastery of Monte Cassino.

Before the Allied attack, Monte Cassino was subjected to massive artillery and air bombardments that, at least in the opinion of J.F.C. Fuller, were "unsurpassed in the history of warfare."[30] As at Passchendaele, the effect of such a "weight of metal" was to create an almost insurmountable obstacle to the movement of attacking Allied forces. As had been the case in the Great War, many of the enterprising German infantrymen defending Cassino survived, in some instances by fitting up to six of their number at a time into two-man shelters called "crabs."[31] When the bombing and shelling ceased, these survivors took full advantage of the tactical truism that "it is only when buildings are demolished that they are converted from mousetraps into bastions of defence."[32]

It was in Italy that the Allies began to suffer their first shortages of infantry. By the end of 1943, every one of the rifle companies in the First Canadian Division had suffered 50 percent casualties.[33] Though the Canadians, volunteers all, resorted to a remustering policy to get more infantrymen, by 1944 the average company strength of some line battalions had fallen to forty-five. The shortage of trained infantrymen (a few replacements arrived in units with a knowledge of elementary platoon and section tactics and some without having fired the Bren) eventually became so serious that it precipitated a political crisis within Canada itself.[34]

The British, faced with a similarly acute shortage of infantry, were forced to break down two divisions. The "rates of wastage" used by the War Office, it turned out, were based on the experience of the North African campaign and bore little resemblance to the requirements of either the Italian or northwest European campaigns. Whereas British infantry in North Africa suffered 48 percent of total casualties (compared to 15 percent for the armored corps and 14 percent for the artillery), in Italy and Normandy, the infantry arm incurred 76 percent of all casualties, with armor artillery accounting for but seven and eight percent, respectively.[35]

While infantry shortages plagued the Allied armies, their logistic trains remained virtual cornucopias of men and material. In this regard it is extremely interesting to compare the "divisional slices" of Allied, German, and Russian armies. A rough and ready method of measuring the efficiency of army organization, the "divisional slice" is determined by dividing the total number of men in an army by the number of divisions it fields. Simply put, it is the total number of personnel required to man, supply, and keep a division in action. For the Canadian Army, the figure was a weighty 93,150; for the British Army, 84,300; and for the more affluent United States Army, a lower 71,000. A certain interpolation is, of course, required before a meaningful comparison can be made since Canadian divisions with strengths of 18,376 (infantry) and 14,819 (armored) were larger than their American equivalents of 14,037 (infantry) and 10,670 (armored). Still, whatever the measurement applied, no nation needed so many men to keep one man in action as did Canada. Taking the fighting arms all together, in the Canadian Army they made up but 34.2 percent of the whole, while in the American and British armies, they constituted 43.5 and 65.3 percent, respectively.[36] By contrast, the German Army divisional slice was roughly 23,000, based on an average divisional strength of 12,000. This meant that a Germany of 85 million inhabitants could mobilize successively 325 divisions, while an America of 140 million could barely maintain eighty-nine divisions. The Soviets, with divisional slices of 22,000 and a population exceeding 170 million, were able to field better than 500 divisions with average strengths of about 10,300 each.[37]

According to Colonel Nicholas Ignatieff, a Russian-born Canadian serving with British intelligence, it took seven noncombatants to keep one man fighting with the British Army, whereas in the Red Army the ratio was little more than two to one. He was particularly struck by the spectacle of one rain-drenched Soviet soldier who arrived on the banks of the Elbe River near Torgau, Germany:

> He was wearing a filthy bandage on his head and he was riding on the back of an ox, which was pulling a small ammunition truck, which had run out of gas. He maintained, with the sense of romance common to all soldiers of experience, that he had been riding the ox and pulling the truck all the way from Stalingrad, and if he hadn't been, the Allies might still be in fairly serious trouble. I asked him what he intended to do with the ox now that the war was nearly over. "Eat it," he said, and there can't be the slightest doubt that he did.[38]

The tendency toward oversupply in the English-speaking armies was literally carried into action. The litter that reportedly accompanied the landing on the beaches of Normandy was caused less by human slothfulness than by slothful thinking. It was also such thinking, or lack thereof, which cost so many infantry lives on the bloody day of assault. Most infantry in the leading waves were, in fact, criminally overloaded. The American soldier carried more than eighty pounds, and any careful examination of photographs of British and Canadian troops waddling ashore on that day will reveal that they, too, were weighted down with roughly the same load. So laden, soldiers wounded before they reached dry land often drowned. Even those that made it to shore were so weighted down by water and kit that they lacked even the strength to keep ahead of the tide, which moved inland at the pace of a slow walk.[39]

At Normandy, getting ashore was only half of the challenge. A few meters inland, the largely English-speaking soldiers of the Allied armies found that, instead of the "green fields beyond," they had run into the *bocage*. Composed of small fields delineated by ditches and thick mounds of earth high as a man's head and crowned by trees and thickets whose roots had been undisturbed for years, the *bocage* was interconnected by numerous narrow roads and dotted with tiny hamlets. It was anything but ideal for armored warfare; in crossing roads and climbing banks, tanks invariably heaved up, thereby dangerously exposing their soft undersides to enemy antitank fire. The hand-held *Panzerfaust* antitank weapons proved an extremely grave threat to any tank caught in such a posture.

The "battle of the hedgerows" thus became an infantry contest, with armor in a supporting role. In this struggle, Allied infantry often discovered that the tactics that it had been taught were less than effective.[40] The 50th (Northumbrian) Division, for example, discovered that normal battle drills for the attack were unsuitable for dealing with German defenses in the hedgerows. Sand was accordingly brought up from the beaches, and through improvising sand models of the countryside, the division was able to devise a new drill for attacking through *bocage*. Taught to all platoon commanders, it was credited with saving many lives.[41]

Despite such expedients, the process of breaking through the *bocage* was very costly for the British infantry. Though comprising only 14 percent of the British force crowded on the Normandy beachhead, the British infantry battalions had suffered 85 percent of the casualties of the first month's fighting. As these were twice as high as had been anticipated by the personnel specialists, the British command was forced to contemplate the breaking up of some battalions in order to keep the others up to strength. This shortage also led the British leadership to continue its policy of attempting to use tanks, artillery, and aerial bombardment as a substitute for, rather than a complement to, infantry.[42]

This tendency was hard to hide from the Germans. One report of the 10th SS *Panzer* Division noted that, in Normandy:

> The morale of the enemy infantry is not very high. It depends largely on artillery and air support. In case of a well placed concentration of fire from our own artillery the infantry will often leave its position and retreat hastily. Whenever enemy is engaged with force, he usually retreats or surrenders.[43]

Beyond the *bocage*, the Normandy countryside was relatively open, with broad fields interrupted only by small woods, fruit orchards, and little clusters of stone houses. Even in this "tank country," however, the British shortage of infantry proved to be a major problem. South and east of the ancient city of Caen, the Germans converted the network of villages that dotted the landscape into a web of antitank fire. Because the handful of British infantry battalions available were unable to clear these villages, the British tank attack of July 18, 1944, proved very costly. In the first seventy-two hours of the attack (Operation Goodwood), over three hundred British tanks, nearly 35 percent of the 877 tanks available to the three British armored divisions taking part, were knocked out by the Germans.[44]

The skill shown by the German infantry in defending the villages south and east of Caen was displayed throughout the battle for Normandy and, indeed, throughout the campaign in Northwest Europe. While there were many reasons for this, the heart of German infantry tactics (and thus the tactical superiority of the German infantry) was the ability of German squads to maneuver. This was a function, not merely of organization and weapons, or even of the tradition of *Stosstrupp* tactics, but of the psychology of the young NCOs and men within them. Contrary to the view promulgated by Allied propaganda, the German soldier was far from an automaton. Less gregarious than either his British or American counterpart, he was highly capable of individual thought and action. Comments such as "the infantry soldier is not trained to fight in twos and threes, whereas the German does so frequently," and "the German is first-class at infiltration, because he will work as a single individual" often appeared in Allied reports.[45] While some of this can be explained by pointing to the high standards of education and strong traditions of craftsmanship in German civil society, a good deal of credit can be given to the German Army practice of training every soldier to take charge of himself and his comrades.[46]

This high level of self-reliance made it possible for the Germans to exploit the Allied shortage of infantry by using infiltration tactics. According to a contemporary German document, the "best countermeasure evolved" against Allied offensive action was "an inconspicuous filtering . . . in numerous small detachments" into an enemy area weakly occupied by infantry.[47] Small group actions were also the building blocks on which German counterattacks were based, as the following Allied after-action report indicates:

> Experience has shown that the Germans will almost invariably launch a counter-attack to break up an attack made by small infantry units. You can expect such a counter-attack, usually by 10 to 20 men, not more than five minutes after you get close to the German positions. They are usually well armed with light machine guns and machine pistols and counter-attack by fire and movement. They keep up a heavy fire while small details, even individuals, alternately push forward. The Germans almost always attack your flank. They seldom close with the bayonet, but try to drive you out by fire.[48]

From the start of the war, German small-unit offensive actions were characterized by incessant talking and shouting. Erroneously interpreted by Allied soldiers as a sign of poor discipline, it was later ascertained that such chatter was, in fact, an effective means of dispelling individual loneliness and heightening group cohesion. The Germans were convinced that the infantryman is, in the word of S.L.A. Marshall, "sustained by his fellows primarily and by his weapons secondarily."[49] That Allied infantry were invariably reluctant "to make use of their own fire to help themselves forward" was less of a technical problem than a human one.[50]

Because of the attention that they paid to the human aspect of war, the Germans had long been aware of the role exhaustion played in diminishing the fighting power of the infantryman. Because of that, they had a longstanding policy of frequently rotating infantry (as well as other combat) units out of line for periods of rest. In addition to allowing the infantrymen to recover their physical strength, these periods were used for training. Lessons learned in recent fighting were discussed, replacements were integrated into squads, and short exercises were held to test new procedures, practice new tactics, and restore skills that had, in the heat of battle, been allowed to atrophy.[51] In short, the Germans used rest periods as a means, not merely of restoring, but also of reforming, their infantry units.

When fighting the British, for example, one German unit discovered a critical weakness of infantry that had placed too little emphasis on the squad:

> NCOs were rarely in the "big picture" so that if the officer became a casualty, they were unable to act in accordance with the main plan. The result was that in a quickly changing situation, the junior commanders showed insufficient flexibility. . . . The conclusion is: as far as possible go for the enemy officers. Then seize the initiative yourself.[52]

The German policies of "custom tailoring" their infantry units and "just in time training" was in keeping with their "artistic" approach to war. "War," German soldiers had been taught to believe, was a "free creative activity," in which leaders and led alike had to constantly adapt themselves to changing situations.[53] "The essential thing" was "the deed," and the processes by which the deed was accomplished were not merely secondary but situational.[54] The doctrine that unified the German Army was not a matter of templates or procedures, but an oral and literary tradition that constantly stressed the importance of resolute and rapid action, cooperation between different arms and units, and the importance of the human element.

The British infantry likewise reflected the larger British tradition of continental (as opposed to colonial) war. The British armies improvised for the life or death struggles of the modern era—the Napoleonic Wars, the Great War, and the Second World War—were largely led by brave but untutored amateurs. Lacking a proper military education, these officers had to be provided with substitutes for tactical judgment. This tended to take the form of rigid rules imposed from above, lists of abstract "principles" advertised as universally applicable, and, increasingly, attempts to substitute mass or gadgetry for clever tactics. Battle drills, devised by a central authority and taught to an entire army, fit in well with this tradition, as did the belief that extravagant use of artillery could economize on the lives of British infantry.

By the end of the war in Europe, this latter idea had become the most obvious characteristic of operating style of the British ground forces. In an attack in the *Reichswald* (Operation Veritable, February 8, 1945), for example, over a thousand artillery pieces and 50,000 shells were assembled to support the attack of a single corps. (This number does not count the light antiaircraft batteries, mortar units, tank squadrons, and infantry machine gun battalions used to provide additional indirect fire against ground targets.) In Italy, on April 9, 1945, an attack of two infantry divisions was preceded by an air strike delivered by 700 bombers and an artillery bombardment produced by 1,200 artillery pieces. (Again, the number of artillery pieces does not include the many light antiaircraft guns, mortars, tanks, and machine guns that allowed the British to "economize" on their artillery.)[55]

Whether this largesse did much to help the British infantryman is hard to say. The bombardment of February 8, for example, seems to have had the effect of disrupting the cohesion of the Germans by keeping leaders from "making the rounds" of the shelters. (This, in turn, indicates that the German division in question lacked the kind of squad leaders that were essential to the German infantry tactics of the period.) In the same attack, the British were unable to silence either the outnumbered German field artillery or the ubiquitous German mortars.[56]

What is certain, however, is that the need to assemble the long rows of guns and mountains of shells for such attacks greatly slowed the tempo of the British campaigns in Italy and northwest Europe. In the former case, the Germans were able to issue a propaganda poster that compared Allied progress up the length of Italy to the pace of a snail.[57] In the latter, the British forces moving from Normandy into the Netherlands and from there into Germany took over six months to cover territory that the Germans of 1940 had, in a supporting operation, plowed through in less than six weeks.

NOTES

1. L. F. Ellis, *The War in France and Flanders, 1939–1940* (London: His Majesty's Stationery Office, 1953), p. 326.

2. Brian Bond, "Arras, 21 May 1940: A Case Study in Counterstroke" in Correlli Barnett et al., *Old Battles, New Lessons, Can We Learn from Military History?* (London: Brassey's Defense Publishers, 1986), pp. 61–83.

3. Arthur Bryant, "The New Infantryman," *Canadian Army Training Memorandum*, No. 44, 1944, p. 32.

4. Bryant, "The New Infantryman," pp. 31–32 and Anthony Farrar-Hockley, *Infantry Tactics* (London: Almark, 1976), pp. 20–24.

5. Robert H. Ahrenfeldt, *Psychiatry in the British Army in the Second World War* (London: Routledge and Kegan Paul, 1958), pp. 198; G. R. Stevens, *Princess Patricia's Canadian Light Infantry, 1919–1957* (Montreal: Southam, 1958), pp. 54–55; and Farrar-Hockley, *Infantry Tactics*, pp. 19–24.

6. Liddell Hart, "The 'Ten Commandments' of the Combat Unit," p. 288.

7. John A. English, *The Canadian Army and the Normandy Campaign, A Study of Failure in High Command* (New York: Praeger, 1990), pp. 114–15. This work contains an entire chapter devoted to the subject of battle drill. For detailed descriptions of such training, see Farley Mowat, *The Regiment* (Toronto: McClelland and Stewart, 1973), pp. 48–49.

8. This opinion was, ironically, reported by Liddell Hart, who argued that his advocacy of battle drill was intended to teach soldiers how to reason as well as react. Liddell Hart, ed., *The Rommel Papers* (New York: Harcourt Brace, 1953), p. 184.

9. Great Britain, War Office, *Current Reports from Overseas*, no. 65, November 29, 1944, p. 13.

10. Sir Howard Kippenberger, *Infantry Brigadier* (Oxford: Oxford University Press, 1949), p. 180.

11. English, *The Canadian Army and the Normandy Campaign*, pp. 112–13.

12. Liddell Hart, *Europe in Arms* (London: Faber and Faber, 1937), p. 36.

13. Field Marshal Albert Kesselring, while refusing to condemn the Italian soldier as naturally poor military material, nonetheless remained convinced that the entire "Italian armed forces were trained more for display than for action." The most soul-destroying aspect of the Italian army, however, and the one that most adversely affected morale was the all-pervading differentiation that existed between officers and men: "An Italian officer led a segregated life; having no perception of the needs of his men, he was unable to meet them as occasion required, and so in critical situations he lost control. The Italian private, even in the field, received quite different rations from the officers. The amount multiplied in ratio to rank. . . . The officers ate separately and were very often unaware of how much or what their men got. This undermined the sense of comradeship which should prevail between men who live and die together." Albert Kesselring, *Memoirs* (London: William Kimber, 1953), p. 107.

14. J.B.A. Bailey, *Field Artillery and Firepower* (London: Oxford University Press, 1989), pp. 171–75.

15. Liddell Hart, *The Rommel Papers*, pp. 91, 130, 133, and 262.

16. Liddell Hart, *The Rommel Papers*, p. 201 and Mellenthin, *Panzer Battles*, pp. 90–109 and 112–17.

17. Ulrich Kleeman, "Streiflichter zur Kriegsführung in Nordafrika," Foreign Military Studies, Manuscript D104, pp. 4–8.

18. The 164th Light Division was provided antitank guns on a similar scale. Tables of organization for the 164th "Afrika" Division microfilmed at the U.S. National Archives, Captured German Records, Series T-78, Reel 861. For a detailed treatment of the history and organization of this formation, see the series "The 164 Light 'Afrika,' " *Tactical Notebook*, July 1992.

19. Farrar-Hockley, *Infantry Tactics*, p. 28.

20. R. M. Orgorkiewicz, *Armored Forces* (London: Arms and Armor Press, 1970), pp. 59–60; and Messenger, *The Art of Blitzkrieg*, pp. 157–58.

21. Ellis and Chamberlain, *Handbook on the British Army*, 1943, pp. 22–25.

22. A. L. Pemberton, *The Development of Artillery Tactics and Equipment* (London: The War Office, 1950), p. 159.

23. "A Few Tips from the Front," *Canadian Army Training Memorandum*, No. 29, 1943, pp. 19–21; and Kenneth Macksey, *Crucible of Power: The Fight for Tunisia, 1942–1943* (London: Hutchinson, 1969), pp. 159, 240, and 262.

24. "A Few Tips from the Front," *Canadian Army Training Memorandum*, No. 29, 1943, pp. 19–20.

25. "A Few Tips from the Front," *Canadian Army Training Memorandum*, No. 29, 1943, pp. 20–21.

26. Pemberton, *The Development of Artillery Tactics and Equipment*, p. 169.

27. "Extracts from a Report Written as a Result of a Tour in the Mediterranean by B.R.A. (Army Artillery Commander), HQ 21 Army Group, Dated 10 Jan. 1944," U.S. National Archives, Record Group 337, Entry 47, Box 92.

28. W.G.F. Jackson, *The Battle for Italy* (London: B. T. Batsford, 1967), pp. 122–23, 138, 139, 141, 167, 238, and 321.

29. "Ortona," *Canadian Army Training Memorandum*, No. 42, September 1944, pp. 31–35; Jackson, *The Battle for Italy*, pp. 152–53; and G.W.L. Nicholson, *The Canadians in Italy* (Ottawa: Queen's Printer, 1956), pp. 325–29, 333, and 681.

30. J.F.C. Fuller, *Thunderbolts* (London: Skeffington and Son, 1946), pp. 54–55.

31. The crabs were steel cylinders, seven feet deep and six feet in diameter. Designed for a two-man machine gun crew, crabs were emplaced so that only thirty inches extended above ground. The above ground portion, however, was provided with armor that was five inches thick. Nicholson, *The Canadians in Italy*, p. 396.

32. Liddell Hart, *The Other Side of the Hill*, p. 374.

33. Nicholson, *The Canadians in Italy*, pp. 338 and 344.

34. Ralph Allen, *Ordeal by Fire: Canada, 1910–1945* (Toronto: Popular Library, 1961), pp. 442–45; and C. P. Stacey, *The Victory Campaign: The Operations in North-West Europe, 1944–45* (Ottawa: Queen's Printer, 1960), p. 385.

35. Stacey, *The Victory Campaign*, p. 284.

36. E.L.M. Burns, *Manpower in the Canadian Army, 1939–1945* (Toronto: Clarke, Irwin, 1956), pp. 14, 18–19, 21 and 23; and Allen, *Ordeal by Fire*, pp. 441–42.

37. Friedrich Otto Miksche, *Atomic Weapons and Armies* (London: Faber and Faber, 1955), p. 163; and Frido von Senger und Etterlin, *Neither Fear Nor Hope*, trans. George Malcolm (London: Macdonald, 1960), pp. 196 and 223.

38. Allen, *Ordeal by Fire*, pp. 439–40.

39. Out of a total of 105 men lost on D-day by Company E, Sixteenth Infantry, which landed on Omaha beach, only one man was killed from the top of the beach inland; the rest perished in the water. It is indeed sadly ironic that many of these soldiers carried on their backs several cartons of cigarettes (the killing kindness of a concerned welfare officer no doubt) and sufficient rations for three days. Subsequent surveys showed that in the excitement of action most men did not even eat during the first day of fighting. S.L.A. Marshall, *The Soldier's Load and the Mobility of a Nation* (Washington, D.C.: The Combat Forces Press, 1950), pp. 11, 22–25, 35, 40, and 47.

40. R. Ernest Dupuy and Trevor N. Dupuy, *Military Heritage of America* (New York: McGraw-Hill, 1956), pp. 535–36; Kenneth Macksey, *Tank Warfare, A History of Tanks in Battle* (London: Rupert Hart Davis, 1971), p. 229; and Charles B. MacDonald, *The Mighty Endeavor: American Armed Forces in the European Theater in World War II* (New York: Oxford University Press, 1969), pp. 282–83 and 293.

41. A.J.D. Turner, *Valentine's Sand Table Exercises* (Aldershot: Gale and Polden, 1955), p. 2.

42. Martin Samuels, "Operation Goodwood—The Caen Carve-Up," *British Army Review*, #96 (December 1990), p. 4.

43. Stacey, *The Victory Campaign*, pp. 119 and 274. At the time of this report, the 10th *SS Panzer* Division had fought against British and American troops, but had had little contact with Canadians.

44. R. H. Liddell Hart, *History of the Second World War* (London: Pan, 1978), pp. 578–579; Chester Wilmot, *The Struggle for Europe* (London: Collins, 1974), pp. 405–11; and Stacey, *The Victory Campaign*, pp. 169–70.

45. *Current Reports from Overseas*, No. 66 (1944), p. 10; and No. 36 (1944), p. 11.

46. Senger und Etterlin, *Neither Fear nor Hope*, p. 219.

47. Great Britain, War Office, *Current Reports from Overseas*, No. 61 (1944), p. 14.

48. "The Germans—How they Fight," *Canadian Army Training Memorandum*, No. 39 (June 1944), p. 39; and *Current Reports from Overseas*, No. 34 (1944), pp. 11–12.

49. Marshall, *Men Against Fire* (New York: William Morrow, 1953), pp. 42–43, 127 and 136.

50. *Current Reports from Overseas*, No. 61 (1944), p. 12.

51. It is interesting to note that German commanders, when queried as to the best technique for increasing the fighting power of their infantry, almost unanimously recommended doubling the home leave accorded each infantryman from the army-wide standard of fifteen days a year to fifteen days every six months. Some commanders even argued that such leave was so important that even major battles (*Großkämpfe*) should not interfere with it. Various reports form infantry division and corps commanders contained in the folder "Hebung der Kampfkraft und Befehl Nr. 15," U.S. National Archives, Captured German Documents, Series T-78, Roll 759.

52. Quoted in Max Hastings, *Overlord* (London: Joseph, 1984), p. 147.

53. "Truppenführung (Troop Leading), The German Field Service Regulations," *Tactical Notebook*, March 1993.

54. Hans von Seeckt, *Gedanken eines Soldaten* (Leipzig: Koehler & Ameland, 1936), p. 159. An English translation of the essay explaining this idea was published as "The Essential Thing," *Tactical Notebook*, November 1993.

55. Pemberton, *The Development of Artillery Tactics and Equipment*, pp. 263–65 and 274–75.

56. Pemberton, *The Development of Artillery Tactics and Equipment*, p. 278.

57. This poster was on display at the Memorial Museum at Caen in January 1991.

7.

A Corporal's Guard

In 1943, a U.S. Army handbook on the British Army excused a rather thin chapter on British tactics by arguing that "British tactical doctrine is essentially similar to that of the U.S. Army." In terms of the American tradition of amateur armies and a consequent tendency towards cumbersome staff procedures, poor coordination between different arms, and an excessive reliance upon artillery, aerial bombardment, and gadgetry, the resemblance was a close one. Nonetheless, there were a numer of important differences between the British and American approaches to the art of war in general and infantry tactics in particular. One of the most important to the infantry was the American effort to make the most of the rifle squad.

Though the squad was not, as is sometimes claimed, an American invention, American soldiers were among the first to recognize the tactical importance of small units. In 1867, for example, General Emory Upton produced a new system of open-order infantry tactics based on eight-man units. As with other open order systems, Upton's squads were essentially a means of controlling fire and movement. They were not capable of maneuvering within themselves or even to serve as the elements of a maneuvering platoon. The corporal who led such a squad, for example, might supervise volley fire and ensure that all members of the squad took part in a rush. He was not, however, given independent missions to perform.

Upton's squad remained with the U.S. Army until 1918.[1] In that year, the American infantry attempted to accommodate the influx of new infantry weapons by designing a platoon that bore a closer resemblance to a child's building set than a cohesive unit. With a strength of fifty-three men, the new platoon consisted of four unequal sections, each of which consisted entirely of one sort of specialist. The hand grenade section, for example, consisted of twelve men trained to use hand grenades in trench warfare. The other three sections were composed of nine rifle grenadiers, fifteen automatic riflemen, and seventeen "ordinary" riflemen. These sections were not combat units in their own right. Rather, they were "pools" that provided the platoon commander with the means to task organize for various combat missions.[2]

One of the more significant aspects of this "modular" organization was the fact that the men in each of the functional sections were further organized into teams. The fifteen automatic riflemen, for example, were divided into four three-man teams, each of which served a single automatic rifle. (The three extra men were NCOs, one sergeant, and two corporals. These permitted teams to be joined together into larger units.) The hand bombers were divided into three squads, each consisting of a leader, a thrower, a scout, and a carrier. The rifle-grenadiers formed a single squad, with six men carrying rifles modified to fire grenades and three men carrying ammunition. The riflemen formed two squads, each with the traditional eight men.[3]

The American experiment with "some assembly required" infantry units was based on two assumptions, both of which turned out to be false. The first was that trench warfare would continue through 1919 and that, as a result, there would be plenty of time for the platoon commander to task organize fighting sections. The second was that an infantryman was more attached to his weapon than his comrades. The first assumption was rendered invalid by the untimely resumption of mobile warfare. The second assumption was called into question by the near disintegration of many American units as they struggled to keep up with the German withdrawals.[4] As a result, to use the words of the U.S. Chief of Infantry of 1938, these platoons "had little cohesion, they attained few marked tactical successes, and they could have had no success at all against fresh, fully trained tactical teams."

In light of this, it is not surprising that the next reorganization of the American infantry made provision for greater supervision. Regulations published in 1919 reduced the size of the platoon and divided it into two equal sections, each of which was further divided into two eight-man squads. In addition to being similar to contemporary French and British organization, this "square" platoon provided for an interesting division of labor. The sergeant who served as the section leader guided the unit. His eyes were therefore to the front. The squad leaders, on the other hand, focused their attention on their squads. They maintained the positions assigned to them, saw to it that the platoon and section leaders' orders were executed and assisted in enforcing fire discipline. Only when platoon and section leaders had lost control over their subordinates were the squad leaders to act on their own initiative.[5]

In keeping with the almost wholesale adoption of French doctrine and methods that characterized the American ground forces of the Great War, the U.S. rifle platoon of the early interwar period bore a strong resemblance to its French counterpart. From 1920 to 1932, for example, it consisted of two sections of two squads each. Though the American eight-man squad was smaller than its French counterpart, it was, like the French squad, an indivisible unit formed around a single automatic rifle. (This was, from the very beginning of the interwar period, the Browning Automatic Rifle (BAR), a weapon that had been introduced in the last weeks of the Great War).[6] As was the case with the French, British, and Soviets, the platoon was seen as the "smallest unit having independent power of maneuver."[7]

Though French-style tactics that were thoroughly consistent with this organization formed the basis for many manuals, and, more importantly, the curricula for the many schools and correspondence courses that sprang up during this period, they had to compete with a domestic school of thought.[8] Associated with men who had been too senior to have been trained by the French in 1917 and 1918, as well as the long-standing "cult of the rifle," this school believed that the skilled marksman was America's secret weapon. Steeped in the belief that American frontiersman had won the American War of Independence and War of 1812 with aimed rifle fire and encouraged by the Great War exploits of the likes of Sergeant Alvin York, these latter-day advocates of "Boer tactics" were reluctant to see the American infantryman converted into the handmaiden of an automatic weapon.

Major General George A. Lynch, who was Chief of Infantry on the eve of the Second World War, expressed the views of this school as follows:

> We ought definitely to reject the theory so current in many armies, that a rifle company is merely a collection of so many automatic rifles. . . . We want the man in the front line to be a fighting man, not an ammunition carrier. We want him to feel that the issue of combat depends on his personal conduct.[9]

It is largely due to the influence of this school that the U.S. infantry obtained, in the mid-1930s, its most salient characteristic—the semi-automatic Garand rifle. This weapon, many influential American infantrymen believed, provided sufficient firepower to free the infantry squad from its previous dependence on the automatic rifle. Thus, in 1939 and 1940, when U.S. rifle platoons were once more reorganized, the BARs were taken out of the rifle squads. In peacetime, this resulted in the exile of the BARs to the company armory. On mobilization, however, each platoon was to draw two BARs and use them to equip a single automatic rifle squad.

At the same time, the number of rifle squads per platoon was reduced from four to three and the rifle section was eliminated. (The section was retained as a designation for a variety of heavy weapons units too small to be platoons but too large to be squads.) This change was made as part of an overall "triangularization" of the American infantry division that, in turn, was part of a comprehensive remolding of the U.S. Army. Just as the reduction in the number of rifle squads from four to three eliminated the section as an echelon of command, the switch from four to three regiments in the division eliminated the brigade. Regiments, battalions, and companies were already triangular and thus underwent fewer changes.

As was the case in most other armies that had adopted the triangular organization, some echelons were provided with what might be called a "heavy" element. For the infantry regiment, there was a platoon of six 37-millimeter antitank guns. For the battalion, there was a heavy weapons company on the French model, with sixteen heavy machine guns, two 81-millimeter mortars, and two .50 caliber machine guns (intended for use against both aircraft and tanks). The company received a mortar section of three 60-millimeter mortars and a section of four "light" machine guns. These were tripod-mounted .30 caliber machine guns similar to the heavy machine guns of the heavy weapons company. (What made them light was the substitution of an air-cooled barrel for the traditional water-cooled one.)[10]

The U.S. Army had been relatively late in jumping on the bandwagon of triangularization. The British, with three infantry brigades to each infantry division, had been triangular from the beginning of the century. French and German infantry divisions, for example, had been composed of three infantry regiments ever since the middle years of the Great War and, like Soviet and Polish infantry divisions, had remained triangular throughout the interwar period. Despite this apparent tardiness, or, perhaps because of it, the American adoption of the triangular form was more than a reshuffling of the organizational deck. It was an integral part of a more fluid approach to infantry tactics that had been slowly developing in the U.S. Army during the 1920s and 1930s.

Though this new approach was often encapsulated by the slogan "two up, one back, hit 'em in the flank," it required, for its complete promulgation, a full book. This book was *Infantry in Battle*, a collection of case studies first published by the Infantry School (at Fort Benning, Georgia) in 1934. Drawn from the experiences of the American Expeditionary Force in 1918, as well as those of the German, French, and even Russian armies of the Great War, these case studies presented a view of infantry that was strikingly different from the "barrage" doctrine that had been borrowed from the French at the end of the Great War. There was, for example, a good deal of emphasis on infiltration, night attacks, and, most importantly, on junior leaders who, in the absence of orders, were capable of making rapid decisions on the basis of "terrain and situation."[11]

One of the most radical changes of the 1939/1940 reforms was the increase in the size of the rifle squad from eight to twelve men. This was justified by the argument that the larger squad would be better able to absorb casualties. What made it acceptable to the army, however, was not this abstract idea but an equally radical change in the infantry drill manual. Since the days of Emory Upton, U.S. infantry squads had formed for drill in two ranks of four men each. Adding or subtracting additional men to this basic formation had the effect of preventing the smooth execution of the complicated close order drill so loved by peacetime regulars. When, however, the squad was formed, as it was after 1940, in a single rank, it could be expanded or contracted as the writers of tables of organization saw fit.[12]

Instead of the traditional corporal, the leadership of General Lynch's expanded rifle squad was to be entrusted to a sergeant. This reflected General Lynch's view that the rifle squad was "the unit of morale":

> For in just the degree that squad physical cohesion becomes relaxed, the necessity for moral cohesion is imposed. It is many years since we could rely on the cohesion of closed ranks or rigid alignment to hold a unit together. Nor can we rely on severe disciplinary measures, sometimes self-imposed, that were once resorted to for maintaining the integrity of a unit. We must rely on other means. The men of a squad must be bound together by ties of comradeship and confidence engendered by long association, by memories of dangers and privations suffered in common, by a patriotic idealism.[13]

This view, which had a lot in common with the German belief in the importance of comradeship, fit in well with the highly cohesive units of the peacetime Regular Army. The way that the U.S. Army expanded itself into the substantially larger "Army of the United States," however, did much to undermine "long association," "memories of dangers and privations suffered in common," and, it might even be argued, "patriotic idealism." In particular, the practice of treating individual soldiers as "interchangeable spare parts" kept in "replacement depots" until "requisitioned" by units, created many situations in which men went into battle alongside strangers. The pernicious effect that this had on the ability of such units to function, let alone triumph, is difficult to overstate.[14]

In April of 1942, the U.S. infantry organization was modified in ways that gave it a superficial resemblance to the contemporary German organization. Infantry regiments were each provided with an antitank company (with twelve German-style 37-millimeter guns) and a cannon company (with self-propelled 75-millimeter and 105-millimeter howitzers). Battalion weapons companies traded some machine guns for additional 81-millimeter mortars and thus became, with eight heavy machine guns and six 81-millimeter mortars, close copies of the machine gun companies of contemporary German infantry battalions. Though German infantry companies had yet to adopt the idea of a separate heavy platoon, the arming of that platoon with three 60-millimeter mortars and two machine guns continued the pattern of superficial imitation.[15]

The 1942 reforms dissolved each platoon's automatic rifle squad and returned the BAR to the rifle squad. This gave the American rifle squad the basic shape that it would have until the end of the war. Though still formally indivisible, the beginnings of what later would be called the "fire team" could be seen in the designation of two of the riflemen as assistants to the man who fired the BAR. A fourth member of the squad was the rifle-grenadier and, as such, was provided with a grenade launcher attachment for his rifle. The squad was completed by the squad leader and assistant squad leader and six "ordinary" riflemen.[16]

As was the case with the German *Schützen* (or, as they were later known, *Panzergrenadiere*), the infantry of American armored divisions started out with roughly the same organization as the "walking" infantry but soon changed to meet the needs of its particular environment. From the beginning, these troops were equipped with armored half-tracked carriers and were thus quite properly known as "armored infantry." The March 1942 organization of the armored division nonetheless called for an armored infantry squad of twelve men commanded by a sergeant. Instead of an automatic rifle, this squad used a .30 caliber air-cooled machine gun as its squads automatic weapon. This could be mounted on the half-track as well as the standard tripod.[17]

The adoption of a German-inspired organization for the infantry battalion did not necessarily lead to the adoption of German-style tactics.

Rather, the new tables of organization, which, with slight modification, would serve for the rest of the war, formed only one of the many forces influencing the formation of American infantry. Some of these, like the widespread recognition that modern war was a new game and a consequent willingness to jettison anything that didn't fit in with the new situation, were largely beneficial. Others, unfortunately, had a largely negative effect. Chief among these was the ill-considered way in which the U.S. Armed Forces were expanded.

Starting on June 30, 1940, with a strength of 456,000 men, the U.S. Army, Navy, and Marine Corps had, by June 30, 1945, grown into a huge force of 11,857,000 men and women. This twenty-five fold growth had many beneficial effects. The skills that the volunteers and draftees brought with them from civilian life resulted in an unprecedented degree of progress in such fields as communications, logistics, aviation, troop entertainment, civil engineering, and the production of training films. The degree to which talented individuals were permitted to avoid service in the infantry, however, ensured that tens of thousands of American squads would go into combat without proper training or leadership.

This lack of new talent could only be partially compensated for by making use of veterans of the 100,000-man interwar army. Though the quality of soldiers in the peacetime infantry had been high, there had been no systematic attempt to train enlisted men for eventual service as officers or NCOs. Even those enlisted men who held reserve commissions received no special training. Once mobilization began, the opportunity for commissioned service in other branches, as well as the immediate promotion to NCO rank that often accompanied transfer to the Air Corps, took many more talented "old soldiers" out of the infantry.[18]

The situation with officers was little better. Those who were most capable soon found themselves rapidly promoted. Many of those remaining lacked either knowledge of modern warfare or the leadership to properly train small units. In 1941, for example, Army Chief of Staff General George C. Marshall reported that junior officers lacked experience, had little confidence in themselves, and hence failed to assume or discharge their responsibilities.[19] As late as November 1944, General Patton would rage, "Our chief trouble in this war is the lack of efficiency and lack of sense of responsibility on the part of company officers."[20]

The traditional American solution to lack of craftsmen—the use of mass production techniques—mitigated this problem to a certain degree. Well understood skills, like rifle marksmanship, could be taught by this "industrial" approach: instructors who did nothing but teach known-distance shooting put trainees through a standard course of instruction. Films, many of which exploited some of Hollywood's greatest talents, could replace much of what had previously been taught by means of lectures delivered by junior officers. Scores of manuals, many of which were far more detailed than anything previously published in the United States and many more of which were clearly intended for the use of small unit leaders and even individual soldiers, were published. Nonetheless, when it came to teaching tactics, or even many of the applied skills (such as the care of heavy weapons) needed to put tactics into practice, there was no substitute for an officer or NCO who knew what he was doing.

The job of training the new American infantry was made more difficult by the practice of assigning men with above average intelligence and education to the Air Corps, the technical branches, and the various programs that kept college men on campus. As a result, the infantry got a disproportionate share of men with below average intelligence and education (and, since mental ability tended to be associated with physical development, the infantry also received large numbers of men with substandard physiques). One commander went so far as to complain that he lacked men with the capacity to serve as instructors because "everybody higher than a moron" had been pulled out of his unit.[21]

General Leslie J. McNair, who, as commanding general of the Army Ground Forces, was responsible for the raising of U.S. infantry units for most of the Second World War, was painfully aware of these problems. His solution, transferring trained men out of the Regular Army and National Guard divisions raised and trained in 1940 and 1941, provided some relief. The cost, however, was high. Units that had strong regional associations lost them. Units which had trained for a year or more lost the habit of working as a team. There is some evidence, moreover, that this move was counterproductive. High quality men who had been part of cohesive units were deprived of the comradeship that many had found to be the chief reward of serving in the infantry. Once these social bonds were destroyed, these men found themselves drawn to forms of service that promised rapid promotion, more glamour, or a chance to learn civilian skills.[22]

The net result of the shortage of instructors, the lack of qualified NCOs and junior officers, and the relatively poor quality of the men assigned was a noticeable inability of the American infantry to practice the tactics associated with the 1942 tables of organization. One solution, advocated by the famous General Patton, was to abandon any hope of having units smaller than battalions (!) attempt to maneuver.

> Today, when the chief small-arms fire on the battlefield and the majority of the neutralizing fire is delivered by machine guns, mortars, and artillery, there is no advantage in advancing by rushes, because, until you get within three hundred yards, small-arms fire has very little effect, whereas when YOU lie down between rushes you expose yourself to the effect of shrapnel. When you get to three hundred yards, your own small-arms fire, which is superior to anything now existing . . . , will neutralize that of the enemy *small-arms fire*, so that you do not have to advance by rushes. I say this very feelingly because I have seen, on many occasions in maneuvers and in battle, troops advancing by rushes when they were defiladed behind hills and could have gone forward in limousines, had they been available, with perfect impunity. The proper way to advance, particularly for troops armed with that magnificent weapon, the M-1 rifle, is to utilize marching fire and keep moving. This fire can be delivered from the shoulder, but it can be just as effective if delivered with the butt of the rifle halfway between the belt and the armpit. One round should be fired every two or three paces. The whistle of the bullets, the scream of the ricochet, and the dust, twigs, and branches which are knocked from the ground and the trees have such an effect on the enemy that his small-arms fire becomes negligible.[23]

A less radical answer to the problem was the adoption of the British practice of battle drill. In the case of Colonel J. C. Fry's 350th Infantry, this involved dividing squads into two teams, one serving the BAR and the other composed of riflemen. This formal subdivision of the squad notwithstanding, Fry's method assumed that most attacks carried out by squads and platoons would be both frontal and stereotyped. Deliberate maneuver was left to higher echelons.[24]

As was the case with the British, the main solution to the overall inability of American infantry to field squads and platoons capable of maneuver was found outside of the infantry. Aerial bombardment, tanks, tank destroyers, and, most of all, masses of artillery served as a second-class substitute for the first-class infantry that was rarely available. This situation caused Patton to recall a comment made to him during the Great War by a French general lecturing to students at the A.E.F. staff college at Langres, "The poorer the infantry, the more artillery it needs; the American infantry needs all that it can get."[25]

As the Second World War dragged on, the German infantry began to suffer from many problems similar to those which plagued the American infantry. Talented men were diverted to the *Luftwaffe*, the technical services, and, increasingly, to the armored formations of the army and SS. Combat losses deprived the infantry of many NCOs and junior officers who, combining extensive peacetime training with recent combat experience, were best able to lead small units. As their places were taken by men who lacked either the talent or the training to maneuver with the same degree of skill, the German Army began to look for ways to make the best of a bad situation.

One approach was to improve the weapons carried by the infantry. Beginning in late 1943, the German infantry began to receive "machine pistol model 43/1," a weapon that we now recognize as the direct ancestor of all modern assault rifles. The most obvious virtue of this weapon was its ability to simplify small unit tactics. This can be seen in the following report from an infantry battalion fighting on the Eastern Front:

> The enemy, who at the beginning had defended himself stubbornly, was obliged to flee as the machine pistol platoon attacked with "hurrah," firing their machine pistols as they ran. The success came through the great moral effect achieved by bursts of fire from 25 machine pistols fired at the run.[26]

Another battalion of the same division had a similar experience:

> Upon the arrival of the other two squads the whole squads attacked the enemy frontally shouting "hurrah," with two squads to the left of the road and one squad to the right of the road. With the fire support of the assault guns and short bursts of fire from the machine pistols, this [attack] succeeded in pushing the enemy back to the most forward [German] trench. Because heavy machine gun, light machine gun, and rifle fire was directed towards the platoon, it was forced to hit the deck. After a short burst of surprise fire (*Feuerüberfall*) from the assault guns and the whole platoon (one magazine per man), the most forward trench was taken by assault.[27]

With this kind of firepower available to each individual soldier, the German Army began to rethink the way that it distributed infantry heavy weapons. In particular, the arrival of the assault rifle permitted the Germans to reorganize their infantry units in a way that reduced the number of different weapons assigned to each squad, platoon, and company and thus reduced the complexity of commanding such units.

One unit responded to the provision of assault rifles by organizing rifle companies as "direct fire companies," with three platoons equipped solely with assault rifles and a fourth platoon of four tripod-mounted machine guns. The former machine gun company was converted into a mortar company, with four 120-millimeter and eight 81-millimeter mortars. How this organization worked in practice can be seen from one of this battalion's after-action reports.

The troops returned to their old position without any special training in their new weapons. The twelve former light machine gun positions were occupied by the four [tripod-mounted] machine guns and machine pistol men. These [positions] did not have to be modified as the fields of fire of the new weapons [at close ranges] were close to those of the light machine guns.[28]

When new tables of organization for the German infantry were issued in 1944, the design of squads, platoons, and companies was altered to make the most of the new assault rifle, as well as to take into account the fact that squad, platoon, and even company commanders were less capable than they once had been. The *Einheitsgruppe* was replaced by two basic types of squad—an "assault squad" (*Sturmgruppe*) and a light machine gun squad. The assault squad was uniformly armed with assault rifles. The light machine gun squad had two MG 42 light machine guns. Two assault squads and one light machine gun squad, plus three rifle-grenadiers, made an "assault platoon" (*Sturmzug*).

There is no evidence that the eight-man assault squads had permanent subdivisions. There was, for example, no provision for the post of "assistant squad leader." That, and the retention of the two light machine guns as "platoon" weapons, seems to indicate that the German authorities of 1944 had lost faith in the ability of their infantry squads to maneuver independently. The division of labor between long range fire (light machine guns) and short range fire (assault rifles) further indicates a degree of specialization (and thus reduction in flexibility) that was absent in the old *Einheitsgruppe*.

Two assault platoons, plus an "old fashioned" platoon of three *Einheitsgruppen* and a small squad of five snipers, made a "grenadier" company. (Hitler had, in 1943, conferred that title on all infantry units that lacked a pre-existing honorific.) The retention of the old-style platoon seems to have been a stop-gap measure intended to buy time until the production of assault rifles was sufficient to equip the entire infantry. The addition of the snipers, on the other hand, was an affirmation of the fact that not all of the hastily-trained German infantrymen of the last year of the war had either the skill or the *sang-froid* needed for long distance killing. The small size of the grenadier company (three officers and 109 men) as well as the absence of heavy weapons, reflect a desire to provide the young lieutenant commanding the company with a unit that was easy to handle.[29]

Three grenadier companies and a heavy company made a grenadier battalion. The heavy company, which had evolved from the long mistitled machine gun company, consisted of four platoons. Two were armed with four heavy machine guns each, one with six 81-millimeter mortars, and one with four 75-millimeter infantry guns. Two battalions, plus an additional infantry gun (150-millimeter infantry guns and 120-millimeter mortars) company and a "tank destroyer" company made a grenadier regiment.[30] Antitank guns were conspicuous by their absence, having been replaced in the tank destroyer company by the *Panzerschreck* rocket launcher and at lower echelons by the *Panzerfaust* rocket-propelled grenade.[31]

Dependent on horse-drawn wagons for almost all of its transport and filled with tired, often desperate, men in ill-fitting rayon uniforms, the German grenadier regiments of 1944 and 1945 were sorry-looking shadows of the young, confident infantry regiments that had made the *Blitzkrieg* possible. In many respects, however, the "peoples' grenadiers" were the model for the bulk of the world's infantry for the rest of the twentieth century. Their chief weapons—the automatic assault rifle and the hand-held grenade launcher—were easy to manufacture and easy to use. Their tactics resembled those of guerillas. And, despite the weight of bombs, shells, tanks, and aircraft thrown against them, these late-war warriors, like their successors in nearly every corner of the world, proved difficult to beat.

The third model for the infantry squad to come out of World War II was the invention of the other ground force fielded by America in that conflict, the United States Marine Corps. Like the U.S. Army, the Marine Corps had entered World War II with a rifle platoon that contained three rifle squads and a BAR squad.[32] Unlike most soldiers, who tended to view automatic rifles as either defensive weapons or little more than a means of bolstering rifle fire, many Marines had a more sophisticated view of their BARs. In particular, jungle fighting in Nicaragua in the 1920s and 1930s had convinced many Marines that the BAR was an important tool for close combat. As a result of this inclination, as well as subsequent experience in the Pacific, each reorganization of the Marine infantry brought additional BARs into the rifle platoon and, in particular, the rifle squad.

In 1942, when the Army restored the BAR to the rifle squad, the Marine Corps added two automatic rifles to each of its rifle squads. This enabled each twelve-man squad to be broken up into two six-man teams, each of which contained an automatic rifleman, his assistant, and four riflemen. During the same period, the Second Raider battalion began to experiment with a nine-man squad divided into three three-man "fire groups." Each squad was equipped with one BAR, five Thompson submachine guns, and three M-1 rifles. This allowed each "fire group" to be armed with one rifle and two automatic weapons. Lieutenant Colonel Evans Carlson, commanding officer of the Second Raider Battalion, argued that this sort of squad could cover a front of from 100 to 300 yards. (A squad armed with bolt-action Springfield rifles and one BAR was supposed to be able to cover a frontage of 50 yards.)[33]

The idea of a triangular squad was not entirely new. As early as 1915, the German Army had experimented with what they called *Musketen* squads. Each twelve-man squad was divided into three four-man teams, each of which served a Madsen automatic rifle. (German soldiers of this period often used the term *Muskete*—meaning "musket"—to designate hand-held automatic weapons.) In the 1930s, Communist guerillas operating in North China used the fire group method imitated by Carlson's Second Raider Battalion. (Indeed, it was while serving as an exchange officer with these guerillas that Colonel Carlson picked up the idea.)

In March 1943, the First Raider Battalion adopted its own version of the triangular squad. As had been the case with the German *Musketen* squads, the chief automatic weapon was the automatic rifle. Each of the three three-man fire teams was thus provided with one BAR, one M-1 rifle, and one M-1 carbine. Another difference was the provision of a squad leader who was freed from membership in any one fire team so that he could more effectively combine the actions of all three teams. The value of such organization was proved in actual combat in New Guinea and elsewhere.[34]

In July 1943, the Marine Corps conducted further experiments at its base at Camp Pendleton, California. Models tested included the twelve-man squads broken down into two, three, and even four fire groups. In March of 1944, the results of this experiment were implemented in an order that called for a squad of thirteen men organized into three four-man fire teams, each of which was to be armed with a single BAR and three M-1 rifles. To emphasize the importance of the fire team, its leader was made a corporal. The squad leader was consequently "promoted" to sergeant. The net result was a squad that had as many automatic rifles and as many NCOs as most European platoons had at the beginning of World War II.[35]

NOTES

1. "The U.S. Army in 1914," *Tactical Notebook*, February 1993.

2. U.S. Army, Tables of Organization, Series A, January 14, 1918, Table 7, Rifle Company, Infantry Regiment, reprinted in U.S. Army, Center of Military History, *United States Army in the World War, 1917–1919, Organization of the American Expeditionary Forces, Volume I* (Washington, D.C.: U.S. Government Printing Office, 1988), p. 347.

3. For the context in which these platoons fought, see "U.S. Infantry," *Tactical Notebook*, May and June 1993.

4. George A. Lynch, "The Tactics of the New Infantry Regiment," *The Infantry Journal*, March-April 1939, p. 112.

5. Virgil Ney, *Organization and Equipment of the Infantry Rifle Squad from Valley Forge to ROAD* (Fort Belvoir: U.S. Army Combat Operations Research Group, 1965), pp. vii, 13–18, 27–38, and 75.

6. Ney, *Infantry Rifle Squad*, pp. 37–42 and 47–48.

7. Walter R. Wheeler, *The Infantry Battalion in War* (Washington, D.C.: The Infantry Journal, 1936), p. 5.

8. "The French Connection," *Tactical Notebook*, February 1993.

9. George A. Lynch, "The Tactics of the New Infantry Regiment," address to the Command and General Staff School, March 14, 1939, quoted in Ronald Spector, "The Military Effectiveness of the U.S. Armed Forces, 1919–1939," in Alan R. Millett and Williamson Murray, eds, *Military Effectiveness, Volume II, The Interwar Period* (Boston: Allen & Unwin, 1988). This speech should not be confused with the article of the same name referenced in other notes to this chapter.

10. Lynch, "The Tactics of the New Infantry Regiment," p. 112. (This is the *Infantry Journal* article, not the speech.)

11. Richard Tindall, et al., *Infantry in Battle* (Washington, D.C.: The Infantry Journal, 1934.) This book has been widely reprinted, most recently by the United States Marine Corps (as Fleet Marine Force Reference Pamphlet 12-2).

12. For an interesting account of rank and file reception of the 1939/1940 reforms, see Victor Vogel, *Soldiers of the Old Army* (College Station, TX: Texas A&M University Press, 1990), pp. 105–6.

13. Lynch, "The Tactics of the New Infantry Regiment," p. 103.

14. The dry details of U.S. Army replacement policy are presented in Robert R. Palmer et al., *The Procurement and Training of Ground Combat Troops* (Washington: U.S. Government Printing Office, 1948). The psychological cost of such a policy is documented in Samuel Stouffer, et al., *The American Soldier, Combat and Its Aftermath* (Princeton, NJ: Princeton University Press, 1949). A comparison between the German and American systems of combat replacement is made in Martin Van Creveld, *Fighting Power, German and U.S. Army Performance, 1939–1945* (Westport, CT: Greenwood, 1982).

15. It is important to note that the German company machine guns were mounted on tripods and provided with spare barrels, long-range sights, and extra ammunition. The American company machine guns were bipod mounted weapons whose air-cooled barrels were not designed to be changed in combat.

16. United States of America, War Department, Table of Organization 7–17, Infantry Rifle Company, April 1, 1942.

17. Virgil Ney, *The Evolution of the Armored Infantry Rifle Squad* (Fort Belvoir, VA: U.S. Army Combat Operations Research Group Memorandum 198, March 1965), pp. 31–39.

18. Palmer, et al., *The Procurement and Training of Ground Combat Troops*, pp. 16–17. For instances where this happened in individual units, see Vogel, *Soldiers of the Old Army*, p. 107, and Alwyn Featherston, *Saving the Breakout, The 30th Division's Heroic Stand at Mortain, August 7–12, 1944* (Novato, CA: Presidio, 1993), pp. 8–9.

19. Kent Robert Greenfield, et al., *The Organization of Ground Combat Troops* (Washington, D.C.: Government Printing Office, 1947), p. 48.

20. Martin Blumenson, *The Patton Papers* (Boston: Houghton Mifflin, 1974), Vol. 2, p. 572.

21. Palmer, et al., *The Procurement and Training of Ground Combat Troops*, pp. 16–19.

22. Featherston, *Saving the Breakout*, pp. 8–9.

23. George S. Patton, Jr., *War As I Knew It* (New York: Pyramid, 1970), p. 293.

24. J. C. Fry, *Assault Battle Drill* (Harrisburg, PA: The Military Service Publishing Company, 1955), pp. vii–xii, 54, and 64–76.

25. Blumenson, *The Patton Papers*, Vol. 2, p. 521.

26. Report of the commanding general of the 35th Infantry Division, U.S. National Archives, Captured German Records, Series T-78, Roll 769.

27. It's worth noting that the term "frontally" was underlined by the staff officer who reviewed the original document. The product of a system with a well developed fetish for flank attacks at all levels, he was no doubt surprised that such an attack would succeed. Report of the commanding general of the 35th Infantry Division, U.S. National Archives, Captured German Records, Series T-78, Roll 769.

28. Report of the 1st Battalion, 43rd Grenadier Regiment, U.S. National Archives, Captured German Records, Series T-78, Roll 769. Additional after action reports dealing with early assault rifle experiments have been translated and printed in the October 1991, issue of *Tactical Notebook.*

29. Inf. B. Chef. Gen. St.d.H. Nr. 3160/44g vom 5.9.44, U.S. National Archives, Captured German Documents, Series T-78, Roll 763. For a complete description see "The German Grenadier Company, 1944," *Tactical Notebook*, October 1991.

30. It is interesting to note that, while there were only ten numbered companies in the German grenadier regiment, the infantry gun and tank destroyer companies retained their traditional numbers of 13 and 14. Whether this reflected a plan to eventually restore the third battalion to each regiment, was an attempt to confuse Allied order of battle analysts, or simply recorded the terms used by soldiers, is unknown.

31. Inf. B. Chef. Gen. St.d.H. Nr. 3160/44g vom 5.9.44, U.S. National Archives, Captured German Documents, Series T-78, Roll 763. For a complete description see "Volksgrenadier: The 13th (Infantry Gun) Company, 1944," *Tactical Notebook*, April 1992, and "Volksgrenadier: The 14th (Tank Destroyer) Company, 1944," *Tactical Notebook*, May 1992.

32. It is interesting to note that, while the explicit justification for taking the BAR out of the rifle squad had been the introduction of the semiautomatic M-1 rifle, the Marine Corps didn't receive significant numbers of such rifles until the middle of 1942.

33. Benis M. Frank and Henry I. Shaw, Jr., *Victory and Occupation: History of the U.S. Marine Corps Operations in World War II* (Washington, D.C.: U.S. Government Printing Office, 1968), pp. 696–700, 720, and 849–50.

34. Frank, *Victory and Occupation*, pp. 696–711.

35. Frank, *Victory and Occupation*, pp. 696–711. It is interesting to note that the order that implemented the triangular squad throughout the Marine Corps made provision for the occasional replacement of BARs with portable flamethrowers.

8.

East of Suez, West of Pearl

In many respects, the Great Pacific War of 1941–1945 was a thoroughly modern conflict dominated by new weapons—aircraft carriers, long range bombers, and, at the very end, atomic bombs. In other respects, the war between Japan and the alliance of China, the United States, Great Britain, Australia, New Zealand, Canada, and the Netherlands had a quality that might best be described as primitive. This was particularly true of the jungle fighting that took place in Burma, New Guinea, and the Philippines, as well as the fierce struggles for the often tiny islands whose seizure played such a big role in the naval struggle.

Despite the big role played by jungle fighting in the Great Pacific War, the Japanese Army was primarily oriented towards the northeast (rather than the southeast) end of the Asian land mass. This can be seen in the disposition of Japanese land forces near the end of the war: 2,115,000 men guarded Japan, to include Sakhalin and the Kurile islands; 1,310,000 were in Manchuria, North China, and Korea; 953,000 were in South and East China, Malaya, Burma, and Indo-China; and 772,000 occupied Formosa, the Philippines, the Mandated Islands, and Indonesia.[1] The Japanese Empire, after all, was not merely fighting a naval war against the Anglo-Saxon world, but was simultaneously trying to conquer China and defend itself against the Soviet Union.

Japanese expansion in China had begun in the late nineteenth century. From then, until the surrender in 1945, some portion of the Japanese Army was engaged in fighting in, or, at the very least, hostile occupation of, some part of China. Even the one "big war" fought by the Japanese Army before

1941—the Russo-Japanese War of 1904–1905, was a war fought largely on Chinese territory over the issue of who would control Manchuria. It is thus not surprising that the Japanese Army of 1941–1945 was largely formed by the experience of fighting in China. What is less obvious is the degree to which the habits gained in China proved useful in other theaters.

The long conflict between the Japanese and the Chinese was largely a guerilla war. The Chinese were lightly armed but elusive. To deal with such enemies, the Japanese infantry placed a great deal of emphasis on mobility, field craft, and small unit tactics. The weapons of choice were rifles, light machine guns, and small caliber mortars. In a country that lacked proper roads, the truck was often less useful than the bicycle. Masses of artillery and tanks were likewise of little use against enemies who rarely waited long enough for these weapons to be deployed. The few tanks that were used were thus light ones. Artillery pieces—many of which were mountain guns and weapons reminiscent of German infantry guns—were employed singly or in pairs.[2]

The suitability of these habits for jungle warfare can be seen in the campaign that culminated in the fall of Singapore. Japanese divisions that had previously been stationed in Manchuria adapted readily to conditions in Malaya. Many of the little tricks for staying alive in the jungle were presented to the individual Japanese soldier in a widely distributed booklet entitled *Read This Alone—And the War Can Be Won.* The rapidity of the Japanese march down the Malayan peninsula, and their frequently demonstrated ability to run circles around the road-bound defenders of Singapore, indicates that the bulk of the habits, skills, and attitudes necessary to such fighting were already in place.[3]

After long periods of training that emphasized the ability to march twenty-five miles a day for days on end, the Japanese soldier in North China "fought and froze and made . . . terrific marches on a ration which . . . consisted of a half-pound of rice and some blackish potatoes."[4] Expected to carry five days' worth of rations and cook for himself, the Japanese soldier rarely had to wait for his food to be brought up. The lack of rolling kitchens also freed the Japanese soldier from the need to operate near a suitable road. Thus, something as simple as messing arrangements contributed to the remarkable operational mobility that permitted General Yamashita's army to walk down the Malay Peninsula in less than two months and the tactical mobility that permitted Japanese units to repeatedly outflank their English-speaking opponents.[5]

Once in contact with his enemy, the individual Japanese infantryman tended to make extensive use of infiltration and camouflage. Many even carried pieces of matting of the same color as the terrain background;

running behind these in a crouching run, they were practically invisible through the sights of a weapon. Thoroughly professional at digging, the Japanese were taught to construct individual foxholes in the shape of an inverted boot, with the "toe" facing the enemy and containing the fire step, the deep "heel" in the rear, providing security from enemy artillery and mortar bombardment. The roof of the boot, if not underground itself, was usually heavily protected by logs and earth.[6]

In the area of individual weapon handling, the Japanese soldier was renowned for his excellence in the bold and efficient employment of the mortar, which appeared to be his favorite weapon. He also used machine guns with imagination and effect, sometimes even positioning them in trees to gain longer fields of fire. In other instances, they were dug in on open ground but protected by rifle fire, in which case assaults on them became virtual death traps for attacking infantry. Surprisingly, however, the Japanese infantryman was discovered to be a "notoriously poor marksman."[7] Even Japanese snipers, expert at camouflage, were only trained up to ranges of 300 yards.[8]

The standard Japanese infantry platoon consisted of forty-two men organized in four squads of ten men each. The first three squads were built around a single light machine gun (usually the 6.5-millimeter Nambu). The fourth squad was armed with included three 50-millimeter grenade launchers, weapons that Allied troops often referred to as "knee mortars." Though each knee mortar was served by a three-man team, the fourth squad was intended to be used as a single "battery." The light machine gun squads were likewise designed as indivisible units. The lieutenant platoon commander was assisted by the uniquely Japanese institution of the *Renrakukashi*, an NCO responsible for maintaining communications by visual means or through runners between sections.[9]

A Japanese rifle company comprised three rifle platoons. Three such companies plus a German-style machine-gun company (with tripod-mounted machine guns and 81-millimeter mortars) made up an infantry battalion, commanded by a major. The regiment, of three battalions, a 75-millimeter infantry gun company and a 47-millimeter antitank gun company, was also on the German model. Divisions were of two types, one "square" (four infantry regiments) and the other "triangular" (three infantry regiments). With practically no Chinese tanks to worry about, Japanese antitank guns were, from the beginning, used primarily as direct-fire field pieces.[10]

The text-book attacks of a Japanese rifle platoon were superficially similar to those of other armies. The two forward light machine gun squads attempted to fix the enemy while the third light machine gun squad attacked from either the left or right flank. The three knee mortars remained under the direct control of the platoon commander and provided him with what contemporary Germans would have called a *Schwerpunktwaffe*. The standard company attack, on the other hand, was a double envelopment, with one platoon attacking each flank and the third platoon fixing the enemy to the front.[11] The danger of the two enveloping platoons shooting each other was reduced through the use of wooden bullets. Once they had flown a hundred meters or so, these bullets would burn up. At closer ranges, however, they were as deadly "as the finest American lead."[12]

As illustrated by their victory against superior numbers in the Singapore campaign, the Japanese infantry were particularly effective when fighting against the British. The first army to completely abandon the horse, the British Army was particularly dependent upon mortar transport and, consequently, upon the kind of roads that were readily available in Western Europe but extremely rare in Burma and Malaya. This made British action predictable, British defenses easy to outflank, and British retreat easy to cut off. These disadvantages were exacerbated by a British tendency to orient both their attention and firepower towards the front—the one direction least likely to be attacked by the Japanese.[13]

The Japanese fondness for night fighting, a tendency already visible in the Russo-Japanese War, was particularly effective against British troops uncomfortable with darkness. British attempts to conduct envelopments of their own were often defeated because their slow pace allowed the Japanese to "encircle the enemy's encircling force" or, at the very least, launch a spoiling attack.[14] The greatest Japanese advantage over the British, however, was their ability to use the jungle as an avenue of approach.

> Tactically we [the British] had been completely outclassed. The Japanese could—and did—do many things that we could not. The chief of these and the tactical method on which all their successes were based was the "hook." Their standard action was, while holding us in front, to send a mobile force mainly infantry, on a wide turning movement round our flank through the jungle to come in on our line of communications. Here, on a single road, up which all our supplies, ammunition, and reinforcements must come, they would establish a "roadblock," sometimes with a battalion, sometimes with a regiment. We had few if any reserves in depth—all our troops were in the front line—and we had, therefore, when this happened, to turn about forces from the forward positions to clear the roadblock. At this point the enemy increased his pressure on our weakened front until it crumbled. Time and again the Japanese used these tactics, more often than not successfully, until our troops and commanders began to acquire a roadblock mentality which often developed into an inferiority complex.[15]

In Malaya and Java, Japanese formations often made sweeps as wide as three miles and as deep as four to six miles. These were normally effected at a slow but steady pace. Advance guards, in the meantime, pressed forward in small groups, usually of platoon and no greater than company strength, attempting to insert themselves between enemy positions in order to get behind any organized defenses. Each group was normally given a definite mission, such as seizing a particular point or attacking a located headquarters or flank. When counterattacked, these groups held their fire until the enemy had passed. On numerous occasions, Japanese companies hid in swamps and rivers, sometimes with water up to their necks, until the enemy had passed through them and could thus be fired on from the rear.[16]

Although the Japanese army was steeped in the offensive, it rapidly gained a reputation for being equally formidable in the defense. Strong believers in active defense, the Japanese were often known to crawl close to enemy lines when bombarded by hostile artillery and mortars, not just to enhance their own security—as such action did—but to bring light mortar fire to bear on the enemy lines as well.[17] The machine gun remained the principal weapon of Japanese defensive operations, and heavy models were often sited well forward to cover main lines of approach. Reverse-slope positions were commonly used, and extensive digging always proved the rule. As the war progressed, the Japanese turned more and more to defensive systems in depth. All positions and trenches throughout the war were made as mutually supporting as possible.[18]

It was something of a wonder to British officers (at Kohima, in Burma) to learn how few men there were in some positions. The secret was that the Japanese did not fight to their front if they could fight to a flank. This meant that they had to rely on neighboring bunkers for protection, that is "to cover them," while they covered their neighbors. This system involved a good deal of training and discipline and a consistently high standard in the siting of posts, but it did make the maximum use of firepower. British and Indian troops were psychologically incapable of such tactics, each man preferring to fight to his front and remaining responsible for his own protection. Also, of course, though recognizing the need for head cover, the British hated being entombed in bunkers and liked the free use of their weapons, denied by Japanese-type bunkers. But these bunkers did allow the Japanese to bring down mortar fire on their own positions, when under attack, and time and again drove the British and Indians from them before they could dig in. And in Burma the Japanese mortarmen were the counterparts of the German machine-gunners in the First World War.[19]

In Burma, the antidote to Japanese tactical superiority was the complete remolding of the British and Indian troops that fought there. The author of this reform, Field Marshall Sir William Slim, believed that the strength of the Japanese Army lay not in its higher leadership but in the spirit of the individual Japanese soldier, who "fought and marched till he died." Under Slim's guiding hand, the British infantrymen learned "to move on his own feet and to look after himself." Mastering the absolutely vital art of patrolling and realizing that mobility and survival were synonymous, the British soldier quickly gained confidence. As a result, the myth of the "natural" superiority of the Japanese soldier was gradually dispelled.

Slim built further on this by launching a series of minor offensive operations in which only attainable objective were assigned to troops participating. Like the Germans on the Eastern Front, who used small-scale, relatively easy attacks as a means of gradually converting rear echelon units into frontline infantry, Slim avoided confidence-sapping defeat by the practice of "sending a man to do a boy's job." He thus often sent brigades to attack companies and battalions against platoons. This "on the job training" was reinforced with a series of courses, exercises, and unit training programs that emphasized firm discipline, physical toughness, leadership by example, and individual weapons skills.

Reduced scales of transport and equipment were accordingly introduced, to the point where an Indian division required but 120 tons of daily supplies in lieu of the 400 per day considered normal for sustaining a standard division in the field.[20] Slim noted with some relish that "as we removed vehicles from units and formations which joined us on European establishments, they found to their surprise that they could move farther and faster without them."[21] In actual operations, greater tactical freedom was given to subordinate commanders. Companies, even platoons, under junior leaders became the basic units of the jungle. Out of sight of one another, often out of touch, their wireless blanketed by hills, they marched and fought on their own. Instead of retreating when outflanked, troops now tended to withdraw into "keeps" or strongholds, dubbed "beehives" by the Japanese; maintained by airborne supply, these functioned somewhat like an anvil on which Japanese intrusions were hammered by mobile reserves. The Japanese army never fully recovered from its defeat in the Imphal-Kohima battle, which, significantly, was inflicted by a regular land force.[22]

Slim was personally very much opposed to the formation of special forces which he considered "wasteful." For a commander who was often critically short of his most important commodity, infantrymen, this observation is not particularly surprising:

The result of these . . . special units was undoubtedly to lower the quality of the rest of the Army, especially of the infantry, not only by skimming the cream off it, but by encouraging the idea that certain of the normal operations of war were so difficult that only specially equipped *corps d'elite* could be expected to undertake them. Armies do not win wars by means of a few bodies of super-soldiers but by the average quality of their standard units. . . . The level of initiative, individual training, and weapon skill required in, say a commando, is admirable; what is not admirable is that it should be confined to a few small units. Any well-trained infantry battalion should be able to do what a commando can do; in the Fourteenth Army they could and did.[23]

Field Marshall Slim's campaign was the only conflict between Japan and the Western Allies that consisted entirely of action on land. The other two major campaigns, General Douglas MacArthur's Southwest Pacific campaign and Admiral Chester Nimitz's Central Pacific campaign, had a pronounced naval character. The way in which the naval character of these campaigns was exploited, however, was very different. In MacArthur's case, the sea was used as a means of operational and tactical mobility, a perenially open flank that offered opportunities to strike the Japanese where they were weakest. In the case of the Central Pacific campaign, the sea was used primarily as a strategic highway that, as often as not, carried landing forces of Marines and soldiers straight into the teeth of the Japanese defenses.[24]

The high cost of the lack of operational maneuver in the Central Pacific was often exacerbated by an unfortunate fondness for frontal attacks. The legendary Marine commander, Lewis B. Puller, went so far as to advise that there was "mighty little room for fancy tactics below division level." In his view, the attack was simply a matter of:

The enemy are on the hill. You go get 'em. In the end you'll save more. There are times when you'll have to flank, but don't forget that the shortest distance between two points is a straight line.[25]

The fruits of this philosophy can be seen in the record of the attack on Peleliu Island in September of 1944, where the three battalions of Colonel Puller's First Marine Regiment lost 56 percent of their strength.[26]

Despite the advantage of the recently introduced fire team organization, a rich provision of machine guns to rifle companies, and a specialized assault platoon in every battalion, Marine infantry tactics were nearly as linear as those used by the British on the Somme nearly thirty years before. The amphibious vehicles landed in regular, predictable waves; squads, platoons, companies, and even battalions formed lines before moving forward; and, instead of being used to exploit success, reserves were used to reinforce portions of the line that had suffered the heaviest casualties. The constant companion of such linearity, the promise that heavy preparatory bombardment would "soften up" the defenders was also present. To an even greater degree than is usual, however, this promise proved false. Though 500 buildings were destroyed, very few, if any, of the Japanese machine guns, mortars, antitank guns, or field pieces were destroyed by the extensive naval gunfire and bomber attacks that had preceded the landing of the Marines.[27]

The Armed Forces of the United States learned the wrong lessons from the Pacific War. Though it rarely admitted it publicly, the Army decided that the atomic bomb had made conventional warfare obsolete and that, as a result, land forces would be used primarily in the constabulary role. (The fact that occupation of the territory of former enemies was the prime activity of the post-war Army helped reinforce this belief.) The Marine Corps, on the other hand, held fast to its belief in the continuing value of infantry capable of close and sustained combat. Unfortunately, this sound insight was coupled with a perverse desire to continue to waste such infantry in frontal attacks against well defended positions.

The Korean War proved the Army wrong and the Marine Corps half right. The unwillingness of the government of the United States to use atomic bombs against a Soviet Union that had recently acquired nuclear weapons of its own made infantry, once again, an arm of great strategic value. For three years, the fate of the Korean peninsula, and with it, the question of whether the West could defend itself without immediate resort to weapons of mass destruction, depended largely on the skill of men in rifle squads and platoons. At the same time, the Marines achieved much in an amphibious operation that was not only conducted according to principles far different from those used in the Central Pacific but was also commanded by a man who had often been critical of the way that the Central Pacific campaign had been carried out.[28]

General MacArthur's landing at Inchon sealed the fate of the North Korean Army and would have led to a quick victory for the American-led United Nations (UN) forces were it not for the intervention, in the fall of 1950, of Communist China. This intervention took the form of a 300,000-man expeditionary force composed almost entirely of light infantry. Marching by night and resting by day, this force had been able to avoid detection by UN aerial observers and, as a result, gain both strategic and tactical surprise. Indeed, the first sign of the Chinese invasion of Korea was a series of attacks against road-bound columns of UN troops.[29]

The infantry arm was (and, for that matter, still is) the pride of the Chinese Communist People's Liberation Army (PLA), an organization that had been fighting steadily since 1927. By the time of the Korean conflict, the PLA had considerable experience in both guerilla and mobile warfare. Its soldiers, though not all ideologically pure, were generally confident and convinced of the righteousness of their cause. Their doctrine emphasized mobility, deception, distraction, surprise, the concentration of superior force at a vital point, a "short attack," and speedy disengagement. A concomitant emphasis on thorough reconnaissance accounted for the almost uncanny Chinese ability not only to strike along boundaries between enemy units but to flow along neglected avenues of approach deep into the rear of enemy positions.[30]

UN artillery units seem to have been the favorite targets of Chinese Communist infantry attacks. As had been the case with the British of the Great War, artillery was the glue that kept isolated platoon and company defensive positions from becoming "unstuck" and, more often than not, was the single critical element in a UN defensive scheme. At the same time, artillery batteries were particularly vulnerable to infantry attacks. With command attention focused on supporting front line infantry units, local defense was often neglected. UN artillery units were thus in the unfortunate position of being both critical and vulnerable.[31]

The Chinese soldiers who crossed the Yalu were armed with every conceivable type of weapon: American M-1 rifles and carbines, old Japanese rifles, and new Soviet submachine ("burp") guns. Individuals carried eighty rounds of rifle ammunition and four or five "potato masher" grenades. In addition to his basic combat load, the PLA soldier carried a few extra clips for automatic rifles and "burp" guns, loaded belts for heavy machine guns, and one or two mortar shells or TNT for satchel charges. (The Chinese had no antitank weapons, so each platoon carried enough TNT to make eight to ten five-pound satchel charges.) The Chinese soldier was reasonably attired for operations in temperate winter conditions inasmuch as he was issued a heavily quilted cotton uniform for wear over his summer dress. Usually mustard brown in color—although some varieties were dark blue—this uniform was white on the inside and often reversed for fighting in the snow. Additional camouflage often took the form of squares of white cloth and straw mats. These allowed individual soldiers (and, thus, units composed of such soldiers) to blend into the terrain and make themselves invisible to aircraft.[32]

The Chinese soldier wore no helmet, only a heavy cotton cap with big ear flaps. His shoes were usually rubber or canvas sneakers fitted over layers of cotton socks, although many of the first men across the Yalu had been issued fur boots. For sustenance, every man carried emergency rice, tea, and salt for five days: an "iron ration," to be supplemented by requisitioning from the natives the Korean staple of millet seed, rice, and dried peas ground into a powder. Whenever possible, the soldier cooked these rations; otherwise, he ate them cold. Combined with tactics that were sparing of ammunition, this practice made it possible for PLA units to do without the administrative tail so prevalent in Western armies.[33]

There are indications that the Chinese army expected a quick and relatively easy victory in Korea. Steeped in the "man-over-weapons" military philosophy of Mao Tse-tung, Chinese leaders launched their major offensives with confidence that the superior doctrine, tactics, and morale of their best armies could defeat the better-equipped foe.[34] While recognizing U.S. superiority in naval, air, and artillery firepower and overall coordination of arms, the Chinese appreciated that the Achilles' heel of the system might lie in the opposing infantry. One Chinese estimate of the American foot soldier was not that favorable:

> Their infantrymen are weak, afraid to die, and haven't the courage to attack or defend. They depend on their planes, tanks, and artillery. At the same time, they are afraid of our fire power. They will cringe when if on the advance, they hear firing. They are afraid to advance further. . . . They specialize in day fighting. They are not familiar with night fighting or hand to hand combat. . . . If defeated, they have no orderly formation. Without the use of their mortars, they become completely lost . . . they become dazed and completely demoralized. . . . They are afraid when the rear is cut off. When transportation comes to a standstill, the infantry loses the will to fight.[35]

After analyzing the strengths and weaknesses of the UN forces, the Chinese refined the essential tactical principles of Mao Tse-tung to accommodate the reality of the Korean situation. The avoidance of highways and flat terrain became central to their operations, which always had as their object the interposition of force on an enemy's line of retreat.[36] Like Chuikov's Russians at Stalingrad, the Chinese chose to adopt "hugging" tactics of getting in as close as possible to the enemy. Night attacks became so much the rule for them that any exception came as a surprise. By this approach, the Chinese army nullified to a substantial degree UN advantages in artillery, heavy infantry weapons, and ground attack aircraft. Chinese avoidance of roads, use of individual camouflage, and lack of vehicles made Chinese movements nearly impossible for UN aircraft to interdict.[37]

In general, the inhospitable terrain of Korea further served to minimize the disparity between forces. Whereas UN troops found the countryside a handicap to their operations, the Chinese turned the rugged hills and desolate valleys to good advantage. The Chinese infantryman was an excellent camoufleur, and many UN troops were often taken under fire at almost pointblank range by skillfully concealed machine guns and automatic weapons. Equally serious, the broken mountainous landscape, particularly on the east coast, severely restricted UN tactical wireless communications while guerrilla remnants of the North Korean army and Communist Chinese infiltrators cut rear-area wire lines almost as fast as linesmen could lay them. An inability to communicate in moments of crisis spelled disaster for many an isolated UN platoon or company. The Chinese were far less dependent on technical means of communication. Radios were limited to echelons above the infantry regiment. Telephones rarely reached below the battalion level. Communications within battalions and companies depended on runners or such signaling devices as bugles, whistles, flares, and flashlights. These latter means had the additional advantage of unnerving the UN troops.[38]

PLA divisions had a triangular structure, with three infantry regiments, a pack-artillery battalion, and a number of specialist companies. An infantry regiment, with a strength of roughly 3,000 men, comprised three battalions, each of three companies of three platoons. Platoons were further divided into three rather large (twelve- to sixteen-man) squads which, in turn, were divided into three small (three- to five-man) teams. This structure served a political as well as military purpose, as most leaders at or above the squad level and even some team leaders were Communist Party members and had, in addition to their military duties, the task of ensuring that their subordinates were "politically correct."

General James Van Fleet, one of the few observers struck by this organization, noted that though most soldiers in the PLA were not Communist at all, their fire team organization played a big role in making them fight well for the Communist cause. Like the fire team organization of the Marines (which, after all, had been copied from it) and the independently derived German emphasis on comradeship, the Chinese system solved the problem of the "emptiness of the battlefield," a problem that had plagued armies since the beginning of the "open order revolution."[39] In solving the problem of combat motivation, the Chinese "three by three" system of triangular squads also made small units very maneuverable.

Like the German *Stosstrupp* tactics of the Great War, the flexible assault tactics of the Chinese infantry in Korea sometimes caused defenders to "see" far more attackers than were actually present. This perception was enhanced by the Chinese night attacks in which individual infantrymen slowly crawled forward until they were within hand grenade range of UN foxholes. At the appointed hour, bugles would blare, whistles would blow, and the Chinese would, quite literally, rise out of the earth to deliver a short but vicious attack. This practice created the Korean War counterpart to ubiquitous British reports of Germans "coming on in crowds," the frequent newspaper accounts of Chinese "human wave tactics." (These were the reports that caused Marines who knew better to ask the facetious question: "How many hordes are there in a Chinese platoon?")[40]

According to one U.S. Army report, the Chinese made excellent use of terrain during their attacks, but unlike their North Korean allies, they were not prepared to defend it to the death. Withdrawal was as important to their tactics as the advance. Attacks were, moreover, habitually launched from more than one direction and frequently preceded by probes. These probes served a number of purposes—they confused the defenders about the size and shape of the attack while causing the defenders to betray the positions of their automatic weapons. Against UN forces moving as columns, Chinese tactics followed a pattern developed earlier by Lin Piao. Known as the "one point-two sides" method, this V-shaped maneuver included a small attack to fix the front of the column and a simultaneous double envelopment executed with great violence. Aimed at destroying isolated columns before other forces could come to their aid, these attacks were characterized by what the Chinese called the "three fierce actions": fierce fires, fierce assaults, and fierce pursuits.[41]

One week after the Chinese armies lashed out at UN forces, the Eighth Army was forced back fifty miles in its center, precipitating the longest retreat in American military history. The effect of surprise and the incredibly high standard of infantry skills among its soldiers enabled the PLA to decisively wrench the initiative away from the UN. Furtive, light of foot, and highly elusive, the Chinese soldier again raised the bogey of the "superman." The lessons of Pacific fighting against a technically inferior but determined Asiatic enemy had evidently, and most unfortunately, been largely forgotten. Generals Ridgway and Puller would afterward remark that the Eighth was a "fleeing army," that "the Communists had seriously defeated UN forces."[42] Puller later recounted his discovery and impressions of a U.S. Army artillery battalion that had been surprised by Chinese soldiers:

> They had fought hardly at all; the Reds had worked so fast that few shots were fired from our weapons. . . . It was a disgrace to American arms . . . this was not

the only such incident. If I saw one shot-up American battalion in Korea I saw fifty, and I mean fifty.[43]

Experience in Korea convinced Puller that "fancy weapons systems could not in themselves guarantee success in war." What was required, in his view, was hard training and the development of a certain attitude, "the fundamental spirit that alone can produce great armed services." The philosophy that Puller espoused was, in fact, very much akin to that of the "man-over-weapons" idea subscribed to by the Communist Chinese. During training at Camp Pendleton in preparation for Korea, Puller spent "most of his waking hours on the range," constantly striving to ensure that firepower would be provided and that it would be accurate. A strong believer in the value of day and night forced march training, he ranted: "I want 'em to be able to march twenty miles, the last five at double time, and then be ready to fight."[44] The one element of Chinese tactical philosophy that Puller was missing, however, was the Chinese emphasis on small unit maneuver. The capabilities of the Marine rifle squad notwithstanding, Marine tactics in Korea were, for the most part, as linear as those used in the Pacific War. The standard formation for attack—two elements in line with the third element following in reserve—was the same as the one recommended by Jackob Meckel in "A Summer Night's Dream" nearly sixty years before.[45]

The linear and predictable nature of most American infantry tactics continued in the second phase of the war, the long stalemate that lasted from July of 1951 through July of 1953. "Two up and one back" remained the basic defensive formation for all echelons above the platoon. Squads were generally sited abreast of each other and machine guns were generally sited to fire to the front. Though some of the non-American contingents in the UN force understood the value of reverse slopes, American units tended to locate their defensive positions on forward slopes. As with the French in 1870, this practice was based on a desire to make the most of long-range infantry fire.[46]

American defensive tactics in Korea thus represented a curious reversion to the tactics of the first half of the Great War. Designed to keep the enemy outside a defended area rather than trapping him within it, these tactics were aimed at postponing, rather than achieving, decisive action. As such, they fit in well with the UN desire for a negotiated peace settlement and American fear that the decisive defeat of Communist forces in Korea might lead to a wider, possibly nuclear, struggle. These antiquated tactics were also made possible by the fact that the Communist forces in Korea were very short of artillery.

Whether Army or Marine, American infantry (and, indeed, most of the infantry of the other UN contingents) fought the Korean War with the weapons used by American troops in the Second World War. The chief exception to this rule was the widespread use of small caliber recoilless rifles. Introduced into a number of armies in 1944 and 1945, these weapons made it possible for infantrymen to carry (rather than drag) guns of comparable performance to the 25-57-millimeter antitank guns and 75-millimeter infantry guns and pack howitzers that played such a large role in infantry tactics between 1918 and 1945. In the absence of large numbers of enemy machine guns, the chief targets for such weapons were the bunkers that the Chinese and North Koreans often built to reinforce their defensive positions. This similarity of mission notwithstanding, the lighter recoilless rifles tended to be assigned at a lower echelon than the infantry guns and antitank guns they replaced. In the United States Army, for example, 57-millimeter recoilless rifles were assigned to the weapons platoon of rifle companies. There, they took the place of the tripod-mounted light machine guns introduced in 1942.[47]

The chief problem faced by the U.S. Army infantry in Korea, however, was not a matter of weapons or tactics but of cohesion. Whether active duty soldiers fresh from their less-than-strenuous constabulary duties in occupied Japan, hastily mobilized veterans of the Second World War, or partially trained conscripts, the U.S. Army infantryman often went into battle in the company of strangers. The chief culprit was, as it had been in the Second World War, the policy of assembling units from, and refilling units with, individual replacements. During the mobile phase of the Korean War, this self-destructive policy was exacerbated by the high tempo of the fighting. The long periods of training that most Second World War infantry units got before being committed to combat were the exception rather than the rule. During the "stalemate" phase, the policy of rotating individuals (rather than units) out of combat after a fixed period of time was a further impediment to the formation of cohesive units.[48]

The Korean War produced a flood of serious literature on infantry tactics and small unit cohesion, as well as a number of attempts to improve the quality of American infantry. The Army, for example, dropped the notion that its chief role was to govern territory conquered by the Air Force and began to build conventional forces for the "next Korea"—a war that most people assumed would take place in Western Europe. The Marine Corps began a period of self-examination and experimentation that would not be matched for a generation. Nonetheless, the overall U.S. reaction to the failure of its infantry to win in Korea was to give up on the idea of producing first-class infantry. Instead, the U.S. Armed Forces looked to a variety of new inventions—from electronic sensors to tactical nuclear weapons—in the hope that these would make infantry combat obsolete.[49]

NOTES

1. Theodore Ropp, *War in the Modern World* (New York: Collier, 1962), p. 250.
2. Ropp, *War in the Modern World*, pp. 360–61; and Phillip Warner and Michael Youens, *Japanese Army of World War II* (Reading: Osprey, 1973), pp. 14–16 and 25.
3. Ivan Simson, *Singapore: Too Little, Too Late* (London: Leo Cooper, 1970), pp. 151–52.
4. Paul W. Thompson, Harold Doud, John Scofield, and Milton A. Hill, *How the Jap Army Fights* (New York: Penguin, 1943), p. 15.
5. "Japanese Tactics and Jungle Warfare," *Canadian Army Training Memorandum*, No. 35, 1944, pp. 6–7 and Simpson, *Singapore*, pp. 150–51.
6. "Know Your Enemy," *Canadian Army Training Memorandum*, No. 33, 1943, pp. 38–39; "Prepared Defenses," *Canadian Army Training Memorandum*, No. 51, 1945, pp. 24–26.
7. "Japanese Mortars," *Canadian Army Training Memorandum*, No. 50, 1945, pp. 38–39; "Japanese Soldier," *Canadian Army Training Memorandum*, No. 51, 1945, pp. 24–26; and "Jungle Fighting," *Canadian Army Training Memorandum*, No. 34, 1944, pp. 27–29.
8. Phillip Warner and Michael Youens, *Japanese Army of World War II*, p. 38.
9. "Organization and Tactics of the Japanese Platoon and Section on the Malayan Front," *Canadian Army Training Memorandum*, No. 14, 1942, p. 212; and Warner, *Japanese Army of World War II*, pp. 3–4 and 18–23.
10. Warner, *Japanese Army in World War II*, pp. 3–4, 19; and Thompson, *How the Jap Army Fights*, pp. 25–26 and 40.
11. "Organization and Tactics of the Japanese Platoon and Section on the Malayan Front," *Canadian Army Training Memorandum*, No. 14, 1942, pp. 21–22.
12. Burke Davis, *Marine! The Life of Lt. Gen. Lewis B. (Chesty) Puller* (Toronto: Bantam, 1964), p. 161.
13. Sir William Slim, *Defeat into Victory* (London: Cassell, 1956), pp. 33, 119–20, 187–91 and 450–51.
14. "How the Japanese See Us," *Canadian Army Training Memorandum*, No. 30, 1943, pp. 10–11; and Slim, *Defeat into Victory*, p. 119.
15. Slim, *Defeat into Victory*, p. 119.
16. "Japanese Tactics in Jungle Warfare," *Canadian Army Training Memorandum*, No. 35, 1944, p. 7.
17. "U.S. Enlisted Men Discuss the Jap," *Canadian Army Training Memorandum*, No. 44, 1944, p. 6.
18. "Japanese Tactics and Jungle Warfare," *Canadian Army Training Memorandum*, No. 35, 1944, p. 8; "Breakneck Ridge," *Canadian Army Training Memorandum*, No. 50, 1945, pp. 24–25; and "Japs Deepen Defenses," *Canadian Army Training Memorandum*, No. 52, 1945, pp. 13–14.

19. Arthur Swinson, *Kohima* (London: Cassell, 1966), p. 187.

20. An Allied division in Europe consumed 650 tons of supplies per day. *Martin Van Creveld, Supplying War: Logistics from Wallenstein to Patton* (Cambridge, MA: Harvard University Press, 1977), pp. 214–15.

21. Slim, *Defeat into Victory*, pp. 187–91, 540, and 549.

22. Slim, *Defeat into Victory*, pp. 33, 293, 368, 376, 542, and 549; Saburo Hayashi and Alvin C. Coox, *Kogun: The Japanese Army in the Pacific War* (Quantico, VA: The Marine Corps Association, 1959), p. 100; and Liddell Hart, *History of the Second World War*, pp. 539–40.

23. Slim, *Defeat into Victory*, p. 547.

24. Ropp, *War in the Modern World*, p. 373; and Samuel Milner, *United States Army in World War II: Victory in Papua* (Washington, D.C.: U.S. Government Printing Office, 1957), pp. 370–77.

25. Davis, *Marine!*, p. 99.

26. Davis, *Marine!*, p. 206.

27. Aircrafts dropped 800 tons of high explosive. Battleships, cruisers, and destroyers fired 20,000 shells, nearly two for each of Peliliu's 10,000 odd Japanese defenders. James Hallas, *The Devil's Anvil, The Assault on Peliliu* (Westport, CT: Praeger, 1994), pp. 13–20, 26, 35, 51, and 75.

28. For General MacArthur's criticisms of the conduct of the Central Pacific Campaign, see William Manchester, *American Caesar* (Boston: Little, Brown, 1978), pp. 336–39.

29. S.L.A. Marshall, *The River and the Gauntlet* (New York: Morrow, 1953), p. 1; Robert Leckie, *Conflict: The History of the Korean War, 1950–53* (New York: G. P. Putnam's Sons, 1962), p. 195; and Roy E. Appleman, *United States Army in the Korean War: South to the Naktong, North to the Yalu* (Washington, D.C.: U.S. Government Printing Office, 1961), p. 60.

30. Harvey W. Nelson, *The Chinese Military System: An Organizational Study of the Chinese People's Liberation Army* (New York: McGraw-Hill, 1967), pp. 56 and 130–31.

31. For examples, see Gudmundsson, *On Artillery*, pp. 144–47.

32. Davis, *Marine!*, p. 276.

33. Appleman, *South to the Naktong, North to the Yalu*, pp. 668 and 719.

34. Alexander L. George, *The Chinese Communist Army in Action: The Korean War and its Aftermath* (New York: Columbia University Press, 1959), pp. vii and 5–7.

35. Appleman, *South to the Naktong, North to the Yalu*, p. 720.

36. Stuart Schram, *Mao Tse Tung* (New York: Simon and Schuster, 1966), pp. 142–45.

37. C. N. Barclay, *The First Commonwealth Division: The Story of British Commonwealth Land Forces in Korea, 1950–1953* (Aldershot: Gale and Polden, 1954), p. 33.

38. Samuel B. Griffith, *The Chinese People's Liberation Army* (New York: McGraw-Hill, 1967), pp. 132 and 142–43.

39. For a detailed treatment of the "empty battlefield" phenomenon of the first half of the nineteenth century, see Paddy Griffith, *Forward into Battle, Battle Tactics from Waterloo to the Near Future* (Novato, CA: Presidio, 1990), pp. 50–75.

40. Lynn Montross and Captain Nicholas A. Canzona, *U.S. Marine Operations in Korea, 1950–1953: The Chosin Reservoir Campaign* (Washington, D.C.: U.S. Government Printing Office, 1957), p. 93.

41. Appleman, *South to the Naktong, North to the Yalu*, p. 720; Walter G. Hermes, *The United States Army in the Korean War, Truce Tent and Fighting Front* (Washington, D.C.: U.S. Government Printing Office, 1966), pp. 79 and 511; Griffith, *The Chinese People's Liberation Army*, pp. 143–44; Davis, *Marine!*, p. 287; and Montross, *The Chosin Reservoir Campaign*, pp. 82–93.

42. Leckie, Conflict, p. 215; Griffith, *The Chinese People's Liberation Army*, pp. 139, 144–48, and 151–52; and S.L.A. Marshall, *Pork Chop Hill: The American Fighting Man in Action, Korea, Spring 1953* (New York: William Morrow, 1956), p. 20.

43. Davis, *Marine!*, pp. 309 and 316.

44. Davis, *Marine!*, pp. 97, 217, 224, 314, and 319.

45. Montross, *The East-Central Front*, p. 38; Leckie, *Conflict*, pp. 208–11 and 218–25; and Griffith, *The Chinese People's Liberation Army*, p. 146.

46. *Tactics and Technique of Infantry* (Harrisburg, PA: The Military Service Publishing Company, 1950), pp. 47, 67, 53, 123–25, and 128.

47. Weller, *Weapons and Tactics*, pp. 128–35.

48. Roger W. Little, "Buddy Performance and Combat Performance," in Morris Janowitz, ed., *The New Military* (New York: Russell Sage, 1964), pp. 195–97, 204–21; and Richard Gabriel and Paul L. Savage, *Crisis in Command* (New York: Hill and Wang, 1978), p. 41.

49. For an overview of this period, see A. J. Bacevich, *The Pentomic Era, The U.S. Army Between Korea and Vietnam* (Washington, D.C.: National Defense University Press, 1989).

9.

Aluminum Tiger

From the vantage point of a century or two, historians will marvel at America's failure to win its war in Vietnam. When placed against the backdrop of the three hundred years of North American military history, the conflict will seem tailor-made for a nation whose experience was so often punctuated by guerilla and counter-guerilla campaigns. It is only when viewed as part of a much smaller story—the tale of how the industrialized nations of the second half of the twentieth century neglected their infantry—that the outcome of America's war in Vietnam will seem natural and even inevitable.

Generalizing about what might best be described as the Second Indochina War is difficult. From the end of the First Indochina War in 1954 to the completion of the Communist conquest of the Republic of Vietnam, ground combat took many forms. In some cases, the fighting was as conventional as in any battle of the world wars, with both sides consisting of units of "regulars" attempting decisive maneuver of, at least, the seizure or defense of terrain. In other cases, both sides were composed of guerillas, each engaging in the timeless cycle of ambush and counter-ambush. Sometimes the Communists played the role of the sharpshooting minuteman, and the Free World forces played the part of the mindless redcoat. At other times the roles were reversed. The one common theme that runs through these very different events is the fact that victory was achieved by the side that devoted the greatest share of its resources, and, in particular, its human resources, to its infantry.

Much has been made of the great material advantages enjoyed by the anti-Communist forces in Vietnam. This is certainly true where creature comforts and all things associated with aircraft were concerned. In most cases, this material advantage also extended into the realm of artillery and armor—though there were a few cases where American gunners found themselves unable to respond to Communist artillery fire and American infantrymen found themselves alone against Communist tanks.[1] When it came to infantry weapons, however, the Communist forces in Vietnam often enjoyed considerable advantages.

The weapons of choice of the Communist infantryman in Vietnam—whether he was a North Vietnamese regular or a member of a "main force" Viet Cong unit—were those of the *Volksgrenadier* infantry of the last year of World War II: the assault rifle and the rocket-propelled grenade. The chief indirect fire weapons were mortars of various sorts. (The range of calibers was from 60-millimeter through 120-millimeter. The bulk of the mortars seem to have been either Soviet-bloc 82-millimeter weapons or 81-millimeter mortars captured from the French or Americans.) These stables were supplemented by small numbers of 57-millimeter and 75-millimeter recoilless rifles—weapons that had been invented during World War II to take the place of infantry guns and the smaller sort of antitank guns.[2]

The chief virtue of the Communist family of infantry weapons—their ability to produce intense (though short lived) concentrations of fire—provided a considerable advantage in close combat. The chief deficiency of these weapons—their lack of accuracy at long range—was, in most situations faced by the Communist infantry in Vietnam, no great vice. In most cases, the density of foliage, the presence of buildings, or the undulations of the earth so reduced the opportunities for effective long-range fire that the deficiency was not noticed. Indeed, even when they had weapons that could be used at long range (such as tripod-mounted machine guns), the Communist infantrymen seem to have preferred to use them at close range.[3]

The American infantry in Vietnam was armed with a completely different set of weapons. The standard infantry weapon was the M-14, a semi-automatic rifle that was basically an improved version of the M-1 rifle of World War II and Korea. The Browning Automatic Rifle had been replaced by M-14 rifles that had been modified to fire automatically. (These modifications included a heavier barrel.) The Browning .30 caliber machine guns had been replaced by the M-60, a general-purpose machine gun that, though it took many features from, and even bore an outward resemblance to, the German MG-42, had a far slower rate of fire. Indeed, the principal small-unit weapons carried by American infantry units at the beginning of the Vietnam War were all characterized by a comparatively slow rate of fire.[4]

During the Korean War, which had provided the context for the development of these weapons, this slow rate of fire had not been seen as a deficiency. Indeed, during the position warfare phase of the Korean War, when the main task of infantry fire was to keep the enemy at a distance so that he could be attacked by artillery or aircraft, a slow rate of fire was seen as a positive means of reducing the chances that the infantry might run out of ammunition.[5] When the terrain and situation in Vietnam approximated those of Korea—such as in the famous defense of the "Rockpile"—this approach worked well enough to prevent disaster.[6] When such fields of fire were lacking, however, the American infantrymen found themselves at a distinct disadvantage. "When American infantry found themselves walking into close range fire from a dug-in enemy," writes Paddy Griffith in his classic *Forward into Battle*, "the only possible response was to hug the ground until the incoming fire abated."[7]

The American infantry compensated for their lack of close-in firepower in a number of ways. Shotguns, which had been made available to units for use by sentries, found their way into the front lines. The M-79 grenade launcher, a 40-millimeter weapon that could fire both high explosive and cannister shells, proved popular and, if photographs and other pieces of anecdotal evidence are any guide, seems to have been used more extensively than is indicated by the official allowance of one or two per rifle squad.[8] Though issued as platoon and company weapons, M-60 machine guns often migrated down to the squad level, where they were used because the modified M-14 rifles were not particularly well suited to serve as automatic rifles. American infantry grew particularly fond of a simple weapon known as the "claymore mine." Essentially a crescent-shaped explosive charge attached to a remote firing device, the "claymore mine" could be command-detonated to produce an effect that might be described as similar to that of a very large shotgun. Because it had to be set up before firing, the use of this weapon was generally confined to ambushes and the defense.

Additional help for the close-in fight was provided to U.S. infantrymen when, in the course of 1966, most M-14 rifles in Vietnam were exchanged for M-16 assault rifles. (A few M-14 rifles were retained for use by snipers.) Though these new weapons experienced serious teething problems and proved difficult to maintain, they gave each infantryman a weapon comparable to the standard Communist assault rifle, the AK-47.

This redress of the balance of intimate firepower, however, did little to change the longstanding American preference for keeping the enemy at arm's length so that artillery and air strikes could inflict casualties.[9]

In contrast to American practice in Korea and World War II, American artillery in Vietnam was rarely used in a manner that brought decisive results in a short period of time. In World War II, U.S. gunners (as well as their German and British counterparts) had learned that a large number of tubes firing a few rounds each at a single target was generally found to be more effective than a large number of rounds fired by a small number of tubes. The first rounds of a bombardment, after all, are more likely to catch the enemy unawares, and thus tend to cause more casualties than subsequent rounds. A short but intense bombardment, moreover, seems to have a greater psychological effect than a less intense but sustained battering. In Vietnam, however, American artillery was generally deployed as single batteries.[10]

This pattern of deployment ensured that artillery was available to fire a few rounds to rescue a small infantry patrol in contact with an even smaller number of enemy infantrymen. Thanks to the radio and what might be called the "customer-service orientation" of U.S. field artillery units, both coverage and responsiveness became so good that some American infantry companies went into battle without their organic heavy weapons. With a battery of 105-millimeter howitzers able to respond to a call for help within minutes (or, in some cases, even seconds), 81-millimeter mortars were often left in the rear.[11]

The one infantry mortar that the American infantry in Vietnam made extensive use of was the 60-millimeter that, ironically, had been declared obsolete in the 1950s. Essentially a copy of the standard French company mortar introduced in the late 1930s, the 60-millimeter mortar had proved useful during World War II. It had been less popular in Korea, and during the inevitable "rationalization" that followed the end of that conflict, it had been retired. Its functions, the responsible American officials believed, could just as easily be fulfilled by the new M-79 grenade launcher and the 81-millimeter mortar. In the close terrain of Vietnam, however, the M-79 grenade launcher was fully employed as a direct fire weapon, while the 81-millimeter mortar proved too awkward for use by patrols consisting entirely of men on foot.[12]

The Marine Corps officially restored the 60-millimeter mortar to its infantry, with an allowance of three tubes for each rifle company, in 1966. These tubes formed a mortar section within the weapons platoon. (The other sections of the weapons platoon were the machine gun section—with three squads of two M-60 machine guns each—and the antitank-assault section—with three small teams, each trained to use bazookas, flamethrowers, and demolition charges.) Army units were not so fortunate and had to "scrounge" both weapons and ammunition. (The official Army response to the cry from the "field" for 60-millimeter mortars was to try to develop a hand-fired version of the 81-millimeter mortar.)[13]

With or without mortars, the firepower organic to American infantry in Vietnam was dwarfed by what was provided to it from the outside in the form of artillery fire, armed helicopters, and ground attack aircraft. That this was sometimes used to good effect is undeniable. In particular, the ability of a single radio message to initiate a chain of events that would, within minutes, bring down the "might of America," was responsible for saving many American ground units from disaster. Reliance on such means, however, was not an unmixed blessing and, whether cause or symptom, was closely associated with the inability of the United States to field first-class infantry units on a consistent basis.

At the lowest levels, the need to give direction to the artillery, helicopters, and aircraft tended to occupy the attention of infantry commanders to the point where actually leading their men in combat became, at best, a secondary consideration. Though each of these arms was, in most cases, represented by an observer or liaison officer, the task of combining their actions into a single maneuver was left to the infantry commander. In large operations, the latter might have been a battalion commander. For the most part, however, it was a rifle company commander, who was often reduced to playing the role of the harried stockbroker of our comic imagination, a man who is desperately trying to carry on two or three earnest telephone conversations at the same time.

What this was like, even in the best of circumstances, is described in a 1970 article in *Infantry* magazine. In the hypothetical case described, the rifle company commander had, in addition to his three rifle platoons, a battery of 105-millimeter howitzers firing from a fire base five kilometers away, three Cobra helicopter gunships, and three F-4 "Phantom" jet fighter bombers.

> The gunships on the company [radio] net and the artillery on the FO [forward observer] battalion fire net are working simultaneously. The rifle platoons on the company net are attempting to define the limits of the target and identify the locations of automatic and heavy weapons. The situation appears to be in order, but to assume that you have matters in hand 10 minutes from now is a step toward disaster. Are you anticipating the arrival of an airstrike? Is the battalion commander on his way out with the artillery liaison officer (LNO)? Have you been able to maneuver one or more of your rifle platoons to a better position?

Let's handle these questions in order. FACs [Forward Air Controllers] flock to contacts like flies to the "pile in the pasture." Thank goodness for these aggressive, eagle-eyed souls! The FAC, too, will want marking smoke lest he inadvertently place some expensive ordnance on you and your hardworking troopers. Once he has been briefed and has, in turn, briefed his mixed-load flight of F-4s, he is ready to apply the pressure.[14]

The inherently difficult task of combining the fire effects of three or four different arms was further complicated by the layers of "management" that were superimposed upon the company commander. Often provided with helicopters and always just a radio call away, battalion, brigade, and divisional commanders were able to take as much or as little of the battle as they wanted. The strategy of attrition freed these commanders from any need to weave company engagements into larger operations. The philosophy of "management by exception" encouraged them to question, second-guess, and otherwise "supervise" the commander of the company in contact. That this was rarely welcome and often a hindrance, can be seen from a single, hypothetical case.

At this point, some commanders, such as ALFA six [the battalion commander] might commit one or more of the unforgivable sins. They will "checkfire" the artillery, assuming that it will interfere with the tac [tactical] air. This is incorrect, though, since the artillery max ord [maximum ordinate] is only 450 feet. Visualizing an artillery round trajectory in our situation, you will quickly realize that close to the target, where the tac air enters the picture, it is even less than 450 feet. Both the HFT [helicopter fire team of three attack helicopters] and tac air would prefer that the artillery be continued to suppress ground fire.[15]

How a company commander in such a situation could spare more than a stray thought for his rifle platoons remains a mystery. Far easier to understand was the growing belief that, in a battle whose only purpose was to inflict casualties upon an elusive enemy, the rifle platoons were actually a hindrance to the employment of ground attack jets, helicopter gunships, and various forms of artillery. After all, if the chief purpose of the man on the ground was merely to identify targets and choreograph the ballet of fire, then it made sense to greatly reduce the size of infantry units. The United States Marine Corps, in a long experiment known as "Project Stingray," pushed this idea to its logical conclusion. Taking the place of larger patrols, "Stingray" teams of four to six men managed, over the course of the four years of heaviest American involvement, to inflict far more physical damage on the enemy at a cost of far fewer Free World casualties than conventional infantry battalions.[16]

The knowledge that inflicting random casualties brought the United States no closer to victory led to another experiment. Rather than using artillery and aircraft to replace infantry, U.S. Army Colonel David Hackworth designed and fielded a very different sort of infantry unit. Though this "guerilla battalion, U.S. style" was built on a foundation provided by a conventional infantry battalion (the Fourth Battalion of the 39th Infantry), it was organized and led according to what, at least for the time, were very unconventional ideas. The first casualties of Hackworth's reforms were creature comforts such as beer and tape players. These luxuries had no place in the rucksacks of soldiers who were attempting to "out guerilla the guerilla."[17]

Next to be thrown out the window were long-cherished ideas about organization. In particular, the notion of interchangeable rifle companies was replaced by the idea that each of the four rifle companies would develop a combat speciality. Company A, consisting of two oversize (sixty-man) platoons, became the long-range ambush company. Company C, made up of four smaller platoons, specialized in short-range ambushes. (The range in "long- and short-range" referred not to the distance between the ambushers and their prey, but between the ambush site and the rest of the battalion.) Companies B and D were organized as patrol units. Though fully proficient in ambush techniques, these two companies were geared more towards finding the enemy than ambushing him. Company B further specialized in cooperating with (and being transported by) helicopters. Company D, on the other hand, developed expertise in moving on the ground.[18]

The specialized companies were assisted by two specialized platoons. A "special action platoon" of twelve "Vietnamese-sized" Americans and six "Tiger scouts" (former Communist soldiers who had changed sides) was dressed in black pajamas and armed with captured weapons. A sniper platoon, which was treated as an elite unit, provided seven two-man teams. Heavy weapons units, whether at the company or battalion level, were entirely absent. The men needed to form them, Colonel Hackworth reasoned, could be better used to fill the rifle units.[19]

Though most of the men in Hackworth's "guerilla battalion" had become close-combat experts who imitated their enemies, Hackworth's tactics made full use of the helicopters, artillery, and armed aircraft available to him. Sniper teams, ambush forces, and patrols were inserted by helicopter. In larger operations, elements of the battalion cooperated directly with full companies ("troops") of air cavalry. Patrols that ran into enemy units larger than a squad would pull back to a well-covered position and call in artillery or air strikes, while other elements of the battalion would deploy to cut off any available escape routes. Indeed, it was the availability of considerable amounts of long-range firepower from sources outside his battalion that allowed Hackworth to dispense with his organic heavy weapons.

From the point of view of the preceding half-century of American practice, the most interesting of Hackworth's innovations was his insistence on pulling units out of combat for frequent periods of rest and training. Like the Germans of both World Wars, Hackworth knew that troops that spend too much time in contact with the enemy lose much of their combat power. He therefore made the sacrifices necessary to have his company commanders spend a four-week apprenticeship with an Australian infantry company, his snipers attend an (otherwise underutilized) division sniper's school, and his platoons spend about one week in six in a training area far away from the battlefields.[20]

Whether by imitation or parallel invention, many of Hackworth's innovations were repeated in other U.S. units. For every American battalion commander who attempted to beat the enemy at his own game, there were several who were eager to practice what they had been taught at Fort Benning or Quantico, regardless of the cost. In some cases—such as that of the U.S. mechanized infantry company that wiped out a Viet Cong platoon defending a poorly designed bunker complex—these tactics worked well.[21] In others—such as that of the airborne company commander who formed his M-79 grenade launchers into a sort of walking "grand-battery"—the result was merely ridiculous.[22] In attack after attack, however, a style of fighting that had been obsolete in the Great War was used, for the simple reason that it was the one with which the leaders were most familiar.

The conventional explanation for the failure of the U.S. forces in Vietnam to properly adapt to local conditions is the fact that most officers spent very little time trying to tackle the problem. Like their men, most American officers in Vietnam spent twelve months "in country" before being returned to the "Land of the Big PX." In contrast to their men, who tended to serve their entire tours with a single unit, officers split their year between command and staff tours. As a result, officers were under a great deal of pressure to get immediate results and lacked the opportunity to make use of any lessons learned by their predecessors. The problems that plagued American infantry in Vietnam were not, however, peculiar to that war. Poor field craft, predictable tactics, over-reliance on artillery and airpower, and indifferent leadership had been common problems in both Korea and World War II. Therefore, any search for the reason why the

United States failed to consistently produce first-class infantry units in the 1960s must also ask the same of the 1940s and 1950s.

A good part of the answer lies in the peculiar nature of American society. Until the first half of the twentieth century, the great achievement of the United States had been mass production. The use of interchangeable parts, assembly lines, and "scientific" management had made America the richest nation on earth. The same techniques had twice made it possible for the United States to rapidly convert its raw economic power into some of the largest armies in history. The skills and attitudes needed to mass-produce automobiles and refrigerators, however, are not those associated with first-class infantry. In particular, the job of fighting at close quarters has, ever since the open order revolution, required abilities and values that are distinctly pre-industrial.

From General Pershing in the Great War to General Lynch on the eve of World War II, American military leaders often sought to preserve the pre-industrial values that, ironically, are more important to twentieth century infantry than to that of previous eras. American military folklore has long celebrated, in the form of such heroes as Sergeant York and Audie Murphy, the myth of rural America as the nursery of natural soldiers. The great multi-layered bureaucracy that grew up to convert America's economic muscle into military might, however, was generally unwilling to take the steps needed to develop soldiers who embodied those values.

This unwillingness took the form of a belief—natural in a society that strove to free line workers from the need to think on the job—that service in the infantry was unskilled labor. "If you have half a mind to joint the infantry," ran a joke current during World War II, "that's all you need." The chief fruit of this belief was a consistent policy of filling infantry units with men of limited intelligence. Even after studies conducted during World War II indicated that above-average intelligence was an important prerequisite for success as a combat infantryman, America consistently refused to put its brighter sons into rifle squads.

An important corollary to this belief was a uniquely American faith in the interchangeability of men. The "Replacement Depot" system of World War II and the individual rotation system that started in the second half of the Korean War and was used for most of the Second Indochina War were both based on the notion that a unit was little more than a management structure for organizing the work of individuals. The idea that a unit must be a social organization before it can become a fighting outfit—an idea associated with all first-class infantry in this century—could not compete with the convenience of treating men like spare parts.

In the Second Indochina War, as in World War II and Korea, the irony of the American attempt to "industrialize" its infantry was that the infantry serving America's totalitarian enemies was, for the most part, handled in a much less totalitarian manner. Like the Germans, the Japanese, and the Red Chinese, the Vietnamese Communists understood the importance of the human element in warfare. They were willing to allow (and indeed required) young men of talent to serve in the infantry and, in a reversal of American practice, they were happy to relegate dullards to supporting roles. (In the case of those armies which had a strong guerilla tradition, the fact that there were lots of "billets" open for porters meant that the rifleman was *not* at the bottom of the military hierarchy.) They understood the importance of learning from the battlefield and, as a result, were more willing than the defenders of democracy to make immediate use of the opinions of common soldiers.

In the years leading up to the Second Indochina War, Communist Chinese propaganda frequently referred to the United States as a "paper tiger." The power of America, this moniker implied, was no more real than the teeth of a predator painted on crepe. The bite of the U.S. forces sent to Vietnam in 1965, however, proved sharper than most Asian Communists had bargained for. A better metaphor for the United States of the time might therefore have been an "aluminum tiger." Like a cut-out cat made from that metal, the U.S. Armed Forces in Vietnam proved reasonably malleable, occasionally brilliant, but ultimately lacking in the sturdiness that can only be provided by enough of the right sort of infantry.

NOTES

1. The story of the North-Vietnamese tank attack on the Special Forces camp at Lang Vei is told in many places. These include Shelby Stanton, *The Rise and Fall of an American Army, U.S. Ground Forces in Vietnam 1965–1973* (Novato, CA: Presidio, 1985), pp. 250–54.

2. United States Marine Corps, *Professional Knowledge Gained From Operational Experience in Vietnam, 1967* (Quantico, VA: U.S. Marine Corps, 1989), p. 193; Anthony V. Neglia, "NVA and VC: Different Enemies, Different Tactics," *Infantry*, September–October 1970.

3. For anecdotes, see, among others, the interviews in Michael Lee Lanning and Dan Craig, *Inside the VC and the NVA, The Real Story of North Vietnam's Armed Forces* (New York: Fawcett Columbine, 1992), Chapters 10 and 11.

4. Thomas G. Johnson, "Recon by Sound," *Infantry*, September–October 1969, pp. 42–45.

5. Robert H. Clagett, "What Good is a Machine Gun," *Combat Forces Journal*, October 1952, pp. 28–29.

6. Robert A. Doughty, *The Evolution of U.S. Army Tactical Doctrine, 1946–76* (Fort Leavenworth, KS: U.S. Army Command and Staff College, 1979), p. 33.

7. Paddy Griffith, *Forward into Battle, Fighting Tactics from Waterloo to the Near Future* (Novato, CA: Presidio, 1992), p. 154.

8. One technique for employing the M-79 against snipers hiding in buildings required the simultaneous firing of two of the weapons. This way, one round would break the window glass the instant before the other flew through the window. Grady A. Smith, "Old Doctrine, New Techniques," *Infantry*, May–June 1971, p. 30.

9. Doughty, *The Evolution of U.S. Army Tactical Doctrine, 1946–76*, p. 36.

10. Robert H. J. Scales, *Firepower in Limited War* (Washington, D.C.: Government Printing Office), pp. 84–85. For more on this theme, see Gudmundsson, *On Artillery*.

11. Shelby Stanton, *Order of Battle, Vietnam* (Washington, D.C.: U.S. News Books, 1981), p. 53; Scales, *Firepower in Limited War*, pp. 89–91; and Jack Stevenson, "Things to Do With an 81mm Mortar," *Infantry*, January–February 1971, p. 60.

12. "The Marine and his Infantry Weapons in Vietnam," *Marine Corps Gazette*, April 1965, pp. 1–5.

13. Gary Rogers, "New Developments in Infantry Mortars," *Infantry*, July–August 1972, p. 15; and John F. Hathaway, "The Handheld 81mm Mortar," *Infantry*, September–October 1967, pp. 40–42.

14. Albert A. Griffith, "Put Them All Together," *Infantry*, July–August 1970, p. 10. This article also contains an argument against the carrying of 81-millimeter mortars by rifle companies.

15. Griffith, "Put Them All Together," p. 10.

16. Francis J. West, Jr., "Stingray '70," *U.S. Naval Institute Proceedings*, November 1969, pp. 27–37.

17. David H. Hackworth, "Guerilla Battalion, U.S. Style," *Infantry*, January–February 1971, pp. 22–24; and David H. Hackworth and Julie Sherman, *About Face, The Odyssey of an American Warrior* (New York: Simon and Schuster, 1990), p. 682.

18. Hackworth, "Guerilla Battalion, U.S. Style," pp. 22–24; and *About Face*, p. 681.

19. Hackworth, "Guerilla Battalion, U.S. Style," pp. 25.

20. Hackworth, "Guerilla Battalion, U.S. Style," pp. 22–25.

21. William E. Klein, "Mechanized Infantry in Vietnam," *Infantry*, March–April 1971, pp. 19–20.

22. George E. Dexter, "Search and Destroy, Vietnam," *Infantry*, July–August 1966, p. 39.

10.

Beyond Neglect

The military history of the half-century following the fall of France in 1940 can, without too much oversimplification, be boiled down to the story of Western armies allowing their infantry to deteriorate until, in the moment of truth, they discover the folly of such neglect. The armies of less affluent nations have been much less susceptible to this temptation. Indeed, with few strategic resources beyond a surplus of intelligent, energetic, and, quite often, angry young men, such nations have found that well trained and determined infantry is a powerful counterweight to the far more expensive, but often less useful, armies of the developed world.

The long Arab-Israeli conflict provides us with a cross-section view of this larger trend. First erupting into "hot war" as a series of battles between infantry forces, it eventually developed into a proving ground for the world's most advanced conventional weapons. This soon led to a belief that infantry had become obsolete. Subsequent fighting proved, however, that infantry was far more than a poor man's substitute for tanks and jets.

Like the Communist Chinese Peoples Liberation Army, the Israeli Army began its life as the guerilla arm (*Palmach*) of an underground political movement (*Haganah*). Consisting almost entirely of infantry, the *Palmach* first took the field in May of 1941, when it cooperated with the British invasion of French-held Lebanon and Syria. Never consisting of more than four battalions, the *Palmach* could not count on either numbers or technology to help win its battles. Instead, it placed its emphasis on unit cohesion, dynamic small unit leadership, and the independent maneuver of squads. From the beginning, the *Palmach* leadership rejected the British concept of battle drill as "an over-schematic and artificial way of acquiring habits in the field."[1] In its place, the Israelis adopted the German idea of the squad leader as a tactical commander who was trained to make rapid decisions and lead by example.[2]

Partially motivated by a desire to replace it with a more regular force on the British model, Prime Minister David Ben Gurion dissolved the *Palmach* in October 1948. Nonetheless, practices carried on in the *Palmach* carried over to the post-independence armed forces of Israel. These include the requirement that all officers come from the ranks, a pronounced stress on "internal" discipline to obtain what other armies achieve by compulsion, and an intellectual (rather than authoritarian) approach to training and education. Specifically, it has meant that courses for squad leaders have tended to be more mentally challenging than those conducted in other modern armies.[3]

Given this emphasis, it is not surprising that Israeli squads were designed for flexible employment. The standard eight-man squad employed in the Sinai campaign of 1956, for example, was provided with two light machine guns. In uncertain situations—such as patrols—this allowed the formation of two similar teams. In the attack, where a great deal of suppressive fire was needed to ensure the safety of squad members attempting to close with the enemy, the two light machine guns could be pushed forward as a single unit. In keeping with a century-long trend toward a reduction in the number of men closing with the enemy, the Israeli assault elements were tiny. With five men detailed to serve and protect the light machine guns, an eight-man squads was left with only three men to form the second claw of the pincer. Thanks to the fact that one of these men was the squad leader and the widespread use of submachine guns and hand grenades as the chief close combat weapons, these small assault elements seem to have sufficed.[4]

In the opinion of Yigael Allon, often listed as the outstanding field commander in the 1948–1949 War, the great battles of that particular war, the Sinai Campaign and the Six Day War, were "won in the non-commissioned officers courses of the *Haganah* and the *Palmach*." Allon rejected the argument that only in an army of partisans, fighting under special conditions and in independent small groups, was it necessary to train a section leader as a tactical commander capable of sizing up situations, making decisions, and putting them into effect on his own authority. He clearly considered the section leader's position to be the linchpin of operational effectiveness:

The most brilliant plan devised by the most capable general depends for its tactical execution on the section-leaders. Poor section-leaders may ruin the best-laid plans; first-rate section-leaders will often save badly devised plans. This for one simple reason: the section-leader is the *sole* level of command that maintains constant and direct contact with the men who bear the brunt of the actual fighting. It follows, then, that the section-leader is to be trained as a tactical commander and as an educator of his men. [In the Israeli Army] . . . section-leaders are trained to command independently in the field in every instance in which they are required to operate alone with their units. In "regular combat", moreover, when the section-leader acts within the framework of his platoon and under orders from his superior officer, he still requires a high standard of knowledge and an ability to sum up the situation. Modern fire-power and the development of tactical atomic weapons may compel armies to operate in small, dispersed formations both in attack and defence. . . . All levels of command must therefore be trained to think and act independently whenever circumstances demand that they should, and section-leaders are no exception to this rule. Besides, modern weapons which provide small groups of men with greater firepower and more flexibility of movement, call for a high standard of command at all levels. The section-leader is therefore to be trained technically as an officer, not as a corporal.[5]

As observed by S.L.A. Marshall in the mid-1950s, Israeli recruit training was rigorous and demanding, "threefold tougher than in the United States Army." Teaching the private soldier to think clearly, observe keenly, and report accurately has received great emphasis, though relatively little importance has been attached to parade square drill and routines familiar to other peacetime armies. Prior to 1956, sharpshooting was strongly stressed and physical training given a high priority, a standard test for NCO candidates being the completion of a forty-mile march in eight and one-half hours. As regards the latter, it is worth noting that the Israelis wasted no time in road marching, preferring to condition troops by cross-country movement.[6]

Since Israel as a nation could not tolerate high casualties, Yigael Yadin and other Israeli leaders were drawn to adopt Liddell Hart's "indirect approach" on the strategic plane, while embracing Rommel's counsels on the importance of small fighting units on the tactical level. Consequently, Israeli commanders were urged to avoid the expensive head-on attack, strategically and tactically, as there was usually a better way. In an associated vein, commanders were also strongly advised to rest exhausted troops as they were generally expected to be at the limits of their endurance. To Yigal Allon, battle was not just a matter of fire and movement but fire and movement *and* "consciousness," the mental preparation of soldiers for action. In the matter of motivating troops, the Israelis have traditionally seen little need for medals; hardly more than a score were awarded for bravery in the Sinai Campaign, and only fifty-one citations were given in the Six Day War. Significantly, almost half the total Israelis killed in both the Sinai Campaign and the Six Day War were officers.[7]

After the 1956 war, the improvement of relations between Israel and such countries as France and the United States led to unprecedented access to modern weapons. In particular, the Israelis began to acquire large numbers of tanks which, in contravention of nearly all of the accepted lessons of the Second World War, were employed in formations that were, by Second World War standards, short of infantry. In the view of Israel Tal, the most influential armor officer in the Israeli Army of the 1960s and early 1970s, the lack of natural cover on the desert meant that tanks had little to fear from hostile antitank weapons. First-class tank gunnery, Tal believed, would allow the Israeli tanks to shoot accurately from long range, thereby enticing the enemy to reveal his position by shooting too soon. Tal even went so far as to forbid the acquisition of modern armored personnel carriers. In his opinion, infantry served merely as a mopping-up force and could thus make do with second-rate equipment.[8]

The astounding success of Israeli arms in the Six Day War of June 1967 appeared on the surface to verify the theories of General Tal. His long-range sniping tactics proved effective as Israeli tank gunners picked off Egyptian antitank guns at ranges of 1,000 meters or more. Except for the Golani brigade on the Syrian front and the paratroop brigade that fought in Jerusalem, no Israeli infantry brigade was given an independent operational role. The mechanized infantry battalions organic to Israeli armored brigades were used mainly for mopping-up operations. With high mobility maintained through a "conveyor belt" logistics system, complete air superiority, and a hefty ingredient of surprise, the Israelis achieved a classic *Blitzkrieg* victory.

As with previous *Blitzkrieg* campaigns, the 1967 war was not without its "retail" fighting. At Um Katef in the Sinai, for example, Ariel Sharon's division (one infantry brigade, one armored brigade, two parachute battalions, and the largest artillery force yet assembled by the Israeli Army) was forced to resort to a deliberate combined arms night attack "with limited objectives." As might be expected, even this attack, (which, by Israeli standards, was characterized by an unusual degree of centralized control) displayed *Blitzkrieg* characteristics. These included the use of ground attack aircraft and helicopter-borne commandos to knock out the

160 or so Egyptian field pieces and close cooperation between the Israeli artillery and the attacking Israeli infantry.[9]

On a smaller scale, Sharon used a remarkable facsimile of Great War *Stosstrupp* tactics to take fortified Egyptian police stations. Using stealth to approach within striking range, the Israeli paratroopers that carried out these operations used bangalore torpedos to create lanes in the Egyptian barbed wire. This done, small teams of paratroopers jumped into the network of communication and firing trenches and, using grenades and hand-held automatic weapons, cleared them "on the double." As had been the case with Great War assaults of this nature, there was a considerable risk of counterattack. For this reason, Sharon ensured that each of the little fortresses was isolated before it was attacked.[10]

Though the stubborn Egyptian defense at Um Katef was not characteristic of the Arab armies of 1967, it was the harbinger of things to come. To the Israeli decision makers, it was the exception rather than the rule. As a result, the aftermath of the 1967 war saw a further reduction in the infantry strength of the Israeli Army. Most infantry brigades were converted into armored brigades. Within the armored brigades, both the organic infantry component and the self-propelled mortars were reduced to make room for additional tanks. With the exception of the paratroopers and the elite Golani brigade, those infantry units that remained were low on the priority list for both personnel and equipment.[11]

In October 1973, the Egyptian surprise attack across the Suez Canal proved the folly of Israel's neglect of its infantry. Lacking the infantry needed to adequately guard the banks of the canal, the Israelis were caught by surprise. Lacking infantry, mortars, and artillery to combat Egyptian antitank weapons, the counterattacking Israeli armored brigade was nearly destroyed by long-range antitank missiles and short-range rocket propelled grenades. These latter weapons, slightly improved versions of the *Panzerfaust* of the Second World War, seem to have accounted for a large number of the Israeli tanks. This, in turn, meant that at least a portion of the Egyptian infantry had developed the particular blend of patience and courage needed to hold their fire until the charging tanks got within the effective range of the rocket propelled grenade.[12]

Another casualty of the Israeli adoption of the "all tank" theory was the virtual abandonment of their traditional specialty of night fighting, a valuable legacy of *Palmach* days, and, in particular, the teachings of Orde Wingate. One result of this decadence was the use of armored forces to solve tactical problems that would have been better left to infantry. A classic example was the unsuccessful and costly attempt of the Israeli Seventh Brigade to take Tel Shams in Syria by frontal armored assault.

(The same position was taken, at the cost of four wounded, by an infantry night attack.)[13] Indeed, were it not for the night fighting skills of the few infantry units that remained in the Israeli Army, the fighting in both the Sinai and the Golan Heights might have taken a different turn.

In the immediate aftermath of the Arab-Israeli War of 1973, the clear winners of the battle of "lessons learned" were the antitank guided missile and a class of upgunned armored personnel carriers known as "infantry fighting vehicles." From the perspective of the mid-1990s, however, it seems that the Egyptian victory along the Suez Canal was the beginning of a worldwide "infantry renaissance." As with other renaissances, there were those who had no need of reawakening. Throughout the post-war period, the major military powers of Asia—Red China, India, and Communist Vietnam—never lost their faith in the value of well trained infantry. The armies of the developed world, on the other hand, followed the Israeli pattern. In the aftermath of the Second World War, the rebuilt armies of the reconstructed nations of Europe were, *faute de mieux*, largely infantry armies. As soon as they could manage it, most of these armies obtained tanks and other heavy equipment and, like the Israelis, progressively dismantled their infantry forces.

European armies of the late 1940s, 1950s, and even early 1960s could count on the services of a large numbers of veterans of the Second World War, many of whom had served in two or three different armies. Many of these leaders had also gained considerable experience in the many guerilla wars that immediately followed the end of the Second World War. The result was a quiet, but obviously widespread, rethinking of the organization and tactics of the smallest infantry units. Though there were notable exceptions, the general trend was towards the replacement of indivisible squads with squads that, at least from the point of view of their organization and armament, were capable of independent maneuver. The subdivision of squads into two or three teams went hand-in-hand with a considerable increase in the volume of fire that each squad was able to produce. Bolt-action rifles were largely replaced by semi-automatic ones. Magazine-fed automatic rifles were either increased in number or replaced by belt-fed light machine guns of the type long favored by the Germans.[14]

The notable exceptions of this trend were the Soviets and the French. Though they followed the general trend towards greater organic firepower, the Soviets retained the indivisible rifle squad up to the collapse of their empire. The French went in an entirely different direction. Finishing the Second World War with an infantry organization similar to that introduced in the U.S. Army in 1942, they began a series of experiments that resulted, in the late 1950s, in the abolition of the squad as a permanently constituted organization. In its place, infantrymen were organized into weapons crews (*pièces*) and small rifle teams (*équipes*) that were, as the situation demanded, assembled into *groupes de combat*. These could, according to the situation and resources be "support groups" (*groupes d'appui*) composed of two or three light machine gun crews, "assault groups" (*groupes de choc*), or "mixed groups" (*groupes mixtes*). The latter might include rocket launcher crews and engineer teams as well as light machine gun crews and/or rifle teams.

Similar to the American "some assembly required" concept of the Great War, this approach had been proposed in France as early as the 1920s. Its virtue was that it made the French infantry organization far more supple than it had been in either of the World Wars. Its chief vice was that it ignored the fact that a properly functioning squad is far more than a collection of specialists. It is, first and foremost, a social organization composed of men who, because of the bonds between them, would literally prefer to die than let their comrades down. By the end of the 1960s, the French realized that it is far easier for most men to learn how to use a new weapon than form such bonds and introduced a squads in which a permanent "support team" (*équipe d'appui*, armed with a belt-fed light machine gun) cooperated with a permanent "assault team" (*équipe de choc*).[15]

Beginning in the 1970s, the post-war recovery of European infantry was cut short by the widespread introduction of infantry fighting vehicles. Essentially small tanks with compartments for a handful of infantrymen, infantry fighting vehicles are useful for such tasks as providing anti-infantry and anti-antitank protection for main battle tanks, reconnaissance for armored formations, and escort services for convoys. Their immediate effect on infantry units equipped with them, however, is to convert those units into something other than infantry. This is done by reducing both the size and number of rifle squads and making the remaining infantry teams dependent on their vehicles for everything from transport to covering fire.

Building on the experience of the armored *Panzergrenadier* units of the second half of the Second World War, the Germans were the first to introduce infantry fighting vehicles. Ironically, the same societies that produced the wealth needed to buy these expensive weapons were also reducing the number and size of the battlefields where they might profitably be employed. Throughout the post-war period, a combination of aggressive reforestation and the rapid growth of built-up areas has transformed the countryside of Western Europe.[16] The open hollow in which the tanks of the 10th *Panzer* Division assembled prior to their attack out of the Amiens bridgehead in June of 1940, for example, is now home to an American-style shopping mall.[17]

In the 1980s, one of the most important advocates for a massive increase in the infantry forces of European armies was the retired *Bundeswehr* general, Franz Uhle-Wettler. Building on his experience at the end of the Second World War and his studies of more recent conflicts (particularly the wars in Korea and Vietnam), Uhle-Wettler recommended that the *Bundeswehr* raise large numbers of quasi-guerilla light infantry units. Armed primarily with assault rifles, light machine guns, and rocket-propelled grenades, the units that Uhle-Wettler proposed bear a superficial resemblance to the 1944 pattern of *Volksgrenadier* infantry.

On closer inspection there are a number of important departures. Uhle-Wettler replaces the traditional German two-team squad with a triangular rifle squad modeled on the one adopted by the Marine Corps in 1944. Rifle platoons consist of three such squads and a small command team (one officer, one NCO, and three messengers). Three rifle platoons, a heavy weapons platoon, and a small "leadership echelon" (*Führungsstaffel*) make a rifle company. Four rifle companies and a "headquarters and supply" company make a battalion. Battalion-level heavy weapons are completely absent. Instead, the few heavy weapons (four mortars and a handful of antitank missiles each) belong to the heavy weapons platoons of four rifle companies.[18]

One of the more interesting features of Uhle-Wettler's proposed organization is the provision of small *Verfügungs* units to both company and battalion commanders. Identical to ordinary rifle units of the same size and consisting of either a squad (at the company level) or a platoon (at the battalion level), these units serve as the commander's reconnaissance unit as well as his "last ditch" reserve. In addition to providing commanders with the means to personally intervene in crisis, these *Verfügungs* units preserve the integrity of the "ordinary" infantry units by freeing them from the need to provide detachments. The transport platoon of the battalion "headquarters and supply" company is also organized as an infantry platoon and thus provides the battalion commander with a second "last ditch" reserve unit.[19]

In sharp contrast to the infantry forces of the first half of this century, Uhle-Wettler's light infantry battalions would be territorial units—assigned to defend a particular neighborhood, supplied by local caches of food and ammunition, and perhaps even recruited from that neighborhood. The territorial nature of these units would have the important side benefit of freeing them from dependence on motor transport. Though a handful of trucks, jeeps, and motorcycles would be retained for internal housekeeping, Uhle-Wettler's units would not have to devote, as many Western infantry units do, two-fifths or so of their men to the task of driving and caring for motor vehicles.[20]

While the army of the recently united Germany has yet to adopt Uhle-Wettler's proposals, the need to conduct operations in contexts other than full-scale war has caused a second post-war revival of interest in foot-mobile infantry. Great Britain, for example, has found such forces necessary to its attempts to keep a lid on the "troubles" in Northern Ireland and has raised them by the expedient of "dismounting" and retraining mechanized infantry and even artillery units. France has a considerable infantry component in its international intervention force, the "Force Action Rapide." The United States Army has gone so far as to raise complete divisions of "light infantry."

Despite these developments, the "cutting edge" of infantry thinking remains with those armies which benefit from long standing traditions of infantry excellence. The armies of the Scandinavian Peninsula have, for example, built upon the solid foundation of the German *Jäger* tradition. The armies of Communist Vietnam and China continue to place their emphasis on "man over machine." The Swiss, who enjoy the fruits of what is probably the most successful defense policy in the world, have yet to fall prey to the notion that high technology can replace the well-led rifle squad.

In the late 1990s and early twenty-first century, the demand for infantry will increase rather than decrease. Fewer and fewer nations will have both the means to raise large armored forces and the will to use them. The Soviet Union has collapsed. The industrialized countries and the oil-rich states of the Middle East can afford large tank armies, but lack the ability to use them. (This, as Saddam Hussein discovered, is less a matter of what the leadership wants than of the leadership's failure to inspire the troops.) The less developed world has, at times, the desire to raise and use such forces, but lacks the material resources.

In addition to being expensive, armored forces may be well on their way to the obsolescence that was prematurely predicted for them in the wake of the 1973 Arab-Israeli War. The first and second generation antitank guided missiles used in that conflict were too vulnerable to countermeasures and capable of using so few firing positions that they failed to deal a death-blow to armored vehicles. The antitank weapons of the next generation of such weapons—the fiber optic guided missiles currently under development in France, Germany and Japan—have no such limitations. Using a combination of cheap television cameras and the soon-to-be ubiquitous fiber optic cable, these missles combine uncanny accuracy and long (30-kilometer) range with a nearly unlimited choice of firing position. Sufficiently cheap so as to be deployable in adequate numbers, these weapons promise to drive tanks far from the open ground that is their natural home.

Once they begin to hide in woods, towns, and the shadows of mountains, tanks become vulnerable to well-trained infantry. Provided with a simple, short range antitank weapon of adequate power, such infantry need fear little from tanks. The mechanized infantry that is sure to accompany the tanks presents more of a problem. Once separated from their vehicles, these latter-day dragoons will, more often than not, lack both the numbers and the light infantry skills needed to deal with full-time infantry protected by infantry-friendly terrain.

It is thus quite possible that the army of the future will consist largely of two only combatant arms—the "long range assassins" of the fiber optic missile troops and the "retail warriors" of a greatly expanded infantry of the type advocated by General Uhle-Wettler. In addition to tanks and armored personnel carriers, both tube artillery and long range rocket weapons (such as the multiple launch rocket system) will be pushed to the margins. While a clever commander might find some limited use for such weapons, they will be relegated to a few specialist units. Even then, they will be less useful than weapons such as 120-millimeter and 160-millimeter mortars, which, as more and more fighting takes place in woods and built-up areas, have the rare virtue of being able to penetrate significant overhead cover before bursting.

All other things being equal, an army composed of properly trained light infantry backed up by fiber optic guided missiles could defend a given area for an almost indefinite amount of time. Using far less fuel than a conventional force of similar combat power and almost completely free of the need for artillery ammunition, its chief needs would be food, small arms ammunition, and replacement missiles. Difficult to defeat in a "fair fight," such a force would also be far less vulnerable to a loss of contact with its source of supply.

The same virtues would give such a force considerable offensive power. While the fiber optic guided missiles would need some mechanical form of transport, their low "weight per kill" and their long range would permit a corps-sized force to use the sort of road currently associated with a mechanized or armored brigade. Marching over secondary roads and, if need be, cross country, the infantry component would be no more dependent on the paraphernalia of modern logistics than General Juin's mountain troops of the Italian campaign of 1943–1945.

Though more at home in woods and cities, such a force would also be able to operate in more open terrain. An extra ration of fiber optic guided missiles as well as a liberal sprinkling of the hand-held anti-aircraft missiles that proved themselves so effective in Afghanistan would enable the force to deal with both armored vehicles and helicopters.[21]

Of more immediate concern to the developed world is the utility of such a force in the "regional" crises that seem to be popping up all over the place. Far easier to move to a "trouble spot" than conventional forces, a fiber optic guided missile/light infantry combination would also be far easier to keep supplied. Once in theater, the force would be far less dependent on the roads that, in the places most likely to require intervention, are all too rare and all too fragile. (The importance of this consideration can be seen in the difficulties currently experienced by UN armored personnel carriers on the mountain roads and bridges of Bosnia.)

In the "neither war nor peace" conditions under which most of these crises occur, the greatest asset of such a force would be its unprecedented discretion. With the knowledge that highly accurate missiles were only minutes away, the infantry would be able to spread itself far more thinly than would otherwise be safe. At the same time, the lack of reliance on "blind" weapons (such as conventional field artillery, tanks, and helicopter gunships) would greatly reduce the chances of the kind of incidents that proved so counterproductive in the recent UN intervention in Somalia.

The nations most likely to field forces of this sort are China, India, Germany, and Japan. The first two nations already have the light infantry component needed for such a force and have been unable to afford to field significant mechanized forces. Both nations have aircraft and consumer electronics industries of sufficient sophistication to build fiber optic guided missiles and a degree of economic success that makes the building of a $20,000 missile far more attractive than a $500,000 tank. Though they currently lack the right sort of infantry, Germany and Japan are already close to fielding their fiber optic guided missiles. Given the high quality of infantry that they were able to raise during the Second World War, and the fact that both nations have a surplus of well-educated but underemployed young men, the potential for a revival of the German and Japanese infantry traditions is high.

This great potential for symbiosis notwithstanding, the future of infantry is not dependent on the fiber optic guided missile or any other particular piece of technology. Whatever weapon dominates the battlefield, there will always be times when and places where vehicles cannot travel, shells and missiles cannot reach, and electronic sensors cannot sense. There will, moreover, always be men who, for reasons of poverty or strategy, prefer to fight their battles at the retail rather than the wholesale level. For this reason, there will always be a place for first-class infantry.

NOTES

1. Yigael Allon, *The Making of Israel's Army* (London: Valentine, Mitchell, 1970), pp. 9–11, and 16–24.

2. The extent of German influence on the Israeli Army is considerable and even extends to such things as tactical symbology. For more on the intellectual history of the Israeli ground forces, see Bond, *Liddell Hart, A Study of His Military Thought*, Chapter 9.

3. Allon, *The Making of Israel's Army*, pp. 125–30.

4. S.L.A. Marshall, *Sinai Victory* (New York: William Morrow, 1958), pp. 239–40.

5. Allon, *The Making of Israel's Army*, pp. 127.

6. S.L.A. Marshall, "Why the Israeli Army Wins," *Harper's Magazine*, October 1958, pp. 39–43, and Marshall, *Sinai Victory*, pp. 21 and 233–34.

7. Allon, *The Making of Israel's Army*, pp. 91–92 and 258–59; Marshall, *Sinai Victory*, pp. 22–23, 90, and 226; Samuel Rolbant, *The Israeli Soldier: Profile of an Army* (Cranbury: Thomas Yoseloff, 1970), p. 108.

8. Edward Luttwak and Dan Horowitz, *The Israeli Army* (London: Allen Lane, 1973), pp. 143–53, 186–89, 192, and 363–68.

9. This battle is also known as Abu Agheila. D. D. Campbell, "The Gunners in the Arab-Israeli Six-Day War of 1967," *Journal of the Royal Artillery*, September 1968, pp. 132–37; Luttwak and Horowitz, *The Israeli Army*, p. 290.

10. Luttwak and Horowitz, *The Israeli Army*, pp. 113–15.

11. Rolbant, *The Israeli Soldier*, p. 101, and Luttwak and Horowitz, *The Israeli Army*, pp. 95–100, 187, and 363–70.

12. Insight Team of the London Sunday Times, *The Yom Kippur War* (New York: Doubleday, 1974), pp. 164–65, 170–72, 191–95, and 489; J.M.E. Clarkson, "Spark at Yom Kippur: Many Surprises in an Eighteen-Day War," *Canadian Defense Quarterly*, No. 3, 1974, pp. 11–13 and 21; *Lessons From the Arab/Israeli War* (London: Royal United Services Institute, 1974), pp. 2–6; L. W. Bentley and D. C. McKinnon, "The Yom Kippur War as an Example of Modern Land Battle," *Canadian Defense Quarterly*, No. 4, 1974, pp. 14–18.

13. Chaim Herzog, *The War of Atonement* (Boston: Little, Brown, and Company, 1975), p. 271.

14. The details of this development can be seen in the tables appended in Weller, *Weapons and Tactics*.

15. France, Ministère des Armées, État-Major de l'Armé, 3ème Bureau, *Manuel du Préparation au Certificat Interarmes*, Tome I (Paris: Berger-Levrault, 1961), pp. 966–73.

16. Uhle-Wetter, *Gefechtsfeld Mitteleuropa, Gefahr der Übertechnisierung von Streitkräften* (Munich: Bernhard & Graefe, 1980), pp. 23–25.

17. Personal observation of Bruce Gudmundsson during his January 1992 visit to the Amiens battlefield.

18. Uhle-Wettler, *Gefechtsfeld Mitteleuropa*, pp. 124–31.

19. Uhle-Wettler, *Gefechtsfeld Mitteleuropa*, pp. 124–31.

20. Uhle-Wettler, *Gefechtsfeld Mitteleuropa*, pp. 19 and 124–31.

21. Those who argue that such a force would be vulnerable to interdiction from the air might want to consider the failure of both UN interdiction efforts in Korea and similar Soviet efforts in Afghanistan.

Bibliography

BOOKS

Addington, Larry. *The Blitzkrieg Era and the German General Staff.* New Brunswick, NJ: Rutgers University Press, 1971.

Ahrenfeldt, Robert H. *Psychiatry in the British Army in the Second World War.* London: Routledge and Kegan Paul, 1958.

Allen, Ralph. *Ordeal by Fire: Canada, 1910–1945.* Toronto: Popular Library, 1961.

Allon, Yigael. *The Making of Israel's Army.* London: Valentine Mitchell, 1970.

Altmayer, Robert. *La Xème Armée sur la Basse–Somme en Normadie et vers "le réduit breton" Mai-Juin 1940.* Paris: Editions Défense de la France, 1944.

Anders, Wladyslaw. *Hitler's Defeat in Russia.* Chicago: Henry Regnery, 1953.

Appleman, Roy E. *United States Army in the Korean War: South to the Naktong, North to the Yalu.* Washington, D.C.: U.S. Government Printing Office, 1961.

Bailey, J.B.A. *Field Artillery and Firepower.* London: Oxford University Press, 1989.

Balck, William. *Modern European Tactics.* Translated by Louis R. M. Maxwell. London: Sands and Co., 1899.

Barclay, C. N. *The First Commonwealth Division: The Story of British Commonwealth Land Forces in Korea, 1950–1953.* Aldershot: Gale and Polden, 1954.

Barnett, Correlli, et al. *Old Battles, New Lessons, Can We Learn from Military History?* London: Brassey's Defense Publishers, 1986.

Berdach, Rudolf, and Erich Dethleffsen. *Der Artillerie gewidmet.* Vienna: Berdach, 1975.

Bidwell, Shelford, and Dominick Graham. *Firepower, British Army Weapons and Theories of War 1904–1945.* Boston: George Allen and Unwin, 1982.

Bischoff, Kurt. *Im Trommelfeuer, Die Herbstschlacht in der Champagne, 1915.* Leipzig: Gebrüder Fändrich, 1939.

Blau, George E. *The German Campaign in Russia: Planning and Operations (1940–1942).* Washington, D.C.: Government Printing Office, 1955.

Blumenson, Martin. *The Patton Papers.* Boston: Houghton Mifflin, 1974.

Bond, Brian. *Liddell Hart, A Study of His Military Thought*. London: Cassel, 1977.

Bruge, Roger. *Faites Sauter La Ligne Maginot*. Paris: Fayard, 1973.

Buffetaut, Yves. *De Gaulle Chef du Guerre*. Bayeux: Editions Heimdal, 1990.

Burns, E.L.M. *Manpower in the Canadian Army, 1939–1945*. Toronto: Clarke, Irwin, 1956.

Carrell, Paul. *Hitler Moves East, 1941–1943*. Translated by Ewald Osers. Boston: Little, Brown, and Company, 1964.

Carrington, Charles Edmund. *A Subaltern's War*. London: Peter Davies, 1929.

Chapman, Guy. *Why France Fell, The Defeat of the French Army in 1940*. New York: Holt, Rinehart and Winston, 1968.

———, ed. *Vain Glory*. London: Cassell, 1937.

Chuikov, Vasili I. *The Beginning of the Road*. Translated by Harold Silver. London: MacGibbon and Kee, 1963.

Clark, Alan. *Barbarossa: The Russian-German Conflict, 1941–1945*. London: Hutchinson, 1965.

Combat Studies Institute. *Selected Readings in Military History: Soviet Military History, Volume I, The Red Army, 1918–1945*. Fort Leavenworth, KS: U.S. Army and General Staff College, 1984.

Davis, Burke. *Marine! The Life of Lt. Gen. Lewis B. (Chesty) Puller*. Toronto: Bantam, 1964.

Doughty, Robert Allan. *The Evolution of U.S. Army Tactical Doctrine, 1946–76*. Fort Leavenworth, KS: U.S. Army Command and Staff College, 1979.

———. *The Seeds of Disaster, The Development of French Army Doctrine 1919–1939*. Hamden, CT: Archon, 1985.

———. *The Breaking Point, Sedan and the Fall of France*. Hamden, CT: Archon, 1990.

Dupuy, R. Ernest, and Trevor N. Dupuy. *Military Heritage of America*. New York: McGraw-Hill, 1956.

Dupuy, Trevor N. *A Genius for War: The German Army and General Staff, 1807–1945*. London: Macdonald and Janes, 1977.

Edmonds, James, and A. F. Becke. *British Official History of the Great War: Military Operations, France and Belgium, 1918*. London: MacMillan, 1937.

Eisenart Rothe, Ernst von, and Martin Lezius. *Das Ehrenbuch der Garde, die preußische Garde im Weltkriege 1914–1919*. Berlin: Wilhelm Kolk and Verlag Oskar Hinderer, n.d.

Ellis, Chris, and Peter Chamberlain. *Handbook on the British Army, 1943*. New York: Hippocrene, 1976.

Ellis, L. F. *The War in France and Flanders, 1939–1940*. London: His Majesty's Stationery Office, 1953.

Ely, Louis B. *The Red Army Today*. Harrisburg, PA: The Military Service Publishing Company, 1949.

English, John A. *The Canadian Army and the Normandy Campaign, A Study of Failure in High Command*. New York: Praeger, 1990.

Erfurth, Waldemar. *Surprise*. Translated by Stephan T. Possony. Harrisburg, PA: Military Service Publishing Company, 1943.

Erickson, John. *The Soviet High Command*. London: Macmillan, 1962.

———. *The Road to Stalingrad*. London: Weidenfeld and Nicholson, 1975.

Farrar-Hockley, Anthony. *Infantry Tactics*. London: Almark, 1976.

Featherston, Alwyn. *Saving the Breakout, The 30th Division's Heroic Stand at Mortain, August, 7–12, 1944*. Novato, CA: Presidio, 1993.

Ferrard, Stéphane, ed. *L'Armement de l'Infanterie Française 1918–1940*. Paris: Gazette des Armes, 1979.

Frank, Benis M., and Henry Shaw, Jr. *Victory and Occupation: History of U.S. Marine Corps Operations in World War II*. Washington, D.C.: U.S. Government Printing Office, 1968.

Fry, J. C. *Assault Battle Drill*. Harrisburg, PA: The Military Service Publishing Co., 1955.

Fuller, J.F.C. *The Reformation of War*. London: Hutchinson, 1923.

———. *Thunderbolts*. London: Skeffington and Son, 1946.

———. *Memoirs of an Unconventional Soldier*. London: Ivor Nicholson and Watson, 1936.

———. *Machine Warfare*. London: Hutchinson, 1941.

———. *Armored Warfare: An Annotated Edition of Lectures on F.S.R. III (Operations Between Mechanized Forces)*. Harrisburg, PA: The Military Service Publishing Company, 1943.

Gabriel, Richard, and Paul L. Savage. *Crisis in Command*. New York: Hill and Wang, 1978.

George, Alexander L. *The Chinese Communist Army in Action: The Korean War and Its Aftermath*. New York: Columbia University Press, 1959.

German Defense Tactics Against Russian Breakthroughs. Washington, D.C.: U.S. Government Printing Office, 1951.

Great Britain, War Office, *Infantry Training: Training and War*. London: H. M. Stationery Office, 1937.

Greene, Jack. *Mare Nostrum, The War in the Mediterranean*. Watsonville, CA: Jack Greene, 1990.

Greenfield, Kent R., et al. *The Organization of Ground Combat Troops*. Washington, D.C.: Government Printing Office, 1947.

Griffith, Paddy. *Forward into Battle, Battle Tactics from Waterloo to the Near Future*. Novato, CA: Presidio, 1990.

Griffith, Samuel B. *The Chinese People's Liberation Army*. New York: McGraw-Hill, 1967.

Gruss, Hellmuth. *Aufbau und Verwendung der deutschen Sturmbataillone im Weltkriege*. Berlin: Junker und Dunnhaupt, 1939.

Gudmundsson, Bruce I. *Storm Troop Tactics: Innovation in the German Army, 1914–1918*. New York: Praeger, 1989.

———. *On Artillery*. Westport, CT: Praeger, 1993.

Guinard, Pierre, et al. *Inventaire Sommaire des Archives de la Guerre, Serie N 1872–1919, Introduction: Organization de l'Armée Française, Guide des Sources, Bibliographie*. Paris: Service Historique de l'Armée de Terre, 1974.

Hackett, Sir John. *The Profession of Arms*. London: Times Publishing, 1963.

Hackworth, David H., and Julie Sherman. *About Face, The Odyssey of an American Warrior*. New York: Simon and Schuster, 1990.

Hallas, James. *The Devil's Anvil: The Assault on Peliliu*. Westport, CT: Praeger, 1994.

Halter, Heinz. *Jäger im Freiheitskampf, Finnlands Jugend im Weltkrieg*. Leipzig: Schwarzhäupter-Verlag, 1941.

Hastings, Max. *Overlord*. London: Joseph, 1984.

Hayashi, Saburo and Alvin C. Coox. *Kogun: The Japanese Army in the Pacific War.* Quantico: VA: The Marine Corps Association, 1959.

Heinrici, Paul, ed. *Das Ehrenbuch des Deutschen Pioniere.* Berlin: Verlag Tradition Wilhelm Kolk, 1932.

Hermes, Walter G. *The United States Army in the Korean War, Truce Tent and Fighting Front.* Washington, D.C.: U.S. Government Printing Office, 1966.

Herzog, Chaim. *The War of Atonement.* Boston: Little, Brown, and Company, 1975.

Hofschröer, Peter. *Prussian Light Infantry, 1792–1815.* London: Osprey, 1984.

Hooker, Richard, ed. *Maneuver Warfare, An Anthology.* Novato, CA: Presidio, 1993.

Insight Team of the London Sunday Times. *The Yom Kippur War.* New York: Doubleday, 1974.

Italy, Esercito, Corpo di Stato Maggiore. *Manuale di Regolamenti Per i Corsi Allievi Ufficiali di Complemento.* Rome: Edizioni delle Forze Armate, 1942.

Jack, J. L. *General Jack's Diary.* Edited by John Terrain. London: Eyre & Spotswoode, 1964.

Jackson, W.G.F. *The Battle for Italy.* London: B. T. Batsford, 1967.

Janowitz, Morris, ed. *The New Military.* New York: Russell Sage, 1964.

———, ed. *Military Conflict: Essays in the Institutional Analysis of War and Peace.* Beverly Hills: Sage, 1975.

Keravouri, Jouni. *The Russo-Finnish War 1939–1940: A Study in Leadership, Training, and Esprit de Corps.* Fort Leavenworth, KS: U.S. Army War College, 1985.

Kesselring, Albert. *Memoirs.* London: William Kimber, 1953.

Kippenberger, Howard. *Infantry Brigadier.* Oxford: Oxford University Press, 1949.

Laffargue, André. *The Attack in Trench Warfare: Impressions and Reflections of a Company Commander.* Washington, D.C.: The United States Infantry Association, 1916.

Lanning, Michael Lee, and Dan Craig. *Inside the VC and the NVA, The Real Story of North Vietnam's Armed Forces.* New York: Fawcett Columbine, 1992.

Leckie, Robert. *Conflict: The History of the Korean War, 1950–53.* New York: G. P. Putnam's Sons, 1962.

Lessons From the Arab/Israeli War. London: Royal United Services Institute, 1974.

Lewis, S. J. *Forgotten Legions, German Army Infantry Policy, 1918–1941.* New York: Praeger, 1985.

Liddell Hart, Basil Henry. *A Science of Infantry Tactics Simplified.* London: William Clowes, 1923.

———. *Paris, or the Future of War.* London: Kegan, Paul, Trench, Trubner, 1926.

———. *The Remaking of Modern Armies.* London: Murray, 1927.

———. *Thoughts on War.* London: Faber and Faber, 1944.

———. *Defense of the West.* London: Cassell, 1950.

———. *Europe in Arms.* London: Faber and Faber, 1953.

———. *The Soviet Army.* London: Weidenfeld & Nicolson, 1956.

———. *The Real War, 1914–1918.* Boston: Little, Brown, 1964.

———, ed. *The Rommel Papers.* New York: Harcourt Brace, 1953.

———. *Memoirs.* London: Cassel, 1965.

———. *History of the Second World War.* London: Pan, 1978.

———. *The Other Side of the Hill.* London: Pan, 1978.

Lucas, Pascal M. H. *L'Évolution des Idées Tacticques en France et en Allemagne Pendant la Guerre de 1914–1918*. Paris: Berger-Levrault, 1923.

Ludendorff, Erich. *Urkunden der Obersten Heeresleitung über ihre Tätigkeit 1916/1918*. Berlin: Ernst Siegfried Mittler und Sohn, 1920.

Luttwak, Edward, and Dan Horowitz. *The Israeli Army*. London: Allen Lane, 1973.

Luvaas, Jay. *Education of an Army, British Military Thought, 1815–1940*. Chicago: University Press, 1964.

Lynch, George A. "The Tactics of the New Infantry Regiment." *The Infantry Journal*. March–April 1939.

Maasen, Heinz. *Par-Dessus la Meuse, Comment fut forcé le passage à Monthermé*. Translated by J. Jamin. Paris: Payot, 1943.

MacDonald, Charles B. *The Mighty Endeavor: American Armed Forces in the European Theater in World War II*. New York: Oxford University Press, 1969.

Mackintosh, Malcolm. *Juggernaut: A History of the Soviet Armed Forces*. New York: Macmillan, 1967.

Macksey, Kenneth. *Crucible of Power: The Fight for Tunisia, 1942–1943*. London: Hutchinson, 1969.

———. *Tank Warfare, A History of Tanks in Battle*. London: Rupert Hart Davis, 1971.

Manchester, William. *American Caesar*. Boston: Little, Brown, 1978.

Marshall, S.L.A. *The Soldier's Load and the Mobility of a Nation*. Washington: The Combat Forces Press, 1950.

———. *Men Against Fire*. New York: William Morrow, 1953.

———. *The River and the Gauntlet*. New York: Morrow, 1953.

———. *Pork Chop Hill: The American Fighting Man in Action, Korea, Spring 1953*. New York: William Morrow, 1956.

———. *Sinai Victory*. New York: William Morrow, 1958.

Mellenthin, F. W. von. *Panzer Battles, 1939–1945*. London: Cassell, 1955.

Melzer, Walther. *Albert-Kanal und Eben-Emael*. Heidelberg: Scharnhorst Buchkameradschaft, 1957.

Messenger, Charles. *The Art of Blitzkrieg*. London: Ian Allen, 1976.

Middlebrook, Martin. *The Kaiser's Battle, 21 March 1918, The First Day of the German Spring Offensive*. Harmondsworth: Penguin, 1983.

Miksche, Friedrich Otto. *Blitzkrieg*. London: Faber and Faber, 1941.

———. *Atomic Weapons and Armies*. London: Faber and Faber, 1955.

Millett, Alan R., and Williamson, Murray, eds. *Military Effectiveness*. Boston: Allen & Unwin, 1988.

Milner, Samuel. *United States Army World War II: Victory in Papua*. Washington, D.C.: U.S. Government Printing Office, 1957.

Montross, Lynn, and Nicholas A. Canzona. *U.S. Marine Operations in Korea, 1950–1953: The Chosin Reservoir Campaign*. Washington, D.C.: U.S. Government Printing Office, 1957.

Moran, Lord. *The Anatomy of Courage*. London: Constable, 1967.

Mowat, Farley. *The Regiment*. Toronto: McClelland and Stewart, 1973.

Nelson, Harvey W. *The Chinese Military System: An Organizational Study of the Chinese People's Liberation Army*. New York: McGraw-Hill, 1967.

Ney, Virgil. *The Evolution of the Armored Infantry Rifle Squad*. Fort Belvoir, VA: U.S. Army Combat Operations Research Group, 1965.

———. *Organization and Equipment of the Infantry Rifle Squad from Valley Forge to ROAD*. Fort Belvoir, VA: U.S. Army Combat Operations Research Group, 1965.

Nicholson, G.W.L. *The Canadians in Italy*. Ottawa: Queen's Printer, 1956.

Niehorster, Leo W. G. *German World War II Organizational Series, Vol 2/I, Mechanized Army Divisions (10th May, 1940)*. Hannover: Niehorster, 1990.

O'Ballance, Edgar. *The Sinai Campaign of 1956*. New York: Praeger, 1959.

———. *The Red Army*. London: Faber and Faber, 1964.

———. *Korea: 1950–1953*. London: Faber and Faber, 1969.

Orgorkiewicz, R. M. *Armored Forces*. London: Arms and Armor Press, 1970.

Ott, Ernst. *Jäger am Feind, Geschichte und Ofergang der 97. Jäger-Division, 1940–1945*. Munich: Selbstverlag Kameradschaft der Spielhahnjäger E. V., 1966.

Palmer, Robert R., et al. *The Procurement and Training of Ground Combat Troops*. Washington, D.C.: Government Printing Office, 1948.

Paret, Peter. *Yorck and the Era of the Prussian Reform, 1807–1815*. Princeton, NJ: Princeton University Press, 1966.

Patton, George S., Jr. *War As I Knew It*. New York: Pyramid, 1970.

Pelet-Narbonne, E., ed. *Von Löbells Jahresberichte über das Heer- und Kriegswesen*. Berlin: E. S. Mittler, 1913.

Pemberton, A. L. *The Development of Artillery Tactics and Equipment*. London: The War Office, 1950.

Prussia, Kriegsministerium. *Ausbildungsvorschrift für die Fußtruppen im Kriege*. Berlin: Reichsdruckerie, 1918.

Regling, Heinz Volkmar. *Amiens, 1940, Die Deutsche Durchbruch Südlich von Amiens, 5 Bis 8 Juni, 1940*. Freiburg im Breisgau: Verlag Rombach, 1968.

Remold, Josef. *Tagebuch eines Bataillons Kommandeurs. Das III./Gebirgsjäger Regiment 99 im Frankreichfeldzug*. Munich: Schild Verlag, 1967.

Rolbant, Samuel. *The Israeli Soldier: Profile of an Army*. Cranbury: Thomas Yoseloff, 1970.

Ropp, Theodore. *War in the Modern World*. New York: Collier, 1962.

Rosinski, Herbert. *The German Army*. Washington, D.C.: The Infantry Journal, 1944.

Rossmann, Karl. *Kampf der Pioniere*. Berlin: Zentralverlag der NSDAP, 1943.

Rothbrust, Florian. *Guderian's XIXth Panzer Corps and the Battle of France, Breakthrough in the Ardennes, May, 1940*. New York: Praeger, 1990.

Sajer, Guy. *The Forgotten Soldier*. Translated by Lily Emmet. London: Weidenfeld and Nicholson, 1967.

Samuels, Martin. *Doctrine and Dogma, German and British Infantry Tactics in the First World War*. Westport, CT: Greenwood Press, 1992.

Scales, Robert H. J. *Firepower in Limited War*. Washington, D.C.: U.S. Government Printing Office, 1990.

Schram, Stuart. *Mao Tse Tung*. New York: Simon and Schuster, 1966.

Seaton, Albert. *The Russo-German War, 1941–45*. New York: Praeger, 1970.

———. *The Battle for Moscow*. London: Jonathan Cape, 1971.

Seeckt, Hans von. *Gedanken eines Soldaten*. Leipzig: Koehler & Amelang, 1936.

Senger und Etterlin, Frido von. *Neither Fear Nor Hope*. Translated by George Malcolm. London: Macdonald, 1960.

Showalter, Dennis. *Railroads and Rifles, Soldiers Technology and the Unification of Germany*. Hamden, CT: Archon Press, 1975.

Simson, Ivan. *Singapore: Too Little, Too Late*. London: Leo Cooper, 1970.

Slim, Sir William. *Defeat into Victory*. London: Cassell, 1956.

Small Unit Actions During the German Campaign in Russia. Washington, D.C.: U.S. Government Printing Office, 1955.

Stacey, C. P. *The Victory Campaign: The Operations in North-West Europe, 1944–45*. Ottawa: Queen's Printer, 1960.

Stanton, Shelby. *Order of Battle, Vietnam*. Washington, D.C.: U.S. News Books, 1981.

———. *The Rise and Fall of an American Army, U.S. Ground Forces in Vietnam 1965–1973*. Navato, CA: Presidio, 1985.

Stevens, G. R. *Princess Patricia's Canadian Light Infantry, 1919–1957*. Montreal: Southam, 1958.

Stolfi, R.H.S. *A Bias for Action, The German 7th Panzer Division in France and Russia 1940–1941*. Quantico, VA: Marine Corps Association, 1991.

Stouffer, Samuel, et al. *The American Soldier, Combat and its Aftermath*. Princeton, NJ: Princeton University Press, 1949.

Suvorov, Victor. *Icebreaker, Who Started the Second World War?* Translated by Thomas Beatie. London: Hamish Hamilton, 1990.

Swettenham, John. *To Seize the Victory, the Canadian Corps in World War I*. Toronto: Ryerson, 1965.

Swinson, Arthur. *Kohima*. London: Cassell, 1966.

Swinton, Ernest D. *Eyewitness*. London: Hodder and Stoughton, 1932.

Tactics and Technique of Infantry. Harrisburg, PA: The Military Service Publishing Company, 1950.

Thompson, Paul W., Harold Doud, John Scofield, and Milton A. Hill. *How the Jap Army Fights*. New York: Penguin, 1943.

Tindall, Richard, et al. *Infantry in Battle*. Washington, D.C.: The Infantry Journal, 1934.

Travers, Tim. *The Killing Ground, The British Army, the Western Front, and the Emergence of Modern Warfare, 1900–1918*. Boston: Allen & Unwin, 1987.

Turner, A.J.D. *Valentine's Sand Table Exercises*. Aldershot: Gale and Polden, 1955.

Uhle-Wettler, Franz. *Gefechtsfeld Mitteleuropa. Gefahr der Über technisierung von Streitkräften, mit ergänzenden Karten und Skizzen*. Munich: Bernhard & Graege, 1980.

United States Marine Corps. *Professional Knowledge Gained From Operational Experience in Vietnam, 1967*. Quantico, VA: U.S. Marine Corps, 1989.

Urban, K., [pseud.] *Kurze Zusammenstellung über die Polnische Armee*. Berlin: Eisenschmidt, 1939.

U.S. Army, Center of Military History. *United States Army in the World War, 1917–1919, Organization of the American Expeditionary Forces*. Washington, D.C.: Government Printing Office, 1988.

Van Creveld, Martin. *Supplying War: Logistics from Wallenstein to Patton*. Cambridge, MA: Harvard University Press, 1977.

———. *Fighting Power, German and U.S. Army Performance, 1939–1945*. Westport, CT: Greenwood, 1982.

Vasselle, Pierre. *La Bataille au Sud d'Amiens, 20 Mai–8 Juin 1940*. Abbéville: Imprimerie F. Paillart, 1963.

Vogel, Victor. *Soldiers of the Old Army*. College Station, TX: Texas A&M University Press, 1990.

Warner, Phillip, and Michael Youens. *Japanese Army of World War II*. Reading: Osprey, 1973.

Weeks, John. *Men Against Tanks*. New York: Mason Charter, 1975.

Weller, Jac. *Weapons and Tactics*. London: Nicholas Vane, 1966.

Wendt, Hermann. *Verdun 1916, Die Angriffe Falkenhayns im Maasgebiet mit Richtung auf Verdun als strategisches Problem*. Berlin: E. S. Mittler & Sohn, 1931.

Wheeler, Walter R. *The Infantry Battalion in War*. Washington, D.C.: The Infantry Journal, 1936.

Wilmot, Chester. *The Struggle for Europe*. London: Collins, 1974.

Winter, Dennis. *Haig's Command, A Reassessment*. London: Viking, 1991.

Witzleben, Herman von. *Taktik-Fibel*. Berlin: Verlag Offene Wort, 1935.

Wood, Herbert Fairlie. *Vimy!* London: Corgi, 1972.

Wray, Timothy A. *Standing Fast: German Defensive Doctrine on the Russian Front During World War II*. Fort Leavenworth, KS: U.S. Army Command and General Staff College, 1986.

Wynne, Graham C. *If Germany Attacks: The Battle in Depth in the West*. Westport, CT: Greenwood Press, 1976.

Zaloga Steven, and Victor Madej. *The Polish Campaign, 1939*. New York: Hippocrene, 1985.

Zhukov, Georgy Konstantinovich. *Memoirs*. London: Jonathan Cape, 1971.

Zoberltitz, Anton Constantin von. *Das Alte Heer, Erinnerungen an die Dienstzeit be allen Waffen*. Berlin: Heinrich Beenken, 1931.

ARTICLES

"Amiens, 1940: The Schwerpunkt in Action." *Tactical Notebook*. December 1991.

Asplin, C. "Surprise in Defence, The Battle of Reims, 15th July, 1918." *Fighting Forces*. April 1939.

Augustin. "Die Minenwerfer des deutschen Heeres (Fortsetzung)." *Technik und Wehrmacht*. Volume 5/6 (1920).

Bentley, L. W. and D. C. McKinnon. "The Yom Kippur War as an Example of Modern Land Battle." *Canadian Defense Quarterly*. No. 4 (1974).

"Breakneck Ridge." *Canadian Army Training Memorandum*. No. 50 (1945).

"A Brief History of the Development of the Fire Team in the United States Marine Corps." *Tactical Notebook*. March 1994.

Bryant, Arthur. "The New Infantryman." *Canadian Army Training Memorandum*. No. 44 (1944).

Campbell, D. D. "The Gunners in the Arab-Israeli Six-Day War of 1967." *Journal of the Royal Artillery*. September 1968.

Clagett, Robert H . "What Good is a Machine Gun." *Combat Forces Journal*. October 1952.

Clarkson, J.M.E. "Spark at Yom Kippur: Many Surprises in an Eighteen-Day War." *Canadian Defense Quarterly*. No. 3 (1974).

"Czechoslovakian Infantry, 1923." *Tactical Notebook*. August 1992.

"Depicting a German Division." *Tactical Notebook*. January and February 1992.

Dexter, George E. "Search and Destroy, Vietnam." *Infantry*. July–August 1966.
Doughty, Robert A. "French Antitank Doctrine, 1940: The Antidote that Failed." *Military Review*. May 1976.
"Einzelschilderungen aus dem Kriege an der Westfront." *Militärwissenschaftliche Rundschau*. 1940, Heft 4.
"Ersatz Divisions in 1914." *Tactical Notebook*. July 1993.
"The Essential Thing." *Tactical Notebook*. November 1993.
"A Few Tips from the Front." *Canadian Army Training Memorandum*. No. 29 (1944).
"The First Polish Division in 1942." *Tactical Notebook*. July 1992.
"Forming New Units." *Tactical Notebook*. October 1992.
France, Ministère des Armées, État-Major de l'Armé, 3ème Bureau. *Manuel du Préparation au Certificat Interarmes*. Tome I. Paris: Berger-Levrault, 1961.
"The French Army Machine Gun Battalion, 1940." *Tactical Notebook*. February 1992.
"The French Connection." *Tactical Notebook*. February 1993.
"The French Infantry Regulations." *Infantry Journal*. February 1926.
"French Offensives in 1915." *Tactical Notebook*. December 1992.
"French Regulations for the Infantry." *Infantry Journal*. January 1927.
"The German 18th Artillery Division (1943–1944)." *Tactical Notebook*. February 1993.
"German Flamethrowers at Verdun." *Tactical Notebook*. April 1993.
"The German Grenadier Company, 1944." *Tactical Notebook*. October 1991.
"The Germans—How They Fight." *Canadian Army Training Memorandum*. No. 39 (June 1944).
Germany, Generalstab. (7. Abteilung). "Die Entwickelung der deutschen Infanterie im Weltkrieg 1914–1918." *Militärwissenschaftliche Rundschau*. Vol. 3 (1938).
Great Britain, War Office. *Current Reports from Overseas*. Nos. 34 (1944), 36 (1944), 61 (1944), 65 (1944), and 66 (1944).
Griffith, Albert A. "Put Them All Together." *Infantry*. July–August 1970.
Hackworth, David H. "Guerilla Battalion, U.S. Style." *Infantry*. January–February 1971.
Hale, Lonsdale. "Glimpses of German Military Life." *Colburn's United Service Magazine*. No. 715 (June 1888).
Hathaway, John F. "The Handheld 81mm Mortar." *Infantry*. September–October 1967.
"How the Japanese See Us." *Canadian Army Training Memorandum*. No. 30 (1943).
Hudson, C. E. "Flanking Machine-Gun Fire." *The Infantry Journal*. February 1925.
"Infantry Tactics, 1914–1918." *Journal of the Royal United Services Institute*. Vol. 64 (1919).
"Japanese Mortars." *Canadian Army Training Memorandum*. No. 50 (1945).
"Japanese Soldier." *Canadian Army Training Memorandum*. No. 51 (1945).
"Japanese Tactics and Jungle Warfare." *Canadian Army Training Memorandum*. No. 35 (1944).
"Japs Deepen Defenses." *Canadian Army Training Memorandum*. No. 52 (1945).
Johnson, Thomas G. "Recon by Sound." *Infantry*. September–October 1969.
"Jungle Fighting." *Canadian Army Training Memorandum*. No. 34 (1944).
Kentish, R. J. "The Case for the Eight Company Battalion." *Journal of the Royal United Services Institute*. July 1912.
Klein, William E. "Mechanized Infantry in Vietnam." *Infantry*. March–April 1971.
"Know Your Enemy." *Canadian Army Training Memorandum*. No. 33 (1943).

Laffargue, André. "Hints to the Foot Soldier in Battle." *The Marine Corps Gazette*. March 1917.
Liddell Hart, Basil Henry. "The 'Ten Commandments' of the Combat Unit—Suggestions on Its Theory and Training." *Journal of the Royal United Services Institution*. No. 64 (1919).
———. "Man-in-the-Dark Theory." *The Royal Engineers Journal*. No. 33 (1921).
———. "A Science of Infantry Tactics." *The Royal Engineers Journal*. No. 33 (1921).
———. "The Soldier's Pillar of Fire by Night: The Need for a Framework of Tactics." *Journal of the Royal United Services Institution*. No. 66 (1921).
"The Main Effort." *Tactical Notebook*. October and November 1991.
"The Many Meanings of Ersatz." *Tactical Notebook*. July 1993.
"The Marine and his Infantry Weapons in Vietnam." *Marine Corps Gazette*. April 1965.
Marshall, S.L.A. "Why the Israeli Army Wins." *Harper's Magazine*. October 1958.
"Mass." *Tactical Notebook*. February 1992.
Meckel, Jakob, "A Summer Night's Dream." *Tactical Notebook*. May, July, and August 1993.
"Military Notes on Foreign Armies." *Infantry Journal*. November 1925.
Neglia, Anthony V. "NVA and VC: Different Enemies, Different Tactics." *Infantry*. September–October 1970.
"The 164 Light 'Afrika' Division." *Tactical Notebook*. July 1992.
"Organization and Tactics of the Japanese Platoon and Section on the Malayan Front." *Canadian Army Training Memorandum*. No. 14 (1942).
"Ortona." *Canadian Army Training Memorandum*. No. 42 (September 1944).
Osterroht. "Über Kampfweise der Infanterie, Betrachtungen zu Heft 1 der A.V.I." *Wissen und Wehr*. 1923.
"Prepared Defenses." *Canadian Army Training Memorandum*. No. 51 (1945).
Ross, G. MacLeod. "Death of a Division." *Infantry Journal*. April 1930.
Samuels, Martin. "Operation Goodwood—The Caen Carve-Up." *British Army Review*. No. 96 (December 1990).
"78th Assault Division: A Paper Battle." *Tactical Notebook*. July 1992.
Smith, Grady A. "Old Doctrine, New Techniques." *Infantry*. May–June 1971.
"A Soviet Motorized-Mechanized Brigade in September 1943." *Tactical Notebook*. July 1992.
Stevenson, Jack. "Things to Do With an 81mm Mortar." *Infantry*. January–February 1971.
Stolfi, R.H.S. "Equipment for Victory in France." *History*. Volume 55 (1970).
"Truppenführung (Troop Leading), The German Field Service Regulations." *Tactical Notebook*. March 1993.
"The U.S. Army in 1914." *Tactical Notebook*. February 1993.
"U.S. Enlisted Men Discuss the Jap." *Canadian Army Training Memorandum*. No. 44 (1944).
"Volksgrenadier: The 13th (Infantry Gun) Company, 1944." *Tactical Notebook*. April 1992.
"Volksgrenadier: The 14th (Tank Destroyer) Company, 1944." *Tactical Notebook*. May 1992.
"Wedge and Kessel." *Military Review*. August 1941.
West, Francis J., Jr. "Stingray '70." *U.S. Naval Institute Proceedings*. November 1969.

Westphal, Siegfried. "Von der 'Bombenkanone' zum Infanteriegeschütz." *Wehrtechnische Monatshefte*. July 1938.

Yekimovskiy, A. "Tactics of the Red Army in the 1920s and 1930s." *Voyenni Vestnik*, No. 3 (March 1967). Translated and reprinted in Combat Studies Institute, *Selected Readings in Military History: Soviet Military History, Volume I, The Red Army, 1918–1945*. Fort Leavenworth, KS: U.S. Army Command and General Staff College, 1984.

———. "Tactics of the Soviet Army During the Great Patriotic War." *Voyenni Vestnik*, No. 4 (April 1967). Translated and reprinted in Combat Studies Institute, *Selected Readings in Military History: Soviet Military History, Volume I, The Red Army, 1918–1945*. Fort Leavenworth, KS: U.S. Army Command and General Staff College, 1984.

UNPUBLISHED DOCUMENTS

After Action Reports of Various German Divisions that Served in the Polish Campaign of 1939. U.S. National Archives, Washington, D.C. Microfilm Series T-78, Roll 861.

Armee-Oberkommando 6 Ic/40. "Feindnachrichtenblatt von 3.6.1940." U.S. National Archives, Washington, D.C. Captured German Records. Microfilm Series T-312, Roll 1379.

"Essai de Reconstitution du J.M.O. du 37ème R.A.D. du 5 Janvier au 16 Juin 1940." Service Historique de l'Armée de Terre, Vincennes, France. Carton 34N568.

"Extracts from a Report Written as a Result of a Tour in the Mediterranean by B.R.A. (Army Artillery Commander), HQ 21 Army Group, Dated 10 Jan., 1944." U.S. National Archives, Record Group 337, Entry 47, Box 92.

1st Battalion, 43rd Grenadier Regiment. Report U.S. National Archives. Washington, D.C. Captured German Records, Microfilm Series T-78, Roll 769.

XIV Armee Korps, Ia. "Fernspruch von HVZ+39," included as appendix 127 to XIV. Armee Korps, "Kriegstagbuch." U.S. National Archives, Washington, D.C. Captured German Records. Microfilm Series T-314, Roll 528.

General der Infanterie beim Chef Generalstab des Heeres IV. Nr. 2886/43 geh. dated 20 October 1943. U.S. National Archives, Washington, D.C. Captured German Records. Microfilm Series T-78, Roll 759.

"Historique Sommaire du 237e R.A.L.H.D. de l'A.D. 16 du 4 Juin au 3 Juillet 1940." Service Historique de l'Armée de Terre, Vincennes, France. Carton 34N660.

Inf. B. Chef. Gen. St. d.H. Nr. 3160/44g vom 5.9.44. U.S. National Archives. Washington, D.C. Captured German Records, Microfilm Series T-78, Roll 763.

Kleeman, Ulrich. "Streiflichter zur Kriegsführung in Nordafrika." U.S. National Archives, Washington, D.C. Foreign Military Studies, MS D-104.

Laffargue, André. Letter of General André Laffargue to Bruce Gudmundsson, October 15, 1987. Institute for Tactical Education, Quantico, VA.

Luttwak, Edward N. "Urban Warfare Task Forces (Kampfgruppen) and Emergency ad hoc Forces (Alarmeinheiten)." Unpublished report for U.S. Army TRADOC, 1 March 1983. (DTIC AD-B085 081.)

9. Infanterie Division Ia. Nr. 300/40 *geheim* dated 4.6.40. U.S. National Archives, Washington, D.C. Captured German Records. Microfilm Series T-315, Roll 508.

9. Infanterie Division Ia. "Tagesmeldung, den Generalkommando XIV. AK." U.S. National Archives, Washington, D.C. Captured German Records. Microfilm Series T-315, Roll 508.

"Normalgliederung Inf. Division (Ost), table included in folder marked 'Ia, KTB, Akte D, Band 2, Kriegsgliederungen.' " U.S. National Archives, Washington, D.C. Captured German Records. Microfilm Series T-312, Roll 783, Frame 785.

"Rapport du Chef d'Escadron Brock." Service Historique de l'Armée de Terre, Vincennes, France. Carton 34 N672.

"Rapport du Chef d'Escadron Charrierre Comandant le 3ème Group du 237ème R.A.L.H.D. pour le periode du 3 Septembre 1939 au 24 Juin 1940." Service Historique de l'Armée de Terre, Vincennes, France. Carton 34N660.

Reports from infantry division and corps commanders contained in the folder "Hebung der Kampfkraft und Befehl Nr. 15." U.S. National Archives, Washington, D.C. Captured German Records. Microfilm Series T-78, Roll 759.

Reports of the various U.S. military attachés in Vienna and Warsaw. U.S. National Archives, Washington, D.C. Record Group 165.

Tables of organization for the 164th "Afrika" Division microfilmed at the U.S. National Archives. U.S. National Archives, Washington, D.C. Captured German Records. Microfilm Series T-78, Reel 861.

35th Infantry Division. Report of the commanding general, U.S. National Archives. Washington, D.C. Captured German Records, Microfilm Series T-78, Roll 769.

United States of America, War Department. Table of Organization 7–17, Infantry Rifle Company, 1 April 1942. U.S. Army Center for Military History, Washington, D.C.

Index

About the Authors

JOHN A. ENGLISH is the author of the classic first edition of *On Infantry* (Praeger, 1984) and of *The Canadian Army and the Normandy Campaign* (Praeger, 1991). He currently teaches at Queen's University at Kingston, Ontario, and is the editor of a new Praeger series, War Studies.

BRUCE I. GUDMUNDSSON is the editor of *Tactical Notebook* and co-host of the weekly television program *Modern War*. His other books include *Stormtroop Tactics* (Praeger, 1989) and *On Artillery* (Praeger, 1993). He is the editor of the Praeger series on the Military Profession.

ISBN 0-275-94588-X
90000>
EAN
9 780275 945886
HARDCOVER BAR CODE